THE JESUIT RELATIONS AND ALLIED DOCUMENTS: TRAVELS AND EXPLORATIONS OF THE JESUIT MISSIONARIES IN NEW FRANCE, 1610-1791. VOL. XLII. [CLEVELAND]

Published @ 2017 Trieste Publishing Pty Ltd

ISBN 9780649617982

The Jesuit Relations and Allied Documents: Travels and Explorations of the Jesuit Missionaries in New France, 1610-1791. Vol. XLII. [Cleveland] by Reuben Gold Thwaites

Edited by Trieste Publishing Pty Ltd.
Cover @ 2017

www.triestepublishing.com

REUBEN GOLD THWAITES

THE JESUIT RELATIONS AND ALLIED DOCUMENTS: TRAVELS AND EXPLORATIONS OF THE JESUIT MISSIONARIES IN NEW FRANCE, 1610-1791. VOL. XLII. [CLEVELAND]

REUBEN GOLD THWAITES

THE JESUIT RELATIONS AND ALLIED
DOCUMENTS: TRAVELS AND
EXPLORATIONS OF THE JESUIT
MISSIONARIES IN NEW FRANCE,
1610-1791. VOL. XLII [CLEVELAND]

Trieste

I. 9641

The Jesuit Relations and Allied Documents

Travels and Explorations of the Jesuit Missionaries in New France

1610-1791

THE ORIGINAL FRENCH, LATIN, AND ITAL-
IAN TEXTS, WITH ENGLISH TRANSLA-
TIONS AND NOTES; ILLUSTRATED BY
PORTRAITS, MAPS, AND FACSIMILES

EDITED BY
REUBEN GOLD THWAITES
Secretary of the State Historical Society of Wisconsin

Vol. XLII
LOWER CANADA, IROQUOIS: 1632–1657

CLEVELAND: The Burrows Brothers
Company, PUBLISHERS, MDCCCXCIX

The Imperial Press, Cleveland

EDITORIAL STAFF

CONTENTS OF VOL. XLII

ILLUSTRATION TO VOL. XLII

PREFACE TO VOL. XLII

Following is a synopsis of the documents contained in the present volume:

XC. The *Relation* of 1655 – 56 is written by Jean de Quen, in the absence of his superior (Le Mercier) at the Onondaga mission recently begun by the Jesuits. This enterprise constitutes the main subject-matter of the *Relation*, and is fully described in the journal of Father Dablon, who, with Chaumonot, began the mission in the preceding autumn (1655). A prefatory note by De Quen outlines the chief events of the year, which are later given in detail.

The spring of 1656 opens most auspiciously for commerce; "for twenty years past, vessels have not reached this country so early,— at the very beginning of the month of June,— or in greater number." An appeal is made for six more missionaries, in view of the new fields of labor which are now opening.

The *Relation* proper begins with an account of Le Moyne's second voyage to the Mohawk country (August to November, 1655). He is welcomed by that tribe; and councils are held, with profusion of speeches and presents. The Father then visits the Dutch settlement at Fort Orange. After returning thence, his life is threatened by a pretended madman, who is only appeased by the offer of a dog for sacrifice. In November, he returns to Montreal, experiencing great hardships on the journey thither.

Soon after Le Moyne's departure on the above errand, an Onondaga deputation, "representing all the upper Iroquois Nations," arrives at Quebec to confirm the peace. At the ensuing council, the envoys give twenty-four presents to Onontio and his allies. They ask for a French colony in their country, and for Christian teachers; also for French soldiers to aid them against their enemies, the Eries. After careful consideration, it is decided to send back Dablon and Chaumonot with these envoys (as we have already seen in Doc. LXXXVII., Vol. XLI.). The greater part of this *Relation* is devoted to an account of their embassy to Onondaga, as recounted in the journal thereof kept by Father Dablon.

The voyage thither is described in detail. The travelers mainly depend for their food upon such game as they encounter. At first, this is scarce, but soon they find abundance,— on one occasion killing thirty bears in one day. "One of the ceremonies of the feast that followed this great slaughter was the drinking of bear's fat after the meal, as one drinks hippocras in France." One night, an Indian suddenly becomes temporarily insane, and imagines that some animal which plunges into the water has leaped down his throat. His tribesmen undertake to cure his delusion by pretending to share it, and mimicking his actions, and a laughable scene ensues. "They too began to cry and sing in imitation of the animals with which they were supposed to be afflicted,— all, in time with their song, beating that wretched man. What confusion!— a score of voices imitating ducks, teals, and frogs; and what a spectacle, to see people counterfeiting madness in order to cure a madman! Finally, they succeeded; for, after our man had perspired well, and become thoroughly tired, he lay down on his mat, and slept as peacefully as if nothing had happened." At the end of ten days, they reach an outpost of the Onondaga country,—a fishing village, where Chaumonot meets several of his former Huron disciples, now captives among the Iroquois. At a little distance from the chief village of the Onondagas, the Fathers are met by the old men of that tribe, who, after speeches of welcome, escort them to the village, where they are hospitably entertained and lodged.

Numerous councils are held, at which a special effort is made by the Jesuits to secure peace for the Algonkins as well as the French,—a point of especial difficulty with the Iroquois. The time outside of these affairs is variously spent,—sometimes in religious labors; sometimes in entertaining discourse with a group of savages, who ask questions about the French and their country across the sea, or "about the beginning of the world." The Frenchmen are taken to visit the salt spring four leagues thence, at which place it is proposed to establish the colony and mission. A child of ten years, captured from the Eries, with whom the Iroquois are at war, is burnt to death; but the Father succeeds in secretly baptizing this boy before his death. His torment lasts "only two hours, because of his youth; and not a tear or a cry escaped him from amid the flames." On Sunday, the Fathers say mass in the cabin of a woman of rank, who was converted to the faith at Quebec and on the homeward journey thence. Cayuga and Oneida deputies arrive, and take part in the ratification of peace. Chaumonot, following the custom of the country, makes numerous presents of

wampum and beaver-skins to accompany his speeches;
and having thus secured the good will of his savage
hearers, preaches to them the Christian faith, to which
they listen attentively.   His eloquence and tact
charm them; and the chief Cayuga deputy adopts
him as a brother.   Some conversions are made, and
the Fathers baptize several children.   They are overcome with delight when, at an important council,
the most influential of the Onondaga chiefs solemnly
announces his conversion to the faith,— a statement
applauded by his people.   A bark chapel is erected
for the missionaries, but it proves too small for the
crowds who come to hear them.   They soon are able
to baptize numerous adults, among them the oldest
woman of the tribe, regarded by her people as a cen-
tenarian.   Most of the leading men, however, refuse
to believe,— especially as they will not give up their
faith in dreams; they also fear that the Christian
religion will bring ruin upon their country, as they
think it has done with the Hurons.   Teotonharason — the woman already mentioned, who offered
her cabin for use as a chapel — and several of her
family are attacked by apparently mortal diseases;
but all are miraculously cured by baptism, which
confounds those who have slandered the faith.   These
last spread many false rumors, accusing the Fathers
of sorcery, and of malice toward the Iroquois tribes.

The Fathers behold and describe many superstitious rites,— among these, some practiced in obedience to dreams, which even involve the sacrifice of
human life; also the Ononhouaroia, or "festival of
fools," as Chaumonot calls it.   One of the men
participating therein, the host of the Fathers, sets
his own cabin on fire; but Chaumonot arrives in time

to put out the flames, and pacifies the frenzied man.

The ceremonies which are annually performed by these savages in preparation for war are also described. This is followed by an explanation of their reasons for attacking the Erie tribe. A captive taken from those enemies is brought to Onondaga, and burned to death at a slow fire.

On the last day of February, 1656, the Onondagas notify the Jesuits that the proposed French settlement among them must be begun at once, or they will break off the peace. After many unsuccessful efforts to send word to Quebec regarding these matters, Dablon himself goes thither, escorted by a score of Indians. This trip, made during the month of March, is full of hardship and suffering. At the end of his journal is inserted a note by the Paris editor, announcing that letters just received from Quebec inform him that Dablon has returned to Onondaga with the superior of the missions, Le Mercier, and two other priests, to join Chaumonot there. These missionaries "are escorted by fifty valiant Frenchmen, who have already begun a good settlement in the very heart of these Nations."

The account of the Onondaga mission being finished for this year, De Quen proceeds to mention the discoveries of two young Frenchmen who return (August, 1656) from a two years' trading and exploring expedition to the upper lake region. Their names are not given here, but recent researches identify these adventurers as Radisson and Groseilliers, and the region explored by them as Wisconsin and the shores of Lake Superior. Not only do they discover new lands and tribes, but they have "sent to heaven about three hundred little children," by baptizing them. They bring back an Ottawa fleet of fifty canoes, loaded with furs,—a joyous sight for the poor colonists. With these Ottawas, upon their return home, depart two Jesuits, Garreau and Druillettes; but the fleet is attacked by the Iroquois, not far from Three Rivers, and Garreau is mortally wounded. The final chapter gives various details of the death and the virtues of this missionary.

XCI. The *Journal des Jésuites* contains a lacuna from February 5, 1654 to October 25, 1656. A record for that time was kept by Le Mercier and others; but, for some unknown reason, it was written upon paper of another size, and detached from the book usually devoted to this purpose. An explanation to this effect is made by De Quen, who continues the *Journal*. It may be added that the MS. above referred to has long since disappeared, with many other valuable documents.

Beginning, then, with October 25, 1656, De Quen continues the record. A cemetery for the hospital nuns is consecrated in their new choir; and on the same day is laid therein the body of Charles de Lauson's young wife. The Iroquois still attempt to seduce the Hurons at Quebec. A council is held, November 3, at which the Oneida envoys offer presents to the Hurons to induce them to settle in the Iroquois country. Le Moyne brings assurances of peace from the Mohawks. On the 17th, Ragueneau makes presents to the Oneidas; one of these is "to grease their Legs, and to welcome them on their arrival." The general purpose of this council is to establish amicable relations with that tribe, who also invite the Jesuits to live with them. The day after Christmas, Mohawk ambassadors come to notify the

Hurons that their warriors will come next spring to escort them to the Iroquois country.

XCII. A separate sheet lying within the MS. volume of the *Journal des Jésuites* gives an account of the death, at the hands of the Iroquois (May 29, 1655), of the Jesuit brother, Jean Liégeois. Commendation is bestowed upon his services to the mission, and his fidelity therein.

XCIII. This curious and interesting document gives "a list of the benefactors of Nôtre Dame de Recouvrance at Kebec," from 1632 to 1657. This was the chapel built by Champlain, who also left in his will a bequest for it. The members of the Hundred Associates, both collectively and individually, gave various ornaments and supplies for the use of the chapel, until it was destroyed by fire in 1640; thereafter, they left "the care of that matter to the charity of the habitants, contenting themselves with paying the pension of 600 livres for two fathers at each Residence." Montmagny was a generous and frequent giver. In 1645, a gift of 1,250 beaver-skins was made by the governor and the habitants for building a church at Quebec in honor of Our Lady of Peace. A year later, the Associates gave to the church, apparently at Montmagny's suggestion, a bell for its steeple.

La Tour, the Acadian exile, gives 100 livres in money (1647); and Robert Hache, the Jesuit brother (1650), a large bell of 1,000 livres' weight. Two of the habitants bequeath by will small legacies. Many devout ladies of the colony bestow gifts,— sometimes money, more often altar-cloths, laces, garments, etc. Prominent among these is Madame de la Peltrie, the foundress of the Ursuline Convent. It is noticed that, since 1651, the Jesuit house has given much aid to the parish church,—maintaining a seminary for children, caring for the sacristy, etc. Various gifts from France are recorded, presented by benefactors of the missions, or by personal friends of Canadian priests and nuns. Most of the prominent habitants of Quebec are mentioned in this list of donations.

R. G. T.

MADISON, WIS., March, 1899.

XC

RELATION OF 1655-56

PARIS: SEBASTIEN ET GABRIEL CRAMOISY, 1657

SOURCE: We follow a copy of the original Cramoisy (H. 126), in Lenox Library, New York.

RELATION
DE CE QVI S'EST PASSE'
EN LA MISSION DES PERES
DE LA COMPAGNIE DE IESVS,
AV PAYS
DE LA NOVVELLE FRANCE,
és Années 1655. & 1656.

Enuoyée au R. P. LOVYS CELLOT,
Prouincial de la Compagnie de IESVS,
en la Prouince de France.

A PARIS,
Chez SEBASTIEN CRAMOISY, Imprimeur
ordinaire du Roy, & de la Reyne,
ET
GABRIEL CRAMOISY, ruë S. Iacques,
aux Cicognes.

M. DC. LVII.
Auec Priuilege du Roy.

RELATION

OF WHAT OCCURRED

IN THE MISSION OF THE FATHERS
OF THE SOCIETY OF JESUS,

IN THE COUNTRY

OF NEW FRANCE,

in the Years 1655 and 1656.

Sent to Rev. Father LOUYS CELLOT,
Provincial of the Society of JESUS
in the Province of France.

PARIS,
SEBASTIEN CRAMOISY, Printer in
ordinary to the King and Queen,
AND
GABRIEL CRAMOISY, ruë St. Jacques,
at the Sign of the Storks.

M. DC. LVII.
By Royal License.

Table des Chapitres contenus en ce Liure.

Table of the Chapters contained in this Book.

Extraict du Priuilege du Roy.

PAR grace & Priuilege du Roy, il eſt permis à
SEBASTIEN CRAMOISY, Marchand Libraire
Iuré en l'Vniuerſité de Paris, Imprimeur ordi-
naire du Roy, & de la Reine, Directeur de l'Imprimerie
Royalle du Louure, Bourgeois & Ancien Eſcheuin de
Paris, d'imprimer ou faire imprimer, vendre & debi-
ter vn Liure intitulé, *La Relation de ce qui s'eſt paſſé*
en la Miſſion des Peres de la Compagnie de IESVS, *au*
Païs de la Nouuelle France, és années 1655. & 1656. &c.
Et ce pendant le temps & eſpace de ſept années con-
ſecutiues.   Auec defenſes à tous Libraires, Impri-
meurs, & autres, d'imprimer ou faire imprimer ledit
Liure, ſous pretexte de déguiſement ou changement
qu'ils y pourroient faire ; aux peines portées par ledit
Priuilege.   DONNÉ à Paris le 23. Decembre 1656.
Signé, Par le ROY en ſon Conſeil,

CRAMOISY.

Extract from the Royal License.

BY grace and License of the King, permission is granted to SEBASTIEN CRAMOISY, Bookseller under Oath in the University of Paris, Printer in ordinary to the King and Queen, Director of the Royal Printing-house of the Louvre, Citizen and Former Alderman of Paris, to print or cause to be printed, sold, and retailed, a Book entitled, *La Relation de ce qui s'est passé en la Mission des Peres de la Compagnie de* JESUS, *au Païs de la Nouvelle France, és années* 1655. *et* 1656. *etc.* And this during the time and space of seven consecutive years, forbidding all Booksellers, Printers, and other persons to print or cause to be printed the said Book, under pretext of any disguise or change that they might make therein, under the penalties provided by said License. GIVEN at Paris, December 23, 1656. Signed, By the KING in his Council,

CRAMOISY.

Permiſsion du R. P. Prouincial.

NOUS Lovys Cellot, Prouincial de la Compagnie de Iesvs, en la Prouince de France, auons accordé pour l'aduenir au ſieur Sebastien Cramoisy, Marchand Libraire, Imprimeur ordinaire du Roy & de la Reine, Directeur de l'Imprimerie Royalle du Louure, Bourgeois & Ancien Eſcheuin de cette Ville de Paris, l'impreſſion des Relations de la Nouuelle France. Fait à Paris ce 28. Decembre 1656.

Signé, Lovys Cellot.

Permission of the Rev. Father Provincial.

W E, LOUYS CELLOT, Provincial of the Society
of JESUS in the Province of France, have
for the future granted permission to sieur
SEBASTIEN CRAMOISY, Bookseller, Printer in
ordinary to the King and Queen, Director of the
Royal Printing-house of the Louvre, Citizen and
Former Alderman of this City of Paris, to print the
Relations of New France. Done at Paris, this 28th
of December, 1656.

Signed, LOUYS CELLOT.

[1] Relation de ce qvi s'eſt paſſé en la Miſſion
des Peres de la Compagnie de I E S V S,
au Païs de la Nouuelle France,
és années 1655. & 1656.

Envoyée av R. P. Lovys Cellot Prouincial de la Compagnie de
I ᴇsᴠs en la Prouince de France.

M ON R. P.
Pax Chriſti,
Comme les Semaines ſont compoſées de iours, &
de nuits: les Saiſons, de froid & de chaud; de pluyes [2]
& de beaux temps: ainſi pouuons nous dire, que noſtre
année n'a eſté qu'vn mélange de ioyes, & de triſteſſes; de
bons & de mauuais ſuccés. De ſçauoir qui des deux a
emporté le deſſus: i'en laiſſe le iugement à V. R. & à tous
ceux, à qui l'eſtat de nos Miſſions, que ie luy enuoye, ſera
communiqué.

On n'auoit point veu depuis vingt ans, les vaiſſeaux
arriuer de ſi bonne heure en ce païs cy, ny en plus grand
nombre. On en a veu cinq ou ſix tout à la fois moüiller à
la rade de Kebec, & cela dés le beau commencement du mois
de Iuin. Voila noſtre ioye, commune auec tous les habitans
du païs. Mais n'ayant rencontré aucun de nos Peres
dans les vaiſſeaux, qui nous vint ſecourir en la conqueſte
des ames, nous en auons reſſenty vne triſteſſe toute
particuliere.

Au mois de Septembre de l'année derniere 1655. *deux*
de nos Peres monterent [3] *au païs des Iroquois Onontae-*
ronons, pour donner commencement à vne nouuelle Miſſion,

[1] Relation of what occurred in the Mission of
the Fathers of the Society of JESUS, in
the Country of New France, in
the years 1655 and 1656.

*Sent to the Rev. Father Louys Cellot, Provincial of the Society of
JESUS in the Province of France.*

M Y REVEREND FATHER,
            Pax Christi.

*As the Weeks are composed of both days and
nights; the Seasons, of heat and cold, of rain* [2] *and
shine; so also we may say, our year has been but a
mingling of joys and sorrows, of successes and failures.
To decide which of the two has predominated, I leave to
Your Reverence and to all those to whom the state of our
Missions — an account of which I send you herewith —
shall be communicated.*

*For twenty years past, vessels have not reached this
country so early, or in greater number.   Five or six at a
time were seen anchored in the roadstead at Kebec, — and
that in the very beginning of the month of June, — to our
own delight and that of the entire country.   But, not
finding in the vessels a single one of our Fathers come to
help us in the conquest of souls, we were very keenly
disappointed.*

*In the month of September of last year, 1655, two of
our Fathers went up* [3] *to the country of the Onontaeronon
Iroquois, to start a new Mission among people who, after
killing, slaughtering, burning, and eating us, came to*

parmy des peuples, qui apres nous auoir tuez, maſſacrez,
bruſlez, & mangez, nous venoient rechercher.   Le ſuccés
de cette entrepriſe, nous a donné de la crainte pendant tout
l'Hyuer; mais le retour de l'vn des deux Peres au Printemps
dernier, accompagné de quelques Capitaines Iroquois, a
changé cette crainte en quelque aſſeurance, qui nous fait
eſperer vn bon ſuccés de cette entrepriſe.

Cette eſperance s'eſt notablement accreuë, par le zele, &
par le courage, de quatre de nos Peres, & de deux de nos
Freres, et de cinquante ieunes François, qui ſont allez ietter
les fondemens d'vne nouuelle Egliſe, en vn lieu où le
Demon, & la cruauté, ont regné, peut-eſtre depuis le
Deluge.   Les Iroquois Onontaeronons qui nous eſtoiẽt venus
viſiter, triomphoient d'aiſe, voyant que nous ſecondions
[4] leurs deſſeins.   La ioye, qui paroiſſoit ſur leur viſage,
& dans leurs paroles, redondoit dans nos cœurs.   Mais
cette feſte fut bien toſt troublée, par le maſſacre, & par la
priſe de ſoixante & onze Hurons Chrétiens, partie enleuez,
partie aſſommez, par les Iroquois Agneronons, dans l'Iſle
d'Orleans, à deux lieuës de Kebec.   Voyla vn grand
mélange de bien & de mal, de ioye & de triſteſſe.

Sur la fin du mois d'Aouſt, nous viſmes paroiſtre
cinquante Canots, & deux cens cinquante Sauuages, chargez
des treſors du païs, qui venoient trafiquer auec les
François, & demander des Peres de noſtre Compagnie, pour
les aller inſtruire, dans les épaiſſes Foreſts de leur païs,
éloignées cinq cens lieuës de Kebec.   A la veuë d'vn ſi beau
iour, on oublie toutes les mauuaiſes nuits paſßées, deux de
nos Peres & vn de nos Freres s'embarquent auec trente
François; mais les Agneronons, [5] que nous appellons les
Iroquois inferieurs, qui n'ont iamais voulu de paix auec
nos Alliez, couperent en vn moment le fil de nos eſperances,
attaquant ces pauures peuples à leur retour, & tuans l'vn

*solicit our services. During the entire Winter, we were
apprehensive of the failure of this enterprise; but last
Spring the return of one of the two Fathers, accompanied
by several Iroquois Captains, changed this fear into some
confidence, which led us to hope for success in the undertaking.*

*This hope was notably increased by the zeal and courage
exhibited by four of our Fathers, two of our Brethren, and
fifty young Frenchmen, who went to lay the foundations of
a new Church in a place where the Evil One and cruelty
have reigned, perhaps, ever since the Deluge. The
Onontaeronon Iroquois, who had come to visit us, exulted
with joy on seeing us favor [4] their purpose; and their
delight, as shown in word and look, overflowed into our
own hearts. But this joyous mood soon became clouded by
the massacre or capture of seventy-one Christian Hurons,
killed or seized by the Agneronon Iroquois on the Island of
Orleans, two leagues from Kebec. Ours was a mingled
portion of good and ill, of joy and sorrow.*

*Toward the end of the month of August, we perceived
fifty Canoes and two hundred and fifty Savages
approaching, laden with the treasures of the country.
They were coming to trade with the French, and to ask for
Fathers of our Society to go and teach them in their dense
Forests, five hundred leagues distant from Kebec. In the
face of so pleasant a day, we forgot all the unpleasant
nights of the past. Two of our Fathers and one of our
Brethren embarked, with thirty Frenchmen; but the
Agneronons —[5] whom we call the lower Iroquois, and
who have never consented to make peace with our Allies —
cut the thread of our hopes in a moment by attacking these
unfortunate people, on their return, and killing one of the
two Fathers who were going to preach the Gospel to them
in their country.*

des deux Peres, qui leur alloient preſcher l'Euangile dans leur païs.

   Vous voyez bien, que nous pouuons dire auec verité, que les iours de cette derniere année ont eſté boni & mali, *bons & mauuais, comme les iours de Iacob. Diſons pluſtoſt, qu'ils ont tous eſté bons, puis qu'ils ſe ſont paſſez en la Croix. Nous auons cette conſolation, que c'eſt la querelle de Ieſus-Chriſt, & ſon Euangile, qui eſt la cauſe de nos trauaux, & qui nous oſte la vie. Nous ne nous eſtonnons point à la veuë de noſtre ſang. Notre douleur & noſtre triſteſſe eſt noſtre petit nombre, nous crions à l'aide, & au ſecours, & nous croyons que V. R. entendra nos cris, & nos voix, quoy que pouſſez* [6] *de bien loin, & qu'elle nous enuoyera ſix braues Peres au prochain embarquement, gens de cœur, qui ne s'effrayent point à la veuë de mille morts, qu'il faut tous les iours ſubir, en cherchant des Barbares dans les tanieres de leurs grands bois. Nous la prions inſtamment de nous accorder noſtre demande, & de nous ſecourir de ſes prieres, & de celles de tous nos Peres & Freres de ſa Prouince.*

      De V. R.

A Kebec ce 7.   Le tres-humble, & tres-obeïſſant
Septembre 1656.   ſeruiteur en Noſtre Seigneur,

                  Iean de Qvens.

You see plainly with what truth we can say that the days of this past year have been boni et mali — "*good and evil,*" *like the days of Jacob. Yet, let us say rather, that they have all been good, since they have been filled with Crosses. We have this consolation, that it is the cause of Jesus Christ and his Gospel that gives rise to our labors and loss of life. We are not startled at the sight of our own blood. Our small number causes us grief and sadness; we cry for help and succor, and we believe that Your Reverence will hear our appeal, although uttered* [6] *from afar; and that you will send us, by the next ship, six valiant Fathers, men of courage, who are not afraid to face a thousand deaths, which danger must every day be undergone in seeking Barbarians in the lairs of their vast forests. We pray you earnestly to grant our request, and entreat that we may receive the aid of your prayers and of those of all our Fathers and Brethren in your Province.*

YOUR REVERENCE'S

Kebec, this 7th of   Very humble and very obedient
September, 1656.   servant in Our Lord,

JEAN DE QUENS.

[7] CHAPITRE I.

VOYAGE DU PERE SIMON LE MOYNE AUX IROQUOIS
AGNIERONNONS.

I L auoit efté iugé neceffaire, dés l'Efté de l'année
derniere 1655, d'enuoyer vn Pere de noftre Compagnie dans le païs des Iroquois Agnieronnons,
pour affermir la paix auec eux; par ce témoignage
de confience & d'amour.   Le fort eftant heureufement tombé fur le Pere Simon le Moyne, il partit
pour cét effet de Montreal, le dix-feptiéme iour
d'Aouft, auec douze Iroquois, & deux François.
  C'eft vn chemin de Precipices, de lacs & de riuieres:
de chaffe, de peche, de fatigue, & de recreation,
felon les lieux où on fe retrouue.   Nos voyageurs
tuërent bien-toft apres leur depart dix-huit Vaches
fauuages, en moins d'vne heure, en des Prairies que
la nature feule a preparées à ces troupeaux, qui font
fans maiftre.   Ils firent naufrage vn peu plus [8]
loin, dans vn torrent impetueux, qui les porta dans
vne baye, où ils trouuerent vn calme le plus doux du
monde.   La faim les accueille à quelques iournées
de là, qui leur fit trouuer bon tout ce qu'ils prenoient
à la chaffe; tantoft vn Loup, ou vn Chat fauuage;
tantoft vn Ours ou vn Renard; en vn mot quelque
befte que ce fut.   Ils font quelquefois obligez de fe
coucher, n'ayant beu que de l'eau boüillie, détrempée
de terre & d'argile: les fruits fauuages n'ont plus
pour lors d'amertume, ils paroiffent delicieux au
gouft, à qui la faim fert d'vn bon fucre.

[7] CHAPTER I.

JOURNEY OF FATHER SIMON LE MOYNE TO THE AGNIERONNON IROQUOIS.

IN the Summer of last year, 1655, it was thought necessary to send a Father of our Society into the country of the Agnieronnon Iroquois, in order that we might, by this show of friendship and confidence, confirm the peace with them. The lot having fortunately fallen upon Father Simon le Moyne, he left Montreal on this errand, on the seventeenth day of August, with twelve Iroquois and two Frenchmen.

The route is one of Precipices, lakes, and rivers, of hunting and fishing, of weariness and recreation, varying in different parts. Soon after their departure, our travelers killed eighteen wild Cows within less than an hour, on Prairies prepared by nature alone for those ownerless herds. They were wrecked, a little farther [8] on, in an impetuous torrent, which carried them into a bay where they found the gentlest calm in the world. Some days' journey, hence, hunger overtook them and made them relish all that they took in hunting, whether a Wolf or a Wildcat, a Bear or a Fox,— in short, any animal whatever. They were sometimes forced to lie down at night with no refreshment but boiled water, mixed with earth and clay. Wild fruits lost their bitterness, and seemed delicious to the taste, hunger serving excellently to sweeten them.

Le Pere arriua dans le bourg d'Agniée le dix-
feptiéme iour de Septembre.   On l'y reçoit auec des
careffes extraordinaires, & on luy prefente à l'abord
trois colliers de pourcelaine.   Le premier, pour
arrefter le fang, qui fe pourroit répandre en chemin,
& qui luy cauferoit des frayeurs: c'eft à dire, qu'il
ne deuoit point craindre qu'on le tuaft traitreufe-
ment.   Le fecond, pour conforter fon cœur, & empefcher qu'aucune émotion ne luy peuft troubler fon
repos.   Enfin, [9] il falloit luy lauer les pieds d'vn
baulme precieux, pour adoucir les fatigues d'vn fi long
voyage: & ce fut le troifiéme collier de pourcelaine.

Le iour fuiuant tout le peuple eftant affemblé dans
la place publique, le Pere expofa les prefens qu'il
apportoit de la part d'Onnontio, Gouuerneur du Païs.
Et au lieu de commencer cette action par vn chant à
leur ordinaire; il adreffa fa parole à Dieu, à haute
voix, & dans la langue du païs, le prenant à témoin
de la fincerité de fon cœur, & le coniurant de prendre
la vengeance de ceux qui faufferoient leur foy, & qui
contreuiendroient à vne parole donnée fi folemnelle-
ment à la veuë du Soleil & du Ciel.   Ce qui agrea
puiffamment à ces peuples.

Vn des Capitaines Iroquois fit paroître à fon tour
de tres-riches prefens, pour refpondre à tous les
articles de paix que le Pere auoit propofez.   Le plus
beau & le premier de ces prefens, eftoit vne grande
figure du Soleil, faite de fix mil grains de pourcelaine; afin, dit-il, que les tenebres n'ayent point de
part à [10] nos confeils, & que le Soleil les éclaire,
mefme dans le plus profond de la nuit.

Ces Nations ne font compofées que de fourbes, &
toutefois il faut fe confier à leur inconftance, &

The Father reached the village of Agniée on the seventeenth of September, and was received with extraordinary cordiality, being presented at the outset with three porcelain collars. The first was to check any possible bloodshed on the way, which might alarm him,— that is, he was not to fear death by treachery. The second was to cheer his heart, and prevent any emotion from disturbing his rest. Finally, [9] they must needs anoint his feet with a precious balm, to allay the fatigues of so long a journey; and such was the purpose of the third porcelain collar.

On the following day, when all the people had assembled in the public place, the Father displayed the presents brought by him from Onnontio, Governor of the Country. Instead of beginning this ceremony with a song, as is their custom, he invoked God in a loud voice and in the language of the country,— calling him to witness the sincerity of his heart; and entreating him to take vengeance on those who should violate their faith, and break a promise given so solemnly in the sight of the Sun and of Heaven. This greatly pleased these people.

One of the Iroquois Captains exhibited, in his turn, some very rich presents, in answer to the various articles of peace proposed by the Father. The first and finest of these presents was a large image of the Sun, made of six thousand porcelain beads,— its purpose being, as he said, to dispel all darkness from [10] our councils, and to let the Sun illumine them even in the deepest gloom of night.

These Nations are composed only of rogues, and yet we must trust ourselves to their fickleness, and surrender ourselves to their cruelty. Father Isaac

s'abandonner à leur cruauté. Le Pere Iſaac Iogues
fut aſſommé de ces perfides, lors qu'ils luy témoi-
gnoient plus d'amour. Mais puis que Ieſus-Chriſt a
enuoyé ſes Apoſtres, comme des Agneaux entre des
loups, pour faire d'vn loup vn Agneau, nous ne deuons
pas craindre d'abandonner nos vies en ſemblables
rencontres, pour mettre la Paix & la Foy, où la guerre
& l'infidelité ont touſiours eſté dans leur regne.

Ce conſeil s'eſtant paſſé dans des agrémens reciproques, le Pere prit deſſein de pouſſer iuſques à la
Nouuelle Hollande, à dix ou douze lieuës de-là. Vne
Chreſtienne Hurone, captiue des Iroquois depuis ſix
ans, l'attendoit en chemin auec vne ſainte impatience,
& le receut auec ioye, luy apportant vne petite innocente à baptizer, que Dieu luy auoit donnée dans ſa
captiuité, & qu'elle nourriſſoit pour le Ciel. C'eſt
[11] vne conſolation bien ſenſible, de recueillir ces
fruits du Sang de Ieſus-Chriſt, dans vn païs barbare,
au milieu de l'infidelité. Le compliment que luy fit
vne bonne femme, ne ſent rien de la barbarie. Ta
venuë, luy dit-elle, nous réjoüit iuſques au fond de
l'ame: nos plus petits enfans en ſont ſi aiſes, qu'ils
en vont croiſtre à veuë d'œil: & ceux meſme qui ne
ſont pas encore nez, ſautent de réjoüiſſance dans le
ventre de leurs meres, & ils veulent en ſortir au
pluſtoſt, pour auoir le bien de te voir.

Le Pere fut receu auec de grands témoignages
d'affection de la part des Hollandois, où nouuellement
il eſtoit arriué vn grand malheur. Quelques Sauuages voiſins de Manathe, qui eſt la place principale
de la Nouuelle Hollande, ayant pris querelle auec vn
Hollandois, & en eſtant venus aux mains, ils furent
aſſez mal traitez; deux ou trois de leurs gens y eſtans
demeurez ſur la place. Pour ſe vanger de cette

Jogues was killed by those traitors while they were showing him the most love.   But, since Jesus Christ sent his Apostles as Lambs among wolves, to convert them into Lambs, we should not fear to lay down our lives in like circumstances, for the sake of establishing Peace and the Faith where war and infidelity have always held sway.

After this council, which passed in many exchanges of courtesy, the Father determined to push on as far as New Holland, ten or twelve leagues beyond.   A Huron woman — a Christian, and for six years a captive among the Iroquois — was awaiting him on the way with holy impatience, and received him with joy, bringing him a little innocent to baptize, whom God had given her in her captivity, and whom she was rearing for Heaven.   It is [11] a very lively satisfaction to pluck these fruits of the Blood of Jesus Christ, in a barbarous country, and in the midst of infidelity.   The compliment paid the Father by a good woman has no savor of barbarism. '' Thy coming,'' she said to him, '' makes us glad in our inmost souls; our smallest children are so rejoiced that they begin to grow before our eyes; and even those not yet born leap with joy in their mothers' wombs, and wish to come forth at the earliest moment, to be blessed in seeing thee.''

The Father was received with great demonstrations of affection by the Dutch, who had recently met with a serious disaster.   Some Savages living near Manathe, the chief town of New Holland, in a quarrel with a Dutchman had come to blows, and had fared ill, leaving two or three of their men upon the spot.   To revenge this grievance, the Savages rallied, to the number of about two hundred, and fired a

iniure, ces Sauuages ſe r'allierent enuiron deux cens,
& mirent le feu à vne vingtaine de Métairies écartées
çà & là; maſſacrant ceux [12] qui faiſoient quelque
reſiſtance, & menant les autres captifs, hommes,
femmes & enfans, iuſques au nombre d'enuiron cent
cinquante. Nous ne ſçauons pas quelle ſuite aura
eu cette affaire.

Au retour de ce voyage de la Nouuelle Hollande,
le Pere ſe vit en grand danger d'eſtre la victime d'vn
demon d'enfer, ou d'vn homme qui contrefaiſoit le
Demoniacle; courant comme vn enragé par les
cabanes, & chantant d'vn ton animé de fureur, qu'il
vouloit tuer Ondeſonk: (c'eſtoit le nom du Pere.) Il
romp, il briſe tout, & approchant du Pere, la hache
en main, l'ayant hauſſée pour ramener ſon coup,
comme voulant luy fendre la teſte, il eſt arreſté au
moment de cet attentat. Il continuë toutefois ſa
fureur, & ſon chant funeſte, iuſques à ce qu'vne
femme Iroquoiſe luy dit, Tuë mon chien, & qu'il
ſoit la victime en la place d'Ondeſonk, car il eſt trop
de nos amys. A ce mot, il s'appaiſe, il fend la teſte
de cét animal d'vn coup de hache, & le porte par
tout, comme en triomphe.

Le lendemain matin, les parens de ce [13] furieux
apporterent vn preſent de pourcelaine au Pere, pour
eſſuyer, luy diſoient-ils, la pouſſiere de la nuit; car
c'eſtoit dans l'horreur des tenebres que cecy eſtoit
arriué.

Il faut parmy ces peuples, eſtre toûjours en crainte,
ſans craindre toutefois, puis qu'vn cheueu ne tombera
pas de nos teſtes, ſans la permiſſion de celuy, qui
nous conſerue entre ſes bras, & qui a le ſoin de nos
vies, d'autant plus que nous les abandonnons pour
les intereſts de ſa gloire.

score of small Farms scattered here and there,
slaughtering those [12] who resisted, and carrying
the rest — men, women, and children, about a
hundred and fifty in all — into captivity. We do not
know how the affair terminated.

Upon his return from this journey to New Holland, the Father was in great danger of falling a
victim to a demon of hell, or a man who pretended
to be possessed by a Demon, who ran through the
cabins like a madman, and sang in a tone of frenzy
that he was bent on killing Ondesonk (for so was the
Father called). Demolishing everything in his path,
he approached the Father, hatchet in hand; he was
stopped in the act of raising it to deal a blow,
apparently intending to split his head. But he continued his frenzy and his direful chant, until an
Iroquois woman said to him: " Kill my dog, and
let him be the victim instead of Ondesonk; for he is
too great a friend of ours."   At these words he grew
calm; and, cleaving the animal's head with a hatchet-
stroke, he bore it around, as if in triumph.

On the following morning, the madman's relatives
[13] brought the Father a present of porcelain,— to
wipe away the dust of the night, as they told him;
for all this had occurred in the dread hours of
darkness.

Among these people one must be ever in fear,
and yet fear nothing; for not a hair shall fall from
our heads without the permission of him who
holds us in his hand and cares for our lives —
and still less, if we surrender them to advance his
glory.

A Huron Christian, captured a year before by the
Iroquois, suffered something worse than fear; his

Vn Chreſtien Huron, captif des Iroquois depuis vn an, n'en fut pas quitte de la ſeule peur. On luy fendit la teſte, ſans autre forme de procez, ſous vn ſimple ſoupçon, qu'il auoit declaré au Pere, quelques deſſeins qu'ils vouloient luy tenir cachez.

Cela n'empeſcha pas le retour du Pere, & des deux François ſes compagnons: à qui trois Iroquois ſe ioignirent, pour leur ſeruir d'eſcorte, & de guide. L'Hyuer eſtant trop auancé, il y eut beaucoup à ſouffrir, principalement depuis le rencontre qu'ils firent de quelques [14] Iroquois Agnieronnõs, qui auoient eſté pourſuiuis par vne bande d'Algonquins, qui auoient pris trois de leurs compagnons captifs. Cette crainte des Algonquins, dont ils redoutoient le rencontre, obligea nos voyageurs à quitter leurs canots, & quaſi tout leur equipage, pour ſe ietter dans vne ſapiniere perduë, où il n'y auoit ny chemin, ny route; tout n'eſtant rien que mareſcages d'eaux croupiſſantes à demy-glacées. Par mal heur, le Ciel ſe couurit, & le Soleil s'eſtant caché, qui ſert de bouſſole & de conduite à tous ces peuples, dans les bois, ils s'égarerent entierement. La nuit les obligea de s'arreſter au pied d'vn arbre, dont les racines & vn peu de mouſſe, les empeſcha de coucher dans l'eau: c'eſtoit le neufiéme iour du mois de Nouembre.

Le lendemain il faut marcher dés la pointe du iour, dans vn temps pluuieux, & à trauers ces mareſcages, dont ils ne trouuent aucune iſſuë, ſinon bien proche de la nuit. Eſtans ſortis de là, ce ne ſont que ruiſſeaux, & que terres mouuantes, où ils enfoncent dans la bouë [15] iuſques au genoüil. Ils ſe voyent enfin arreſtez d'vne grande riuiere & profonde. Ils couppent

head was split without ceremony, upon a mere sus-
picion that he had revealed to the Father certain
purposes of theirs which they wished to conceal
from him.

The occurrence did not hinder the return of the
Father and of the two Frenchmen, his companions,
three Iroquois joining them as escort and guides.
As the Winter was far advanced, much suffering was
experienced, especially after meeting with some [14]
Agnieronnon Iroquois, who had been pursued by
an Algonquin band that had captured three of their
companions. This fear of the Algonquins, whom
they dreaded to encounter, compelled our travelers
to abandon their canoes and almost all their baggage, and to take refuge in a pathless fir forest, where
they found nothing but marshes of stagnant and
half-frozen water. Unluckily, the Sky became
clouded; and, as the Sun, the universal compass and
guide of these peoples, was hidden, they utterly lost
their way in the woods. Night compelled them to
halt at the foot of a tree, but for whose roots and a
little moss they would have lain in the water. This
was on the ninth day of November.

The next day, they were forced to proceed at
daybreak, in the rain, across those marshes, whence
they found no outlet until very near night-time.
Issuing thence, they encountered only streams and
boggy ground, where they sank in the mud [15] up
to their knees. At the end, they found their way
obstructed by a wide and deep river. Immediately
they felled five or six trees of suitable size, and
pushed them into the water, where they lashed them
together, making therefrom a raft,—as it were, a
floating bridge; on this they crossed the river, using

incontinent cinq ou fix arbres d'vne iufte grandeur, qu'ils pouffent en l'eau; & les ayant liez enfemble, ils en font vn cayeux, & comme vn pont flottant, fur lequel ils paffent cette riuiere, auec de longues perches, qui leur feruent de rames & d'auirons; tout cela, fans auoir dequoy faire vn demy-repas.

Le iour d'apres, ils ne voyent pas plus clair dans leurs égaremens, quoy que de temps en temps, ils montent au haut des arbres, pour reconnoiftre le païs: finon fur le foir, qu'ils arriuerent au bord d'vn ruiffeau, qui leur eftoit connû; mais où toutefois ils ne trouuerent rien de quoy manger.

Enfin, le quatriéme iour de leur long égarement, de leurs grandes fatigues, & de la cruelle faim qui les fuiuoit par tout, ils arriuerent à la veuë de Montreal, de l'autre bord de la riuiere, où ayant fait du feu, & ayant tiré trois ou quatre coups de fufil, pour donner aduis de leur retour, la charité de nos François fut [16] prompte à leur porter quelque fecours, & à les repaffer en canot, au lieu d'où ils eftoient partis depuis prés de trois mois.

long poles which served as oars or paddles,— all this without having had a morsel to eat.

On the next day, although they occasionally climbed trees, to reconnoiter the country, they were just as much at a loss as ever. But, toward evening, they came to a stream that was known to them,— where, however, they found nothing to eat.

At length, on the fourth day of their long wandering, of their sore weariness, and of the cruel hunger which ever pursued them, they came in sight of Montreal, on the opposite bank of the river. When they had made a fire and discharged three or four musket-shots in announcement of their return, our French people's charity was [16] prompt to succor them, and to convey them by canoe back to the place whence they had started, nearly three months before.

CHAPITRE II.

AMBASSADE DES IROQUOIS ONONTAERONNONS, QUI
DEMANDENT DES PERES DE NOSTRE COM-
PAGNIE POUR SE FAIRE CHRESTIENS.

L ORS que le Pere Simon le Moyne fut enuoyé
aux Iroquois Agnieronnons, qui font plus
voifins de Montreal & de Kebec, & qui faifans
la Paix auec nous, ont toufiours continué dans les
deffeins de guerre, auec les Algonquins & les Hurons :
en mefme temps les Iroquois Onontaeronnons, qui
font plus éloignez, vinrent en Ambaffade de la part de
toutes les Nations Iroquoifes d'en-haut, pour l'affer-
miffement de la Paix, non feulement auec les Francois;
mais auffi auec les Algonquins & les Hurons.

[17] Ils eftoient dix-huit de compagnie en cette
ambaffade, qui pafferent par Montreal & par les trois
Riuieres, pour venir à Kebec, & pour y trouuer Monfieur de Laufon Gouuerneur du païs, & en fuite les
fauuages Algonquins & Hurons, qui y font leur
demeure.

Le temps du confeil eftant pris au douzieme de
Septembre 1655. iour de Dimanche, à l'heure de
midy, vn grand monde s'y trouua. Au milieu de
cette affemblée, le principal Ambaffadeur, qui portoit la parole, fit paroiftre vingt-quatre colliers de
pourcelaine; qui aux yeux des Sauuages, font les
perles & les diamans de ce païs.

Les huit premiers prefens s'adreffoient aux Hurons & aux Algonquins, dont les principaux chefs

CHAPTER II.

EMBASSY OF THE ONONTAERONNON IROQUOIS WHO
ASK FOR SOME FATHERS OF OUR SOCIETY TO
CONVERT THEM TO CHRISTIANITY.

A T the time when Father Simon le Moyne was
sent to the Agnieronnon Iroquois,—who are
nearer Montreal and Kebec, and who, while
making Peace with us, have never desisted from their
hostile designs on the Algonquins and Hurons,—the
Onontaeronnon Iroquois, who are more distant, came
on an Embassy representing all the upper Iroquois
Nations, to confirm the Peace, not only with the
French, but also with the Algonquins and Hurons.

[17] The delegation consisted of eighteen men,
who came to Kebec by way of Montreal and three
Rivers, to see Monsieur de Lauson, Governor of the
country, and also the Algonquin and Huron savages
living here.

A great crowd assembled on the date fixed for the
council,—Sunday, the twelfth of September, 1655,
at noon. In the midst of this assembly the chief
Ambassador, who acted as spokesman, displayed
twenty-four collars of porcelain—the pearls and
diamonds of this country, in the Savages' eyes.

The first eight presents were designed for the
Hurons and Algonquins, whose foremost chiefs were
in attendance. Each gift has a separate name of its
own, according to the impression which they wish
to produce upon the minds and hearts of others.

s'eftoient trouuez à l'affemblée. Chaque prefent a
fon nom different, felon les diuers effets qu'ils pre-
tendent imprimer dans les efprits & dans les cœurs.

C'eft trop pleuré, dit l'Ambaffadeur aux Hurons
& aux Algonquins, il eft temps d'effuyer les larmes,
que vous verfez en abondance, pour la mort de [18]
ceux que la guerre vous a enleuez. Voila vn mouchoir pour cét effet. Ce fut là fon premier prefent.

Le fecond, fut pour effuyer le fang qui auoit rougy
les montagnes, les lacs, & les riuieres, & qui crioit
vengeance contre ceux qui l'auoient refpandu.

I'arrache de vos mains la hache, les arcs, & les
fleches, dit-il, faifant paroiftre fon troifiéme prefent,
& pour couper le mal iufques à fa racine, i'arrache
toutes les penfées de guerre de voftre cœur.

Ces peuples croyent que la trifteffe & la colere, &
toutes les paffions violentes, chaffent l'ame raifonnable du corps, n'y ayant que l'ame fenfitiue, que
nous auons commune auec les beftes, qui y refte
durant ce temps-là. C'eft pourquoy en ces rencontres
ils font d'ordinaire vn prefent, pour remettre l'ame
raifonnable dans le fiege de la raifon, & ce fut le
quatriéme prefent.

Le cinquiéme, eftoit vn breuuage medicinal, pour
chaffer toute l'amertume de leur cœur, & les reftes
du fiel & de la bile, dont ils pourroient eftre irritez.

[19] Le fixiéme prefent, pour leur ouurir les oreilles
aux paroles de la verité, & aux promeffes d'vne
vraye paix, fçachant bien que la paffion rend lourds
& aueugles, ceux qui s'y laiffent emporter.

Le feptiéme prefent, pour donner affeurance que
les quatre Nations Iroquoifes d'en-haut, eftoient
dans les fentimens de la Paix, & que leur cœur ne
feroit iamais diuifé.

" You have wept too much," said the Ambassador
to the Hurons and Algonquins; " it is time to wipe
away the tears shed so plentifully by you over the
death of [18] those whom you have lost in war. Here
is a handkerchief for that purpose." Such was his
first present.

The purpose of the second was to wipe away the
blood which had crimsoned mountains, lakes, and
rivers, and which was crying for vengeance against
those who had shed it.

" I wrest from your hands hatchet, bows, and
arrows," said he, exhibiting his third present; "and,
to strike the evil at its root, I take away all thoughts
of war from your hearts."

These people believe that sadness, anger, and all
violent passions expel the rational soul from the
body, which, meanwhile, is animated only by the
sensitive soul which we have in common with animals.   That is why, on such occasions, they usually
make a present to restore the rational soul to the seat
of reason.   Such was the purpose of the fourth
present.

The fifth was a medicinal draught to expel from
their hearts all the bitterness, gall, and bile with
which they might still be irritated.

[19] The sixth present was to open their ears to the
words of truth and the promises of a genuine peace,
in the knowledge that passion stupefies and blinds
those who yield to it.

The seventh, to give assurance that the four upper
Iroquois Nations were Peacefully inclined, and that
their hearts would never be divided.

" There remains only the lower Iroquois, the
Agnieronnon, who cannot restrain his warlike spirit.

Il n'y a que l'Iroquois d'en-bas, **Agnieronnon**, qui
ne peut arrefter fon naturel guerrier.   Son efprit
eft toufiours en fougue, & fes mains fe nourriffent
de fang.   Nous luy ofterons la hache d'armes de la
main.   Nous reprimerons fa fureur: car il faut que
la Paix regne par tout en ce païs.   Ce fut là le
huictiéme prefent, & la derniere des paroles adreffées
aux Algonquins & aux Hurons.

Les fuiuantes eftoient pour les François, adreffées
à Monfieur noftre Gouuerneur, qu'ils nomment Onnontio.   Pour effuyer les larmes des François.   Pour
nettoyer le fang, qui auoit efté [20] refpandu.   Pour
calmer nos efprits.   Pour nous feruir de medecine,
& d'vn breuuage plus doux que le fucre & le miel.

Le treifiéme prefent fut, pour inuiter Monfieur
noftre Gouuerneur, à enuoyer vne efcoüade de François en leur païs, pour ne faire qu'vn peuple auec
nous, & affermir vne alliance femblable à celle que
nous contractafmes autresfois auec la Nation des
Hurons, nous y eftans habituez.

Le quatorziéme prefent.   Pour y auoir des Peres de
noftre Compagnie, qui enfeigneroient leurs enfans,
& en feroient vn peuple tout Chreftien.

En outre, ils demanderent des Soldats François,
qui deffendroient leurs bourgades contre l'irruption
de la Nation des Chats, auec lefquels ils font en
grande guerre.   Et ce fut là leur quinziéme prefent.

Le feiziéme eftoit.   Pour nous deftiner vne place
dans le centre de toutes leurs Nations, où nous efpe-
rons, fi Dieu fauorife nos entreprifes, d'y eriger vne
nouuelle fainte Marie, femblable à celle que nous
auons autrefois veuë fleurir au [21] milieu du païs
des Hurons.

His mind is ever inflamed, and his hands delight in blood. We will take the war-hatchet out of his hands, and check his fury; for the reign of Peace must be universal in this country." That was the eighth present, and the last of the words addressed to the Algonquins and Hurons.

The following were for the French, being addressed to Monsieur our Governor, whom they call Onnontio; one, to dry the tears of the French; another, to wash away the blood that had been [20] shed; another, to soothe our feelings; and the last, to serve us as a medicine, and as a draught sweeter than sugar and honey.

The thirteenth present was an invitation to Monsieur our Governor to send a company of Frenchmen to their country, in order to make but one people of us, and to confirm an alliance like that formerly contracted by us with the Huron Nation during our residence there.

The fourteenth was a request for some Fathers of our Society, to teach their children and make of them a thoroughly Christian people.

They further asked for French Soldiers, to defend their villages against the inroads of the Cat Nation, with whom they are at open war. That was their fifteenth present.

The object of the sixteenth present was to assign us a place in the center of all their Nations, where we hope, if God favor our undertakings, to build a new sainte Marie, like that whose prosperity we formerly witnessed in the [21] heart of the Huron country.

But, that the annoyances commonly attending the founding of a new settlement might not deter us,

Mais afin que les mefaifes qui accompagnent d'ordinaire les commencemens d'vne nouuelle habitation,
ne nous en détournaffent point, ils nous y eftendirent
vne natte, & des lits de campagne; fur lefquels nous
peuffions repofer plus doucement.

Le dix-huictiéme prefent, eftoit vn May, qu'ils
éleuoient iufques aux nuës, deuant cette maifon
nouuelle de faincte Marie.   Ils vouloient dire par ce
prefent, que le centre de la Paix, & le lieu où tous
les efprits deuoient fe reünir, feroit en cette maifon,
deuant laquelle ce grand May feroit erigé fi haut,
que l'on pourroit le voir de tous coftez, & que toutes
les Nations les plus éloignées y viendroient aborder.

Le dix-neufiéme prefent.   Pour attacher le Soleil
au haut du Ciel, au deffus de ce May, afin qu'il y
battit à plomb, & qu'il n'y euft point d'ombre : que
tous les confeils & les traitez qui s'y feroient, ne
fuffent point dans les tenebres de la nuit; mais que
tout y fuft en plein iour, éclairé du Soleil, qui voit
tout, & qui [22] n'a que de l'horreur pour les trahi-
fons, qui fe plaifent à l'obfcurité.

En fuite, ils allumerent vn feu, pour tous ceux
qui iroient en ce lieu là nous vifiter.

Le vingt-vniéme prefent, affermiffoit les bras d'Onnontio.   C'eft à dire, que Monfieur noftre Gouuerneur, ayant cy-deuant protegé dans fon fein les
Algonquins & les Hurons, auec autant d'amour
qu'vne mere tient fon enfant entre fes bras; il eften-
dit auffi fur eux des foins & des amours de Pere.
C'eft toy, Onnontio, dirent-ils, à Monfieur le Gouuerneur, qui as fouftenu la vie à toutes les Nations
qui te font alliées, & qui fe font iettées entre tes
bras.   Serre-les étroitement, & ne te laffe pas de les

they spread out a mat and some camp-beds for our greater comfort and repose.

The eighteenth present was a May-tree, which they erected in front of that new house of sainte Marie, so high that it reached the clouds. By this they meant that the center of the Peace, and the place for general reunions, would be in that house, before which should be erected this great May-tree, so lofty that it could be seen from every direction, and all the Nations, even those most distant, could come to it.

The purpose of the nineteenth present was to fix the Sun high in the Heavens above this May-tree,— so as to shine directly down upon it, and admit of no shadow,— in order that all councils held and treaties concluded there might take place, not in the obscurity of night, but in open day, lighted by the Sun, which sees all things and [22] has only abhorrence for trea- sonable plots, which court darkness.

They next lighted a fire for all who should visit us in that place.

The twenty-first present strengthened Onnontio's arms,— that is, as Monsieur our Governor had hitherto cherished the Algonquins and Hurons in his bosom, with all the love of a mother holding her child in her arms, he now extended to the Iroquois also a Father's care and love. "Thou, Onnontio," they said to Monsieur the Governor, "hast sustained life in all the Nations that became thy allies and took refuge in thy arms. Clasp them more firmly, and weary not of embracing them; let them live within thy bosom, for thou art the Father of the country."

The twenty-second present assured us that the

embraffer; qu'elles viuent en ton fein, car tu es le
Pere du païs.

Le vingt-deuxiéme prefent, nous affeuroit que les
quatre Nations Iroquoifes d'en-haut, n'eftoient qu'vn
cœur, & n'auoient plus qu'vne penfée, dans vn defir
fincere de la Paix.

Apres cela, ils demanderent des armes contre la
Nation des Chats.

[23] Enfin, le dernier des prefens, fut fait par vn
Capitaine Huron, ancien captif des Iroquois, & maintenant Capitaine chez eux.   Cét homme fe leua, le
Chef de l'Ambaffade ayant finy.   Mes freres, dit-il
aux Hurons, ie n'ay point changé d'ame pour auoir
changé de païs: & mon fang n'eft pas deuenu Iroquois, quoy que i'habite parmy eux.   Mon cœur eft
tout Huron, autant que ma langue.   Ie me tiendrois
dans le filence, s'il y auoit quelque fourbe en cette
Paix, dont on vous porte la parole.   L'affaire eft
bonne, embraffez-la fans deffiance.   Difant cela, il
leur donne vn collier, comme le feau de fa parole,
pour affeurance qu'ils n'eftoient pas trompez.

Il euft fallu refpondre à tous ces prefens par d'autres reciproques, n'eftoit que nous eftions dans le
deffein d'enuoyer en leur pays deux de nos Peres,
pour entrer plus auant dans leur cœur, & pour ne
rien épargner en vne affaire de telle confequence.
Cét heureux partage tõba fur le Pere Iofeph Chaumont, & fur le Pere Claude Dablon: le premier [24]
poffede la langue, le cœur & l'efprit des Sauuages.
Le fecond eft nouuellement venu de France, dans le
deffein & dans les defirs de cette Miffion.

Nos efprits auoient efté puiffamment partagez, fi
nous expoferions nos Peres à cette nouuelle occafion,

four upper Iroquois Nations had but one heart and one mind in their sincere desire for Peace.

After that, they asked for weapons against the Cat Nation.

[23] Finally, the last of the presents was offered by a Huron Captain, formerly a captive of the Iroquois, and now a Captain among them. This man, rising after the Chief of the Embassy had finished, addressed the Hurons as follows: '' My brothers, I have not changed my soul, despite my change of country; nor has my blood become Iroquois, although I dwell among them. My heart is all Huron, as well as my tongue. I would keep silence, were there any deceit in these negotiations for Peace. Our proposals are honest; embrace them without distrust.'' Thus speaking, he gave them a collar, as the seal of his pledge, and to assure them that they were not deceived.

A response in kind to all these presents would have been necessary, had we not purposed sending to their country two of our Fathers to enlist their more cordial support, and to spare no effort in promoting so important an enterprise. This blessed lot fell on Fathers Joseph Chaumont and Claude Dablon, of whom the former [24] knows the language and commands the sympathies of the Savages; while the latter has recently come from France, with heart and soul bent upon this Mission.

Our minds had been greatly divided regarding the propriety of exposing our Fathers to this new risk before the return of Father Simon le Moyne, who was still in the hands of the Agnieronnon Iroquois. For nothing would have been more in accord with the disposition of those Nations,— treacherous as they

auant le retour du Pere Simon le Moyne, qui eſtoit
encore entre les mains des Iroquois Agnieronnons.
Car comme ces Nations ſont perfides, il n'y a rien de
plus conforme à leur genie, qu'ayant ſur nous de ſi
grands auantages, en des perſonnes qu'elles ſçauent
bien nous eſtre cheres & precieuſes, elles viennent
fondre ſur nous, ſur nos Hurons & ſur nos Algonquins, lors que l'on ne ſeroit plus dans la crainte, &
que les penſées de la Paix, auroient oſté à la pluſpart
les deffiances de la guerre.   Toutefois le ſentiment
de Monſieur noſtre Gouuerneur, fut qu'il falloit tout
hazarder, pour tout gagner, eſtant à craindre que ſi
nous perdions cette occaſion, ce ne fut vne rupture
de la Paix, témoignant trop nos deffiances.   Son conſeil ſe trouua dans les meſmes penſées; & nos Peres,
ſur leſquels deuoit [25] tomber cét heureux ſort, ne
doutoient point qu'il ne fallut partir, y allant des
intereſts de la gloire de Dieu, & du ſalut des ames,
dont les Anges nous appelloient à leur ſecours, &
pour leſquels la charité de Ieſus-chriſt nous doit
preſſer.

Enfin nos Peres & ces Ambaſſadeurs; nous quit-
terent le dix-neufiéme de Septembre.   Ie ne ſçaurois
plus fidelement expoſer la ſuitte de leur voyage, &
les fruits que Dieu en a tirés, que par le iournal que
le Pere Dablon nous en a écrit.

are, and having such an advantage over us in the
possession of men whom they well knew to be dear
and precious to us,—than to fall upon us and our
Hurons and Algonquins, when we were no longer
fearing them and when thoughts of Peace had, in
most minds, displaced hostile distrust. Nevertheless, Monsieur our Governor was of opinion that we
must risk all for the sake of winning all, as it was to
be feared that, if we allowed this opportunity to pass
by, our course would cause a rupture of the Peace,
as showing too evident distrust on our part. His
council agreed with him; the Fathers, likewise,
upon whom [25] this blessed lot had fallen, doubted
not that it was their duty to depart upon this Mission, since they were undertaking it for the glory of
God and for the salvation of souls whose Angels were
calling us to their aid, and in whose behalf the
charity of Jesus Christ must solícit our help.

Finally, on the nineteenth of September, our
Fathers and these Ambassadors left us. I cannot
more faithfully set forth the successive events of
their journey, and the fruits which God has reaped
therefrom, than by giving the journal sent us by
Father Dablon.

CHAPITRE III.

VOYAGE DU PERE IOSEPH CHAUMONT, & DU PERE
CLAUDE DABLON, À ONONTAGUÉ; PAÏS DES
IROQUOIS SUPERIEURS.

LES Peuples nommés Agneronnons, s'appellent
les Iroquois d'enbas, ou les Iroquois Inferieurs;
& nous prenons [26] les Onontaeronons, &
autres Nations, qui leurs font voifines, pour les Iroquois d'en-haut, ou les Iroquois Superieurs; pource
qu'ils s'auancent dauantage en montant ver la fource
du grand fleuue Saint Laurent, & qu'ils habitent vn
païs plain de montagnes. Onontaé, ou bien, comme
les autres prononcent, Onontagué, eft la principale
demeure des Onontaeronnons, & c'eft en ce lieu, où
s'eft fait noftre voyage.

Eftant donc partis de Kebec le 19. Septembre
1655. de Montreal le 7. d'Octobre; nous montafme le
faut de Saint Loüys; ce font des courrans d'eau, &
des brifans, qui durent enuiron vne lieuë. Comme
ce paffage eft affés rude, & difficile, nous ne fifmes
que quatre lieuës cette premiere iournée. Le lendemain nous allafmes trouuer, à vn quart de lieuë de
noftre gifte, quelques-vns de nos Sauuages, qui nous
auoient precedés, pour auoir le loifir, en nous atten-
dant, de faire des Canots. Nous paffafmes le refte
du iour auec eux, pour les attendre.

Le 9. nous trauerfames le Lac nommé [27] de Saint
Loüys, qui fe rencontre au beau milieu du lict du

CHAPTER III.

JOURNEY OF FATHERS JOSEPH CHAUMONT AND
CLAUDE DABLON TO ONONTAGUÉ, A COUNTRY
OF THE UPPER IROQUOIS.

THE People named the Agneronnons are called
the Iroquois of the lowlands, or the Lower
Iroquois; while we speak of [26] the Onontaeronons, and other Nations near these, as the Iroquois
of the highlands, or the Upper Iroquois, because
they are situated nearer the source of the great Saint
Lawrence river and inhabit a country full of mountains. Onontaé — or, as others pronounce it, Onontagué — is the chief town of the Onontaeronnons;
and thither our course was directed.

Having, then, left Kebec on the 19th of September, 1655, and Montreal on the 7th of October, we
ascended the Saint Louys rapids; these are formed
by currents of water intercepted by rocks that extend
for about a league. The passage being rather rough
and difficult, we made only four leagues that first
day. On the next, we walked a quarter of a league
from our halting-place, to join some of our Savages,
who had started out ahead of us, in order to have
time, while waiting for us, to make some Canoes.
We passed the rest of the day with them, waiting for
them.

On the 9th, we crossed the Lake named [27] after
Saint Louys, and situated in the very middle of the

fleuue de Saint Laurent.   Ce grand fleuue forme des
Lacs en quelques endroits, répandant fes eaux dans
des lieux plus plats, & plus bas, puis les referrant
dans fon canal.

Le 10. qui étoit vn Dimanche, nous eufmes la confolation de dire la Sainte Meffe: comme nos guides
attendoient le refte de leurs gens, nous eufmes bien-
toft drefsé vn Autel, & vne Chapelle viuante, puis
qu'elle étoit bâtie de feüillages.   Nous fifmes du vin
des réfains du païs, que les Lambruches portent en
affés grande abondance.   Nos deuotions faites, nous
nous embarquâmes, & à peine auions nous fait vne
lieuë, que nous trouuâmes des chaffeurs Sonontoua-
ronnons, qui nous dirent que leur Nation deuoit
enuoyer vne Ambaffade aux François, fur l'Automne, ce qu'ils ont executé.

Le 12. nous paffons quantité de rapides à force de
rames; & fur le foir, au lieu de nous repofer, ayant
bien trauaillé dans ces courans, qui s'étendent enuiron cinq-lieuës, il nous fallut faire le [28] guet, &
nous tenir fur nos gardes: pour ce que nous apper-
ceufmes des Agneronons, grands ennemis des
Hurons, dont noftre bande étoit en partie compofée.

Le 13. nous ne fifmes pas grand chemin, pour ce
que nos prouifions manquant, nos chaffeurs & nos
pefcheurs; alloient chercher leur vie & la noftre,
dans les bois, & dans les riuieres.

Le 14. la pefche, ny la chaffe ne nous fauorifant
point, & nos viures fe trouuant bien-courts, & nos
dents allongées par la faim, nous fifmes curée d'vne
vache fauuage, c'eft à dire d'vne efpece de biche,
car ces animaux ont le bois fait comme ceux des
cerfs, & non comme les cornes de nos taureaux

bed of the Saint Lawrence river. This great stream
forms Lakes in some places, by expanding its waters
over flats and shallows, and then gathering them
together again into its channel.

On the 10th, which was Sunday, we had the consolation of celebrating Holy Mass. While our guides
were waiting for the rest of their number, we quickly
erected an Altar and what might be called a living
Chapel, since it was formed of foliage. Wine we
made from the native grapes, borne in considerable
abundance by the wild Vines. Our devotions
finished, we embarked; we had proceeded scarcely
a league, when we met some Sonontouaronnon
hunters, who told us that their Nation was to send an
Embassy to the French toward Autumn — which
they did.

On the 12th, we ascended many rapids by dint of
hard paddling; and in the evening, instead of resting after our conflict with these currents, which extend for about five leagues, we were forced to watch
[28] and keep guard; for we had caught sight of
some Agneronons, great enemies of the Hurons,
of whom our band was partly composed.

On the 13th, we made small progress, because,
our provisions failing, our hunters and fishers went
to seek their living and ours in the woods and
streams.

The 14th. Both fishing and hunting failing, our
provisions being very short, and our appetites sharp-
ened by hunger, we devoured a wild cow, or species
of hind,— these animals having horns like the stag's,
and not like those of our European bull. That poor
animal had drowned, and her flesh smelled very

d'Europe; cette pauure befte s'eftoit noiée, & fa
chair fentoit bien mal: mais l'appetit eft vn braue
Cuifinier: il ne mit dans ce mets ny fel, ny poiure,
ny cloux de giroffle; & cependant il nous le fit trouuer
de haut gouft. Difons pluftoft, que le zele & l'ardeur qu'on a de gagner ces pauures gens à Dieu,
répand vn fucre fi doux fur toutes les difficultés
qu'on y [29] rencontre, qu'on trouue en verité *dulcedinem in forti* la douceur dans l'amertume.

Le 15. Dieu nous fit paffer de la difette dans
l'abondance. Il donna huiçt ours à nos chaffeurs.
Auffi-toft, nous vifmes quafi tous nos gens deuenus
bouchers, & cuifiniers. On ne voioit que chair, que
greffe, que peaux tout à l'entour de nous, quatre
marmittes boüilloient inceffamment, & quand il en
fallut venir aux coufteaux & aux dents, iamais perfonne ne demanda ny pain, ny vin, ny fel, ny faulce.
Il eft vray que la chair d'ours eft fort bonne en ces
rencontres, fans faupiquets. La pluie furuenant là
deffus obligea nos affamés à fe refaire tout le iour,
fans douleur de perdre le beau-temps.

Le 17. l'abondance continuë, nos gens tuent trente
ours, vn feul en tua dix pour fa part. L'vne des
ceremonies du feftin, qui fuiuit ce grand carnage,
fut de boire de la greffe de ces ours, apres le repas:
comme on boit de l'hypocras en France: & enfuitte
ils fe frotterent tous, depuis les pieds iufques à la
tefte, [30] auec cette huile; car en verité la greffe
d'ours fonduë paroît de l'huile.

La nuiçt du 18. au 19. nous eufmes le diuertiffe-
ment d'vn accident aggreable. Vn de nos Sauuages
s'éueille à minuiçt tout hors d'haleine, palpitant,
criant, fe tourmentant comme vn infenfé. Nous

badly; but appetite is an excellent Cook, who, although he flavored this dish with neither salt, pepper, nor cloves, yet made us relish it highly. Let us say, rather, that the zeal and ardor which we feel for winning these poor people to God, imparts to all difficulties encountered a savor so sweet [29] that we find, in truth, *dulcedinem in forti*—"sweetness in bitterness."

The 15th. God made us pass from scarcity to abundance by giving our hunters eight bears. Straightway, we saw almost all our men turned butchers and cooks, while all around us was to be seen nothing but meat, fat, and skins. Four pots were boiling constantly; and, when knives and teeth were called into service, no one asked for bread or wine, salt or sauce. True, bear's flesh is very good in such circumstances without condiments. Rain coming on at this point forced our famished company to spend the whole day in recuperating, which they did without the grief of losing fine weather.

On the 17th, the plenty continued; our men killed thirty bears, one man killing ten as his share. One of the ceremonies of the feast that followed this great slaughter was the drinking of bear's fat after the meal, as one drinks hippocras in France. Then they all rubbed themselves from head to foot [30] with that oil—for, in truth, bear's fat when melted resembles oil.

During the night of the 18th and 19th, we were diverted by an amusing incident. One of our Savages awoke at midnight, all out of breath, trembling, crying out, and tossing about like a maniac. We thought at first that he had the falling sickness, so

crûmes d'abord qu'il étoit tombé du haut mal, tant
il auoit de conuulſions violentes.   On court à luy, on
l'encourage, mais il redouble ſes cris, & ſa furie: ce
qui iettoit déja la crainte dans les eſprits, en ſorte
que l'on cacha les armes, de peur qu'il ne s'en ſaiſiſt:
pẽdant que les vns preparent vn breuuage pour le
guerir, les autres l'arreſtent le mieux qu'ils peuuent;
mais il s'échappe de leurs mains, & ſe va ietter dans
la riuiere, où il ſe démenoit étrangement; on court
apres luy, on le retire, & on luy prepare du feu.   Il
dit qu'il a grand froid: mais pour ſe chauffer, il ſe
retire du feu, & ſe va placer aupres d'vn arbre, on
luy preſente la medecine preparée; il ne la iuge pas
propre à ſon mal.   Qu'on la donne à cét enfant (dit-
il) monſtrant la peau d'vn ours [31] remplie de paille.
Il fallut luy obeïr, & la verſer dans la gueule de
cét animal.   Iuſques alors tout le monde étoit dans
l'apprehenſion, enfin apres auoir eſté bien interrogé,
quel étoit ſon mal, il dit, qu'il auoit ſongé qu'vn
certain animal, dont le propre eſt de ſe plonger dans
l'eau, l'auoit eueillé, & s'étoit mis dans ſon eſtomach;
que pour le combattre, il s'étoit allé ietter dans la
riuiere, qu'il en vouloit eſtre victorieux; pour lors,
toute la crainte ſe changea en riſée.   Il falloit pourtant guerir l'imagination bleſſée de cét homme: c'eſt
pourquoy ils font tous ſemblant d'eſtre inſenſés
comme luy, & d'auoir à combattre des animaux qui
ſe plongent en l'eau.   Là deſſus ils ſe diſpoſent à
faire ſuerie, pour l'obliger à la faire auec eux, comme
il crioit, & chantoit à gorge deployée dans le petit
tabernacle où ils font cette ſuerie, imitant le cry de
l'animal qu'il combattoit: ils ſe mirent auſſi tous
tant qu'ils étoient à crier, & à chanter ſelon les cris

violent were his convulsions. We ran to him and tried to soothe him; but he so redoubled his cries and his frenzy that the rest were frightened and hid the weapons, lest he might gain possession of them. While some prepared a potion for his cure, the others held him as well as they could; but he escaped from their hands and, running away, leaped into the river, where he acted most strangely. He was followed and dragged out, and a fire was made for him. He said he was very cold, yet to get warm he withdrew from the fire, and took his position near a tree. The medicine that had been prepared was offered to him, but he did not think it suited to his ailment. "Give it to that child," (said he,) pointing to a bear's skin [31] stuffed with straw. They had to obey him, and pour it down the animal's throat. Up to that time, every one had been anxious; but finally, when he had been thoroughly questioned concerning his ailment, he said that he dreamed that a certain animal, whose nature it is to plunge into water, had awakened him and jumped into his stomach; that, in order to fight the creature, he had leaped into the river; and that he was determined to vanquish it. Then all fear was changed to laughter. Still, it was necessary to cure the man's diseased imagination; they all, therefore, pretended to be mad like him, and to have to fight animals which plunge into the water. Thereupon, they prepared to take a sweat, in order to induce him to do so with them. While he was crying and singing at the top of his voice in the little tent used as a sweat-box, and imitating the cry of the animal with which he was contending, they too began, every man of them, to cry and sing in

des animaux à qui ils croyoient auoir affaire, frappant tous ce miferable à la cadence de leur chant.
[32] Quelle confufion d'vne vingtaine de voix contrefaifant les canards, les farcelles, & les grenoüilles, &
quel fpectacle de voir des gens qui font des fous,
pour guerir vn fol.   Et apres tout, ils reüffirent, car
noftre homme ayant bien fué, & s'étant bien lafsé,
fe coucha fur fa natte, & dormit auffi paifiblement,
qui fi rien ne fuft arriué.   Son mal venu par vn
fonge, s'en alla en dormant comme vn fonge.   Qui
conuerfe auec les Sauuages païens, eft en danger de
perdre la vie par vn fonge.

   Le 19. nous n'auançons que de 3. petites lieuës.

   Le 20. nous paffons le faut du Lac, apres auoir
traifnés nos canots par quatre ou cinq rapides
pendant vne demi-lieuë.   La rapidité y eft grande, &
les boüillons fort éleués.

   Le 24. nous arriuons de bon-heure au Lac Ontario.
On tua fur le foir, cinq cerfs dans l'entrée du Lac.
Il n'en falloit pas d'auantage pour arrefter noftre
équipage.   Nous confiderons à l'oifir la beauté de
ce Lac, qui eft à my chemin de Montreal, & d'Onontagué.   C'eft [33] neantmoins la moitié la plus difficile fans comparaifon.   Il faut paffer vn rapide
furieux, qui fait comme l'ambouchure du Lac, en
fuitte on entre dans vne belle plaine d'eau, femée de
diuerfes Ifles diftantes, l'vne de l'autre, d'vn petit
quart de lieuë.   C'eft chofe agreable de voir les
trouppeaux de vaches, ou de cerfs, nager d'ifles
en ifles.   Nos chaffeurs leur couppent le chemin,
lors qu'ils retournent en terre ferme, & en bordent
tout le riuage ; les conduifant à la mort, au lieu qui
leur plaift.

imitation of the animals with which they were
supposed to be afflicted,—all, in time with their song,
beating that wretched man.   [32] What confusion!—
a score of voices imitating ducks, teals, and frogs;
and what a spectacle, to see people counterfeiting
madness in order to cure a madman!   Finally, they
succeeded; for after our man had perspired well and
become thoroughly tired, he lay down on his mat
and slept as peacefully as if nothing had happened.
His ailment, coming in a dream, disappeared like a
dream in his sleep.   He who deals with pagan
Savages is in danger of losing his life through a
dream.

On the 19th, we advanced barely 3 leagues.

On the 20th, we passed the falls of the Lake, after
dragging our canoes through four or five rapids in
the space of half a league.   The current here is
strong, and extremely turbulent.

Early on the 24th, we reached Lake Ontario, at the
entrance to which five stags were killed, toward
evening.   Nothing further was needed to arrest our
company's progress.   We contemplated at leisure the
beauty of this Lake, which is midway between
Montreal and Onontagué.   It marks, [33] however,
the end of by far the more difficult half.   Furious
rapids must be passed, which serve as the outlet of
the Lake; then one enters a beautiful sheet of water,
sown with various Islands distant hardly a quarter of
a league from one another.   It is pleasant to see
the herds of cows or deer swimming from isle to
isle.   Our hunters cut them off, on their return
to the mainland, and lined the entire shore with
them, leading them to death whithersoever they
chose.

Le 25. nous auançons 8. lieuës dans l'entrée du Lac, large de trois petits quarts de lieuës.

Le 26. nous y entrons tout de bon, faifant fept à huict lieuës. Ie n'ay rien veu de fi beau, ny de fi affreux. Ce ne font qu'ifles, que gros rochers grands comme des villes; tous couuerts de cedres, & de fapins. Le Lac mefme eft bordé de groffes roches efcarpées, qui font peur à voir, cachées de cedres; pour la plus part. Etant fur le foir du côté du Nord, nous paffons à celuy du Sud.

[34] Le 27. nous auançons 12. bonnes lieuës par vne infinité d'Ifles grandes & petites. Apres quoy, on ne découure que de l'eau de tous côtés. Le foir nous faifons rencontre d'vne bande de chaffeurs Sonontouaronons, qui ont paffion de nous voir: Et pour le faire plus à leur aife, ils nous inuiterent à vn feftin compofé de bled-d'inde, & de febues cuites dans la belle eau toute claire. Ce mets affaifonné d'vn petit filet du veritables amour à fes delices.

Le 29. nous arriuafmes fur les 9. heures du matin à Otihatangué. On nous prefente la chaudiere de la bien-venuë. Tout le monde eft l'vn fur l'autre pour nous voir manger. Otiatangué eft vne riuiere qui fe décharge dans le Lac Ontario: elle eft étroitte en fon emboucheure, mais bien large dans fon lict ordinaire. Elle eft riche en prairies, qu'elle fertilize, & qu'elle partage en quantité d'ifles hautes & baffes, toutes propres à femer du bled. La fecondité de cette riuiere eft telle, qu'en tout temps, elle porte diuerfes fortes de poiffons. Au printemps, fi-toft que les neiges font [35] fonduës, elle eft pleine de poiffons dorés, les carpes les fuiuent, l'achigen vient apres; c'eft vn poiffon plat, & long d'vn demy pied, d'vn gouft tres excellent; apres luy viennent les

On the 25th, we advanced 8 leagues up the Lake's mouth, which is barely three-quarters of a league wide.

We entered the Lake itself on the 26th, proceeding seven or eight leagues. Such a scene of awe-inspiring beauty I have never beheld,— nothing but islands and huge masses of rock, as large as cities, all covered with cedars and firs. The Lake itself is lined with high crags, fearful to behold, for the most part overgrown with cedars. Toward evening, we crossed from the North to the South side.

[34] On the 27th, we proceeded 12 good leagues through a multitude of Islands, large and small, after which we saw nothing but water on all sides. In the evening, we met a party of Sonontouaronon hunters, who were eager to see us; and, in order to do so more at their ease, they invited us to a feast of indian corn and beans, cooked in clear water, without seasoning. This dish has its charms, when flavored with a bit of genuine love.

Toward 9 o'clock on the morning of the 29th, we arrived at Otihatangué,[1] where we were offered the kettle of welcome, and all crowded about to see us eat. Otiatangué is a river emptying into Lake Ontario, narrow at its mouth but very wide, as a rule, for the rest of its course. It flows through meadows, which it fertilizes and cuts up into many islands, high and low, all suitable for raising grain. Such is the richness of this stream that it yields at all seasons various kinds of fish. In the spring, as soon as the snows [35] melt, it is full of gold-colored fish; next come carp, and finally the *achigen*.[2] The latter is a flat fish, half a foot long, and of very fine flavor. Then comes the brill; and, at the end of May, when

barbuës: Et à la fin de May, quand les fraifes font
meures on y tuë l'efturgeon à coups de hache.   Tout
le refte de l'année iufques en hyuer, le faumon four-
nit dequoy viure au Bourg d'Onontaé.   Nous
couchafmes hier fur les riues d'vn Lac, où fendant la
glace fur la fin de l'hyuer, on pefche ou pluftoft on
puife du poiffon à feaux.   C'eft icy le premier gifte
que nous ayons fait dans le païs des Onontaeronnons.
Nous y auons efté receus auec de grands témoignages
d'amitié.   Vne vingtaine de Hurons, qui étoient icy
à la pefche, firent paroiftre le contentement qu'ils
auoient de voir le Pere Chaumonot.   Les vns fe
iettent à fon col, les autres l'inuitent au feftin,
d'autres luy enuoyent des prefens.   Il faut, dit l'vn
d'eux, que la Priere fe faffe en public, la cabane eft
trop petite, & ce n'eft pas chofe dont il fe faille
cacher.   En effet les infidelles, qui étoient prefens,
[36] ne s'en formaliferĕt pas.   Le Pere entend les
Confeffions, inftruit ces pauures gens, qui n'auoient
pas oüi parler de Dieu, depuis leur captiuité, les
Hurons du Village de Contareia, qui n'auoient iamais
efté inftruits; pour ce qu'ils auoient de grandes auer-
fions de la Foy, ont déja commencé à fe rendre,
preftant l'oreille auec attention aux difcours du Pere.
Tant il eft vray que *afflictio dat intellectum.*
   Le Pere rencontra icy, Otohenha, l'hofte du feu
Pere Garnier, & du Pere Garreau, dans la nation du
Petun.   Il fut fi faifi de ioye à la veuë du Pere, qu'il
ne peut parler d'abord, & fut obligé de differer à vn
autre temps, à luy raconter toutes fes auantures; qui
font, que comme il eftoit en chemin, luy, toute fa
famille, & la fille du bon René nommée Ondoafkoua,
menant vn canot chargé de pelteries, & portant des
prefens de la part de deux Capitaines de fon païs,

strawberries are ripe, sturgeon are killed with
hatchets. All the rest of the year until winter, the
salmon furnishes food to the Village of Onontaé. We
made our bed last night on the shore of a Lake where
the natives, toward the end of winter, break the ice
and catch fish,— or, rather, draw them up by the
bucketful. This was our first lodging in the country
of the Onontaeronnons, who received us with profuse
demonstrations of friendship. A score of Hurons,
who were here fishing, showed their joy at seeing
Father Chaumonot, some throwing themselves upon
his neck, others inviting him to a feast, and still others
sending him presents. "Public Prayers must be
held," said one of them; "the cabin is too small, and
it is not a thing to be kept secret." And, indeed,
the infidels present [36] took no offense. The Father
hears Confessions, and instructs these poor people,
who have not heard God's name since their capture. The Hurons of the Village of Contareia, who,
because of their strong aversion to the Faith, never
allowed themselves to be instructed, are already
beginning to yield, lending an attentive ear to the
Father's words. So true is it that *afflictio dat intellectum*.

The Father met here Otohenha, the host of the
late Father Garnier and of Father Garreau, when
they visited the Tobacco nation. He was so over-
joyed at seeing the Father that at first he could not
speak, and was obliged to defer until another time
the narration of his adventures, which were as follows: When, with all his family and Ondoaskoua,
daughter of the good René, he was on a journey,—
conveying a canoe laden with skins, and bearing
presents from two Captains of his country, who asked

qui demandoient place pour demeurer à Kebec, il fut
malheureufement rencontré par les Onontaheronons,
toute fa famille fut prife, & difperfée en [37] diuerfes
cabanes, dont vne femme, ayant efté aduertie fous-
main, que les parens de celuy, pour qui elle auoit
efté donnée, vouloiẽt la brufler : s'enfuit dans les bois
auec fon enfant, apres que René l'euft Baptizé.

Ce n'eft pas chofe moins funefte, ce qu'il racompta
de la mort, de cette fameufe Marthe Gohatio, fa fain-
teté eft affez connuë.   Dieu a voulu l'éprouuer bien
rudement.   Il dit donc que l'an paffé, eftant allé en
guerre contre la nation du Chat, auec les Onontaheronons, & pris, & faccagé vne Bourgade : il trouua
parmy les morts le bon René Sondiouanen, & fa fille
parmy les captifs, auec cette Marthe, dont nous parlons.   Ce fut à s'entr'encourager, à garder à Dieu
leur promeffe, & à mourir dans la profeffion de la
Foy.   La pauure Marthe, qui ne pouuoit pas fi bien
fuiure le victorieux, à caufe d'vn genoüil enflé, & d'vn
petit enfant, qu'elle auoit bien de la peine à porter,
fut cruellement bruflée en chemin.   Deux de fes
enfans, fe font bien échappés de la main des Onontaheronons : mais on n'en a eu [38] aucune nouuelle.
C'eft vne pitié d'entendre ces pauures gens touchant
leur feruitude ; plufieurs d'entre eux ont efté tués,
par ceux mefme, qui leur auoient donné la vie.   Il ne
faut qu'vne petite d'efobeïffance, ou vne maladie, pour
leur faire décharger vn coup de hache fur la tefte

Le 30. nous quittafmes l'eau, pour nous difpofer à
aller par terre à Onontagué.   L'apres-midy parurent
60. Guerriers Oneoutchoueronons qui s'en alloient au
de là du faut contre les Peuples, qu'on appelle les
Neds percés, Atondatochan les conduifoit, c'eft celuy
qui fut à Montreal en la feconde Ambaffade, qui

for a dwelling-place at Kebec,— he unluckily met with the Onontaheronons. His entire family was captured, and scattered in [37] different cabins. A woman of their number, being secretly warned that the relatives of him for whom she had been given intended to burn her, fled into the woods with her child, after René had Baptized it.

No less sad was his account of the death of that famous Marthe Gohatio, whose piety is so well known. It was God's will to try her very severely. Having gone to war last year, our narrator said, against the Cat nation, in company with the Onontaheronons, upon taking and sacking a Village, he found the good René Sondiouanen among the dead, and his daughter among the prisoners, together with this Marthe of whom we are speaking. It was an occasion for mutual encouragement to keep their promise to God and to die in the profession of the Faith. Poor Marthe, who, because of a swollen knee, and a little child, whom she had much difficulty in carrying, was hardly able to keep pace with the victors, was cruelly burnt on the way. Two of her children escaped, indeed, from the Onontaheronons; but they have never been [38] heard of. It is pitiful to hear these poor people tell about their servitude. Many were killed, even by those who had given them their lives,— only a slight disobedience or an illness being necessary to provoke a hatchet-stroke on the head.

On the 30th, we left the water, and prepared for our trip overland to Onontagué. In the afternoon, there appeared 60 Oneoutchoueronon Warriors, on their way to fight the so-called Neds percés,[3] beyond the rapids. They were led by Atondatochan, the

[*sc.* qu'y] enuoia le bourg d'Oneout. C'eſt vn homme bien fait, & éloquent. Il nous pria de reſter icy encor vn iour afin d'apprendre ce qui nous amenoit.

Le 31. ces Guerriers s'aſſemblent tous. Et apres les ceremonies ordinaires en tel rencontre, le Pere Chaumonot s'adreſſant à Atondatochan; luy dit en premier lieu, qu'il ſe rejoüiſſoit & remercioit Dieu, de voir ce grand homme, dont la voix auoit retenti ſi haut à Montreal, [39] qu'elle s'y faiſoit encor entẽdre tant elle eſtoit fort. En ſecond lieu, que le ſujet qui l'amenoit en ce païs là, c'étoit pour faire executer ſa parolle donnée, pour ne parler plus qu'vn meſme langage, n'auoir plus qu'vn meſme Soleil, & vn meſme cœur: eſtre freres déſormais. A ces deux articles, ſe firent les acclamations ordinaires, & tous firent paroiſtre par leur contenance, la ioye qu'il auoient de ce diſcours; & par ce que le bruit auoit couru icy, qu'on auoit conclud la paix entre les François & les Annieronons, ſans y comprendre les Algonquins & les Hurons, le Pere adiouta en troi-ſiéme lieu qu'il venoit pour faire & conclure vne bonne paix vniuerſelle. Et en quatriéme lieu il fit vn preſẽt de 1500. grains de porceline, pour les inuiter à bien traitter les deux François, qui eſtoient parmy ceux qu'ils alloient combattre; & qu'au reſte, il prioit celuy qui a tout fait, d'auoir ſoin de ſon entrepriſe. Nous auions reſolu de luy faire vn pre-ſent conſiderable, pour arreſter ſes ſoldats; mais nous apriſmes ſous main, qu'aſſeurément nous euſſions [40] eſté refuſez: pource qu'ils étoient viuement piqués de la mort de quelques-vns des leurs, qu'ils vouloient vanger, à quelque prix que ce fuſt. Apres que le Pere eut parlé, l'eſpace d'vne demy-heure: le Chef commença la chanſon de réponce, & tous

same who came to Montreal in the second Embassy
sent by the village of Oneout. He is a man of fine
appearance, and an eloquent speaker. He begged us
to stay here one day longer, that he might learn
our errand.

These Warriors having all assembled on the 31st,
Father Chaumonot, after the ceremonies customary
on such occasions, addressed Atondatochan; he said,
first, that he congratulated himself and thanked God
at seeing that great man, whose voice had rung out
so loud at Montreal [39] that it was still to be heard
there, so great was its strength. In the second
place, he said that he was led to visit that country
in order to secure the fulfillment of his promise, to
speak from that time but the same language, to have
but one Sun, and one heart,— in short, to be thence-
forth brothers. These two clauses were received
with the customary applause, and the faces of all
showed how much they enjoyed this speech. In the
third place, as the report had spread hither that
peace had been concluded between the French and
Annieronons without including the Algonquins and
Hurons, the Father added that he had come to
negotiate a genuine peace between all parties. And,
in the fourth place, he presented 1500 porcelain
beads, in order to solicit kind treatment for the two
Frenchmen who were among those whom they were
going to fight. He also prayed the maker of all
things to watch over Atondatochan's expedition. We
had determined to make him a considerable present
to induce him to stop his soldiers; but learned
privately that we would certainly have [40] been
refused, because of their keen resentment at the loss
of some of their number, which they were bent on

s'accordans merueilleufement bien, fe mirent à chanter
d'vne façon femblable en quelque façon à noftre plain-
chant.   La premiere chanfon difoit, qu'il emploiroit
tout le refte du iour, pour remercier le Pere, d'vne fi
bonne parolle qu'il leur auoit portée.   La feconde
fut, pour le congratuler de fon voyage, & de fon arriuée.   On chanta la troifiéme fois pour allumer vn
feu au Pere, afin qu'il en prift poffeffion.   Le quatriéme chant nous faifoit tous parens, & tous freres.
Le cinquiéme iettoit la hache dans le fond des
abifmes : pour faire regner la paix dans toutes ces
contrées.   La fixiéme chanfon étoit, pour rendre le
François maiftre de la riuiere de Ontiahantagué.
C'eft icy où ce Capitaine inuita les faumons, les barbuës, & les autres poiffons à fe ietter dans nos rets,
& à ne remplir cette riuiere, [41] que pour noftre
feruice.   Il leur difoit qu'ils feroient bien-heureux,
de finir fi honorablement leur vie.   Il nomma tous
les poiffons de cette riuiere iufques aux plus petits,
les apoftrophãt tous auec fon trait d'efprit.   Il
adiouta mille autres chofes, qui firent rire tous les
affiftans.   La feptiéme chanfon nous fut encor plus
agreable.   C'eftoit pour ouurir leurs cœurs, & nous
faire lire le contentement de noftre arriuée, & à la fin
de leurs chanfons ils nous firent vn prefent de deux
milles   grains   de   porcelaine.   Là-deffus le Pere
éleuant fa voix luy dit, que la bonté de fes parolles
alloit toujours croiffant, que iufques à prefent elle
auoit retenti par tous les confins du Lac d'Ontario ;
mais que d'orénauant, elle alloit voler au delà du
plus grand de tous les Lacs, & qu'elle s'entendroit
comme vn tonnerre par toute la F[r]ance.   Cela plut
extremement à ce Capitaine, & à tous fes gens.   Qui

revenging at any cost.   After the Father had spoken
for half an hour, the Chief began the song of
response; and all commenced to sing, in wondrous
harmony, in a manner somewhat resembling our
plain-chant.   The first song said that it would take
all the rest of the day to thank the Father for so good
a speech as he had made them.   The second was to
congratulate him upon his journey and his arrival.
They sang a third time to light him a fire, that he
might take possession of it.   The fourth song made
us all relatives and brothers; the fifth hurled the
hatchet into the deepest abyss, in order that peace
might reign in all these countries; and the sixth was
designed to make the French masters of the river
Ontiahantagué.   At this point the Captain invited
the salmon, brill, and other fish, to leap into our
nets, and to fill that river [41] for our service only.
He told them they should consider themselves fortunate to end their lives so honorably; named all the
fishes of that river, down to the smallest, making a
humorous address to each kind; and added a thousand things besides, which excited laughter in all
those present.   The seventh song pleased us still
more, its purpose being to open their hearts, and let
us read their joy at our coming.   At the close of
their songs, they made us a present of two thousand
porcelain beads.   Then the Father raised his voice,
and told the Chief that his fine powers of speech
would ever increase in volume; that, hitherto, they
had resounded through all the confines of Lake
Ontario, but, in future, they would speed across the
greatest of all Lakes, and be heard as thunder
throughout France.   At this the Captain and all
his followers were extremely pleased.   They then

en fuitte nous inuiterent au feftin, qui acheua la fefte.

Le 1. iour de Nouembre nous partons par terre pour Onontagué: nous rencontrafmes vne bonne Huronne nommée [42] Therefe Oïonhaton. Cette pauure femme ayant apris l'arriuée du Pere vint de trois lieuës, où elle demeuroit pour l'attendre au paffage. Sa ioye fut grande, de ce qu'elle voyoit encor vne fois deuant que de mourir, les Robbes noires. Le Pere luy demanda fi le petit enfant qu'elle tenoit entre fes bras étoit Baptizé, & par qui? elle répond qu'elle mefme l'a Baptizé, par ces parolles, Iefus aye pitié de mon enfant; ie te Baptize mon enfant, afin que tu fois bien-heureux au Ciel. Le Pere l'inftruit là deffus, la Confeffe & la confole. Nous paffons la nuict fur le bord d'vn ruiffeau apres auoir fait cinq bonnes lieuës. Nous en delogeons dés la pointe du iour le 2. de Nouembre. Et apres auoir fait fix à 7. lieuës, nous logeons à la même enfeigne, où nous auons toufiou[r]s logé, fçauoir eft à la belle Etoille. Le 3. nous la quittons deuant le Soleil. Le Pere fait rencontre en chemin de la fœur de cette Therefe dont nous venons de parler, qui luy raconta fes infortunes les larmes aux yeux. l'auois, difoit-elle, deux enfans dans ma captiuité, mais helas! ils ont efté maffacrés, [43] par ceux, à qui ils auoient efté donnés. Et ie fuis tous les iours dans l'apprehenfion d'vn femblable malheur. l'ay à toute heure la mort deuant les yeux. Il fallut la confoler, & puis la Confeffer, & la quitter promptement pour fuiure nos guides, qui nous conduifoient ce iour là à Tethiroguen; c'eft vne riuiere, qui fort du Lac appellé Goienho. Oneïout, Bourgade de l'vne des

invited us to the feast which concluded the ceremonies.

We started overland for Onontagué on the 1st of
November, meeting on the way a good Huron woman
named [42] Therese Oionhaton.   This poor woman,
upon learning of the Father's arrival, came from her
home, three leagues distant, to wait for him as he
passed.   Her joy was great at seeing the black Gowns
once more before her death.   The Father asked her
whether the little child whom she held in her arms
were Baptized, and by whom.   She replied that she
herself had Baptized it, with these words: '' Jesus,
take pity on my child.   I Baptize thee, my little one,
that thou mayst be blessed in Heaven.''   Thereupon
the Father instructed her, Confessed her, and com-
forted her.   At the end of five good leagues, we
passed the night by the side of a brook, and broke
camp at dawn on the 2nd of November.   After making six or 7 leagues, we lodged at our invariable
hostelry, namely, the beautiful Star, leaving it on
the 3rd, before Sunrise.   On the way, the Father
met the sister of that Therese of whom we have just
spoken; with tears in her eyes she told him her misfortunes.   '' I had two children in my captivity,'' said
she; '' but alas! they were slaughtered [43] by those
to whom they had been given; and I am in daily
fear of a like fate, having death ever before my eyes.''
We had to console and Confess her, leaving her very
soon in order to follow our guides, who were leading
us that day to Tethiroguen, a river which has its
source in the Lake called Goienho.   Oneiout, a Village of one of the Upper Iroquois Nations, is at the
head of this Lake, which, narrowing, becomes the
river Tethiroguen, and, further down, forms a water-

Nations des Iroquois Superieurs, eſt au deſſus de ce Lac, qui ſe retreſſiſant fait la riuiere Tethiroguen, & en ſuitte vn ſaut ou vne caſcade d'vne pique de haut appellée Ahaoueté. Auſſi-toſt que nous fûmes arriués à cette riuiere, les plus remarquables d'entre vn bon nombre de peſcheurs, que nous y recontraſmes, nous vindrent faire compliment, & puis nous condui-ſirent dans les plus belles cabanes. Le 4. Nouembre nous fiſmes enuiron ſix lieuës touſiours à pied, & embarraſsés de noſtre petit bagage nous paſſames la nuiƈt dans vne campagne à 4. lieuës d'Onontagué.

fall or cascade, a pike's length in height, called Ahaoueté.[4]   As soon as we had reached this stream, the more notable men among a large number whom we found fishing there came to salute us, and then led us to the most comfortable cabins.   On the 4th of November, we covered about six leagues, still on foot and encumbered with our small baggage.   We passed the night in a field, 4 leagues from Onontagué.

[44] CHAPITRE IV.

ARRIUÉE DES PERES À ONONTAGUÉ.

L E 5. iour de Nouembre de l'an 1655. comme nous
continuions noſtre chemin, vn Capitaine d'importance appellé Gonaterezon, fit vne bonne
lieuë pour venir au deuant de nous. Il nous fait
faire alte, nous complimente agreablement ſur noſtre
arriuée.   Se met à la teſte de noſtre Eſcouade, &
nous mene grauement iuſques à vn quart de lieuë
d'Onontagué, où les Anciens du païs nous attendoient.
Aiant pris place aupres d'eux, ils nous preſenterent
les meilleurs mets qu'ils euſſent, ſur tout des
Citroüilles cuites fous la braiſe.   Pendant que nous
mangeons, vn Ancien Capitaine nommé Okonchiarennen, ſe leue, fait faire ſilence, & nous harangue,
vn grand quart-d'heure, diſant entre autres choſes,
que nous eſtions les tres-bien venus, fort ſouhaités,
& attendus depuis long-temps, que puiſque [45] la
ieuneſſe, qui ne reſpire que la guerre, auoit elle
meſme demãdé, & procuré la paix, c'eſtoit à eux, qui
étoient les Anciens, à ne manier plus les armes, à la
ratifier, & à l'embraſſer de tout leur cœur, comme
ils faiſoient.   Qu'il n'y auoit que l'Agnieronnon, qui
vouloit obſcurcir le Soleil, que nous rendions ſi beau
par noſtre approche, & qui faiſoit naiſtre des nuages
en l'air, à même temps que nous les diſſipions; mais
que tous les efforts de cét enuieux, tomberoient par
terre, & qu'enfin ils nous poſſederoient; qu'à la

[44] CHAPTER IV.

THE FATHERS ARRIVE AT ONONTAGUÉ.

ON the 5th of November, 1655, as we were continuing our journey, a Captain of note, named Gonaterezon, came a good league to meet us. He made us halt, pleasantly congratulated us upon our arrival, put himself at the head of our Company, and gravely led us to a spot a quarter of a league from Onontagué, where the Elders of the country awaited us. When we had seated ourselves beside them, they offered us the best dishes they had, especially some Squashes cooked in the embers. While we were eating, one of the Elders, a Captain named Okonchiarennen, arose, imposed silence, and harangued us a good quarter of an hour. He said, among other things, that we were very welcome; our coming had been earnestly desired and long awaited; and, since [45] the young men, who breathed only war, had themselves asked for and procured peace, it was for them, the Elders, to lay aside their arms and to ratify and embrace it in all sincerity, as they did. He added that only the Agnieronnon was bent on darkening the Sun, which we made so bright by our approach; and he alone generated clouds in the air, at the very time when we dissipated them; but all the efforts of that envious one would fail, and they would finally have us in their midst. Courage, then; we were to take possession of our domains, and enter our new home with all assurance. After

bonne-heure donc nous priſſions poſſeſſion de nos
terres, & que nous entraſſions chez nous, auec toute
aſſeurance.   Apres auoir étendu ce diſcours, & parlé
d'vne façon, qui ſembloit étudiée, le Pere repliqua,
que ſa parolle nous étoit vn breuuage bien agreable,
qui nous oſtoit toute la fatigue du chemin; qu'il
venoit de la part d'Onnontio pour ſatisfaire à leurs
pourſuites, & qu'il ne doutoit point qu'ils ne duſſent
eſtre contents, quand ils apprendroient ſa commiſſion.
Tout le Peuple écoutoit auec attention, & [46] auec
admiration, rauy d'entendre vn François ſi bien parler
leur langue.   Enſuite noſtre Introducteur ſe leue,
donne le ſignal, & nous conduit au trauers d'vn grand
peuple, dont les vns étoient rangés en haye, pour
nous voir paſſer au milieu d'eux, les autres couroient
apres nous, les autres nous preſentoient des fruits,
iuſqu'à ce que nous arriuaſſions au Bourg, dont les
ruës étoient bien nettoyées, & les toits des cabannes
chargez d'enfants.   Enfin nous entrons dans vne
grande cabanne, qui nous étoit preparée, & auec
nous, tout ce qu'elle pouuoit contenir de monde.

Apres nous eſtre vn peu repoſés, on nous appelle
pour vn feſtin d'ours, nous nous excuſaſmes à cauſe
du vendredy.   Ce qui n'empeſcha pas, que nous
ne fuſſions traités, tout le reſte du iour, en diuers
endroits, en caſtors, & en poiſſons.

Le ſoir bien tard, les Anciens tiennent Conſeil
dans noſtre cabanne; vn d'eux, nous ayant fait
ciuilité de la part de toute la nation, nous fit deux
preſents; vn de 500. grains de pourcelaine, pour [47]
nous eſſuier les yeux, qui etoiẽt trempés, des larmes
répandues pour les meurtres arriués chez nous cette
année, & comme la douleur fait perdre la voix, ayant

the speaker had dilated upon this theme, and spoken
in what seemed a rather affected manner, the Father
made answer, that his speech was a very agreeable
draught to us, and took away all the fatigue of our
journey; that he came on Onnontio's behalf, to satisfy
their demands; and that he doubted not that they
would be content when they learned his errand. All
the People listened with attention and [46] admiration, delighted to hear a Frenchman speak their
language so well. Then he who had Introduced us
arose, gave the signal, and led us through a great
crowd of people,— some of whom were drawn up in
rows to see us pass through their midst, while others
ran after us, and still others offered us fruit, until
we came to the Village, the streets of which were
carefully cleaned and the cabin-roofs crowded with
children. At length, a large cabin which had been
prepared for us received us, and also all the people
it could hold.

After resting a little, we were invited to a feast of
bear's meat, but excused ourselves on the plea that
it was Friday. This, however, did not prevent us
from being treated, in different places, all the rest of
the day, to beaver and fish.

Very late in the evening, the Elders held a Council
in our cabin, where one of them, after greeting us on
behalf of all the nation, made us two presents. One
of these was 500 porcelain beads, to [47] wipe our
eyes, wet with tears shed over the murders com-
mitted in our country that year; and, as grief causes
loss of voice, having, he said, clearly perceived our
weakness of utterance upon our arrival, he added a
second present of 500 beads, to strengthen our lungs,
to remove the phlegm from our throats, and to make

bien reconnu, difoit-il, à noftre arriuée qu'elle étoit
foible, il adioufta vn fecond prefent de 500. grains,
pour fortifier noftre eftomach, & netoyer les flegmes
de noftre gorge, afin de nous rendre la voix bien
claire, bien libre & bien forte.   Le Pere les remercia
de leur bonne volonté, & leur dit, qu'Onnõtio &
Achiendasé, ce font les noms de Monfieur le Gouuerneur, & du Pere Superieur de nos Miffions, auoient
les yeux tournés du cofté d'Onontagué pour voir de
Kebec l'état où nous eftions, & qu'il leur faifoit vn
prefent de 2000. grains, pour leur faire ouurir la
porte de la cabanne où ils nous auoient logés, afin que
tous les François puffent voir le bon traitement que
nous y receuions; les belles nattes fur lefquelles nous
étions; & le bon vifage qu'ils nous faifoient.   Ils
furent rauis de ce compliment.

Le l'endemain 6. de Nouembre, on nous inuite dés
le point du iour pour aller [48] à diuers feftins, qui
durerent tout le matin.   Ce qui n'empefcha pas le
Pere, d'aller voir des malades, qui promirent de fe
faire inftruire, s'ils retournoient en fanté.

Le 7. Iour de Dimanche, fe tint vn Confeil fecret
de 15. Capitaines, où il fut appellé apres auoir fait
prier Dieu, à vne 20. de perfonnes qui fe prefen-
terent.   On dit donc au Pere, dans cette affemblée.
1. que Agochiendagueté, qui eft comme le Roy du
païs; & Onnontio, auoient la voix égallement forte &
conftante, & que rien ne pourroit rompre vn fi beau
lien, qui les tenoit fi étroitement vnis par enfemble.
2. qu'ils donneroient de leur plus lefte ieuneffe pour
remener les Ambaffadeurs Hurons, qui étoient venus
traiter de Paix auec nous.   En troifiéme lieu ils
prierent, qu'on fit fçauoir à Onnontio, que quoy que

our voices clear, free, and strong.   The Father
thanked them for their good will, saying that Onnontio and Achiendasé — the names of Monsieur the
Governor and of the Father Superior of our Missions,
respectively — had their eyes turned toward Onontagué, in order to see our condition from Kebec.   He
then presented to them 2000 beads, that they might
open the door of the cabin where they had lodged
us, in order that all the French might see the kind
treatment we received, the beautiful mats upon which
we reposed, and the pleasant faces greeting us.   They
were delighted with this compliment.

On the following day, November 6th, we were
invited at dawn to [48] various feasts, which lasted
all the morning; but this did not prevent the Father
from visiting some sick persons, who promised to
receive instruction if they recovered.

On the 7th, Sunday, a secret Council of 15 Captains was held, to which he was called, after he had
directed the prayers of 20 persons who presented
themselves to him.   In this assembly, they said to
the Father: 1. That Agochiendagueté — who is, as it
were, the King of this country — and Onnontio had
voices of equal power and firmness, and that nothing
could sever so suitable a tie, which held them in such
close union.   2.   They would give some of their
most active young men to conduct home the Huron
Ambassadors who had come with us to treat of Peace.
Thirdly, they begged that Onnontio might be
informed that, even if some one of their own people
should be ill-treated or even killed by the Annieronnons, yet that would not hinder the alliance; and
they desired the same assurance on Onnontio's part,
in case any ill befell [49] the French from the same

quelqu'vn de leur gens receut quelque mauuais
traitement, ou mefme fut tué par les Annieronnons,
cela n'empefcheroit pas pourtant l'alliance, qu'ils
defiroient, qu'il en feroit de mefme du cofté d'Onnontio, s'il arriuoit du malheur à [49] quelques
François du mefme cofté.   En quatriéme lieu, ayant
appris que la chofe la plus agreable qu'ils pouuoient
faire à Onnontio, eftoit de luy faire fçauoir dés cet
Automne, qu'ils auoient erigé vne Chapelle pour les
Croyants, que pour luy complaire, ils y pouruoiroient
au pluftoft.   A cet Article, le Pere ayant pris la
parole leur dit, qu'ils auoient trouué le fecret d'enleuer le cœur de Monfieur le Gouuerneur, & de le
gagner tout à fait.   Tous firent vn cry d'approbation, par lequel finit le Confeil.

Sur le foir, parlant familierement au Pere, ils le
prierent de les entretenir vn peu de la France.   Le
Pere trouuant vne fi belle occafion de cõmencer fon
coup, leur reprefente, comme la France auoit autresfois efté dans le mefme abus, dans lequel ils font:
mais que Dieu nous auoit ouuert les yeux, par le
moyen de fon Fils; furquoy expliquant le grand
myftere de l'Incarnation, refuta toutes les calomnies,
qui auoient couru dans leur païs contre la Foy.   Il
fit cela fi bien, & fi agreablement, que pendant
l'efpace d'vne bonne heure & demie qu'il parla, [50]
ils ne firẽt paroiftre aucun figne d'ennuy: l'iffuë du
confeil fut vn feftin, & vne excufe de ce que les
traitements d'Onontagué, n'eftoient pas fi bons, que
ceux qu'on fait à Kebec à leurs Ambaffadeurs.   La
iournée fe termina par vn grand concours, tant de
ceux qui venoient pour prier Dieu, que des autres
que la curiofité attiroit.

quarter.   In the fourth place, as they had learned
that the most acceptable thing they could do, in
Onnontio's eyes, would be to inform him that Autumn that they had erected a Chapel for the Believers, they said that, to please him, they would take
steps to that end at the earliest moment.   In reply
to this Clause, the Father took the word, and told
them that they had discovered how to win the heart
and the entire good will of Monsieur the Governor.
All gave a shout of approval, with which the Council ended.

Toward evening, conversing familiarly with the
Father, they asked him to tell them a little about
France; and he, embracing an opportunity so favorable to his designs, showed them that France had
formerly been subject to the same errors as themselves, but that God had opened our eyes through
the mediation of his Son.   Then, in explaining the
great mystery of the Incarnation, he refuted all the
calumnies current in their country against the Faith.
So skillfully and agreeably was this done that, though
he spoke for a good hour and a half, [50] they showed
no sign of weariness.   The council was followed by
a feast, and an apology for the inferiority of Onontagué's entertainment compared with that given to
their Ambassadors at Kebec.   The day closed with
a large gathering of people who came, some to pray
to God, and others to satisfy their curiosity.

CHAPITRE V.

LES PERES TRAITENT AUEC CES PEUPLES.

TOUT le premier iour ſe paſſe, partie en feſtins, partie à traiter de la paix pour les Algonquins : & comme cette affaire eſtoit la plus épineuſe, elle demandoit de plus grandes deliberations. C'eſt pourquoy le Pere fit aduertir les Anciens qu'il auoit quelque choſe à leur communiquer en particulier. Eſtans aſſemblez il leur dit 1. Que l'affaire des Hurons eſtant toute concluë, il n'en parloit point dauantage, mais qu'il aſſeuroit, que les Algonquins viendroient en [51] Ambaſſade le Printemps prochain, s'ils voyoient les eſprits diſpoſez à la paix. 2. Que quand les Hurons auroient eſtably leur Bourgade prés de nous, les Algonquins eſtoient pour nous y venir auſſi voir. En troiſiéme lieu, Que pour auoir vne entiere aſſeurance du deſir qu'auoient les Onnontaeronnons de faire la paix, les Algonquins eſperoient reuoir quelques-vns de leurs neveux captifs, puis qu'eux-meſmes auoiẽt ſi liberalement relaſché leurs priſonniers à la requeſte du Gouuerneur de Montreal, & les auoient renuoyez auec des preſens, à quoy neantmoins on n'auoit pas ſatisfait. En quatriéme lieu, Qu'ils deuoient ceſſer de leuer la hache contre la Nation des Nez percez, s'ils vouloient que la paix fuſt vniuer[ſ]elle. La reſponſe fut ; qu'on deliberoit ſur ces quatre Articles.

Le ſoir du meſme iour, vne trentaine d'Anciens

CHAPTER V.

THE FATHERS TREAT WITH THESE PEOPLES.

A LL the first day was spent, partly in feasting, partly in negotiating peace for the Algonquins; and, as this was the most difficult matter, it demanded the most serious deliberation. For that reason, the Father notified the Elders that he had a private communication to make to them. When they were assembled, he addressed them to the following effect: 1. The Huron question being closed, he said no more about it; but he assured them that the Algonquins would send an [51] Embassy the next Spring, if they saw their minds inclined to peace. 2. When the Hurons should have planted their Villages near us, the Algonquins also would wish to visit us. In the third place, in order to be fully assured of the Onnontaeronnons' desire for peace, the Algonquins hoped to see some of their captive nephews returned, since they themselves had so freely released their prisoners, at the request of the Governor of Montreal, and had sent them back with presents,— to which, however, no response had been made. In the fourth place, if they wished the peace to be general, they must cease to raise the hatchet against the Nation of the Nez percez. The answer was, that they would deliberate on these four Points.

On the evening of the same day, some thirty Elders, who had gathered in our cabin, invited the

s'eftans affemblez chez nous, inuiterent le Pere,
comme pour le diuertir, à leur raconter quelque belle
chofe. Le Pere les entretint pendant vne groffe
heure, fur la Conuerfion de [52] S. Paul, dont ils
furent fi rauis, qu'ils le prierent de continuer, & fur
tout de leur dire quelque chofe du commencement
du monde. Il le fit, & prefcha en outre, fur les
principaux myfteres de noftre Religion, auec tel
fuccez, qu'à la fin vn d'eux fe mit à prier publiquement celuy qui a tout fait, & deux autres demanderent, ce qu'il falloit faire pour eftre du nombre
des croyans.

Le 9. le Pere confeffant vn Sauuage dans vne
cabanne, aperceut vis à vis de luy, vn enfant de
quatre ans bien malade, il le voit, luy fait prendre
quelques remedes, & le baptife, cueillant ce premier
fruit que Dieu luy mit entre les mains. L'apres-
midy deux Deputez arriuerẽt de la part des Iroquois
du Bourg d'Oneïout, pour auoir liberté d'affifter au
Confeil. Ils firent le foir grande affemblée chez
nous, & apres vn long difcours, vn d'eux s'adreffant
au Pere, luy fit prefent d'vn collier de mil grains,
pour nous faire part, de la ioye qu'ils auoient, de
noftre arriuée. La refponfe fut, que puis qu'Onnontio & Agochiendaguefé n'eftoient plus qu'vn, il
falloit [53] que les Onneioutchoueronons fuffent
enfans du premier, comme ils l'eftoient du fecond.
On fit dont vn prefent pour les adopter; ce qui leur
agrea plus qu'on ne peut dire.

L'onziéme, pendant que le Pere trauailloit, à rele-
uer les anciens fondements de l'Eglife Huronne, on
fut vifiter la Fontaine fallée, qui n'eft qu'à quatre
lieuës d'icy, proche du Lac appellé Gannentaa; lieu

Father, as if by way of diverting him, to tell them
something entertaining.   For a full hour the Father
talked to them on [52] St. Paul's Conversion, with
which they were so delighted that they begged him
to continue,—and, above all, to tell them something
about the beginning of the world.   He did so; and
he also preached on the chief mysteries of our Religion, with such success that, at the close, one of the
company began to pray in public to the maker of all
things; while two others asked what they must do
to become believers.

On the 9th, while the Father was confessing a
Savage in a cabin, he perceived opposite him a child
of four years, who was, as he saw, very ill.   He
administered some remedies and baptized it, thus
gathering the first-fruit which God put into his
hands.   In the afternoon, there came two Deputies
from the Iroquois of the Village of Oneiout, asking
leave to be present at the Council.   In the evening,
a large assembly was held in our cabin; and, after
a long speech, one of the company, addressing the
Father, presented to him a collar of a thousand
beads, in order to make us share their joy at our
coming.   The answer was that, as Onnontio and
Agochiendaguesé were now one, [53] the Onneioutchoueronons must be children of the former as well
as of the latter.   A present was made for their
adoption, which pleased them beyond measure.

On the eleventh, while the Father was laboring to
restore the ancient foundations of the Huron Church,
the others visited the salt Spring, four leagues
distant and near the Lake called Gannentaa.   This is
the site chosen for the French settlement, on account
of its central position among the four Iroquois

choifi pour l'habitation Françoife, parce qu'il eft le
centre des quatre Nations Iroquoifes, que l'on peut
de là vifiter en canot fur des Riuieres, & fur des Lacs
qui en font le commerce libre, & fort facile. La
pefche, & la chaffe, rendent cet endroit confiderable :
car outre le poiffon, qui s'y prend en diuers temps
de l'année, l'anguille y eft fi abondante l'Efté, que
tel en prend au harpon, iufques à mille en vne nuict ;
& pour le gibier, qui n'y manque pas l'Hyuer, les
tourtes de tout le Païs s'y ramaffent fur le Printemps
en fi grand nombre, qu'on les prend auec des rets.
La fontaine dont on fait de tres-bon fel, couppe vne
belle Prairie, [54] enuironnée de bois de haute fuftaye.
A 80. ou 100. pas de cette fource falée, il s'en voit
vne autre d'eau douce ; & ces deux contraires,
prennent naiffance du fein d'vne mefme colline.

Le 12. fut amené vn captif pris fur la Nation de
Chat, qui va eftre l'objet de la rage de ces peuples,
qui ne fe donnent plus de quartier l'vn à l'autre ;
c'eft vn ieune enfant de neuf à dix ans, qui doit eftre
bruflé dans peu : & c'eft ce qui fit prendre refolution
au Pere, de tafcher à tirer des feux d'enfer, l'ame de
celuy, dont il ne pouuoit pas fauuer le corps : mais
comme la haine de ces barbares va iufqu'à tel excez,
qu'ils ne veulent pas mefme que leurs ennemis foient
heureux en l'autre monde, il fallut vfer d'adreffe
pour inftruire & baptifer en cachette ce pauure mal-
heureux. Le Pere l'ayant donc veu, & luy ayant
parlé, fit femblant d'auoir foif, on luy donna de l'eau.
Il en boit, & en fait tout exprés couler quelques
gouttes dans fon mouchoir ; il n'en falloit qu'vne
pour luy ouurir la porte du Ciel. Il le baptifa
deuant que d'eftre bruflé   Il ne [55] fut que deux

Nations,—being accessible to them by canoe, over
Rivers and Lakes which make communication free
and very easy. Hunting and fishing render this
position an important one; for, besides the fish caught
there at different seasons, eels are so abundant
in the Summer that a man can harpoon as many as
a thousand in one night; and, as for game, which is
always abundant in the Winter, turtle-doves from
all the Country around flock thither toward Spring,
in so great numbers that they are caught in nets.
The spring, from which very good salt is made,
issues within a beautiful Prairie, [54] surrounded by
full-grown forests. At a distance of 80 or 100 paces
from this salt spring is found another of fresh water;
and these two, though of opposite characters, have
their sources in the bosom of the same hill.

On the 12th, a prisoner from the Cat Nation was
brought in, to bear the brunt of these people's rage,
no quarter being now given between the two tribes.
He was a child of nine or ten years, and was to be
burnt in a short time, which made the Father resolve
to attempt the rescue of his soul from the fires of
hell, not being able to save his body. But, the
hatred of these barbarians being so excessive that
they are unwilling that their enemies should be happy even in the other world, it required adroitness
to instruct and baptize this poor unfortunate in secret.
The Father, accordingly, after seeing and speaking
with him, feigned thirst and was given some water.
In drinking, he purposely allowed some drops to run
into his handkerchief,—one was enough to open
Heaven's gates,—and baptized the boy before he
was burnt. He [55] was only two hours in torment,
because of his youth; but he displayed such fortitude

heures dans les tourmens, parce qu'il eſtoit ieune,
mais il fit paroiſtre vne telle conſtance, qu'il ne ietta
ny larmes, ny cris, ſe voyant au milieu des flâmes.

Le 14. qui eſtoit vn Dimanche, ne pût mieux commencer, que par le Saint Sacrifice de la Meſſe, que
nous celebrâmes ſur vn petit Autel, dans vn Oratoire
pratiqué en la cabane de Teotonharaſon; c'eſt vne
des femmes, qui eſtoient deſcenduës à Kebec, auec
les Ambaſſadeurs.   Elle eſt icy conſiderée pour ſa
nobleſſe, & pour ſes biens; mais notamment pource
qu'elle s'eſt hautement declarée pour la Foy, en
faiſant Profeſſion publique, inſtruiſant tous ceux qui
luy appartiennent, ayant déja preſſé, & ſouuent
demandé le Bapteſme pour ſoy, pour ſa mere, & pour
ſa fille, apres leur auoir expliqué elle-meſme, les
myſteres de noſtre Religion, & appris les Prieres.

Sur les 10. heures du meſme iour, deſtiné pour
faire les preſents, toutes choſes eſtant preparées,
aprés auoir publiquement, & à genoux, recité les
Prieres, [56] auec vn grand ſilence de toute l'aſſem-
blée; nouuelles arriuerent, que les Deputez d'Oio-
goïen entroient dans le Bourg.   Il fallut briſer là,
& ſe diſpoſer à les receuoir ſortablement à leur qualité.   Le Pere leur fit deux preſents de compliment,
ils répondent par deux autres, & en adiouſtent vn
troiſiéme, pour le prier de differer au lendemain la
ceremonie, à cauſe que le iour eſtoit bien auancé; ce
qui fut accordé.

that not a tear or a cry escaped him from amid the flames.

The 14th, which was Sunday, could not have been better begun than with the Holy Sacrifice of the Mass, which we offered on a little Altar in an Oratory contrived in the cabin of Teotonharason, one of the women who had gone down to Kebec with the Ambassadors. She is esteemed here for her rank and her possessions, but especially because she has declared herself openly for the Faith, Professing it publicly and instructing all her family. Already she has made urgent request for Baptism for herself, her mother, and her daughter, having explained to them the mysteries of our Religion and taught them to Pray.

Toward 10 o'clock of the same day, which had been assigned for making the presents, when all was ready,—and when we had said Prayers, publicly and on our knees, [56] while all the assembly maintained a profound silence,—word came that the Deputies from Oiogoien were entering the Village. We were forced to break off there, and prepare to receive them in a manner becoming their rank. The Father made them two presents, by way of greeting; they responded with two others, and added a third as a petition that he would postpone the ceremony to the morrow, as the day was far advanced. This was granted.

CHAPITRE VI.

LES PERES FONT LEURS PRESENTS.

L E Lundy 15. de Nouembre, fur les neuf à dix
heures du matin, apres auoir mis fecrettement
en Paradis vn petit moribond par les eaux du
Baptefme, tous les Anciens s'eftans affemblez auec
le peuple, dans vne place publique, comme nous
l'auions demandé, pour contenter la curiofité de tout
le monde.   Nous commençons par les Prieres publiques, comme le iour precedent, [57] puis le Pere
adopta ceux d'Oiogoën pour enfans.   Apres quoy,
il eftala vn grand collier de pourcelaine, pour dire
que fa bouche eftoit celle d'Onnontio, & que les
paroles, qu'il alloit prononcer, eftoient les paroles des
François, Hurons & Algonquins, qui parloient tous
par fa langue.

Le premier prefent appaifoit les cris que le Pere
entendoit par tout, & effuyoit les larmes, qu'il voyoit
couler fur leur vifage: mais parce que ce n'étoit rien
de les effuyer, & qu'il ne pouuoit pas tarir ce fleuue,
tandis que la fource dureroit, il fit le fecond prefent,
pour leur remettre l'efprit, d'où venoient toutes ces
douleurs: & parce que le fiege de l'efprit eft dans la
tefte, il leur fit vne couronne du collier qu'il leur
prefentoit, & leur appliqua fur la tefte l'vn apres
l'autre.   Ils furent d'abord furpris de cette nouueauté, à laquelle ils fe plûrent, quand ils virent que
le Pere tenoit en main vne petite chaudiere, pleine

CHAPTER VI.

THE FATHERS MAKE THEIR PRESENTS.

ON Monday, November 15th, between nine and ten o'clock in the morning,—after a little dying infant had been secretly sent to Paradise by the waters of Baptism,—all the Elders and the people assembled in a public place, in compliance with our request, as we wished to satisfy the general curiosity. We began, as on the preceding day, with public Prayers. [57] Then the Father adopted the people of Oiogoën as his children. After this, he displayed a large porcelain collar, saying that his mouth was Onnontio's, and the words he was about to utter were the words of the French, Hurons, and Algonquins, who all spoke through him.

The first present was intended to hush the cries heard everywhere by the Father, and to wipe away the tears that he saw coursing down their cheeks. But, since it did not suffice to wipe them away, and as he could not dry up this stream while the source was still running, he offered a second present to calm their minds, the seat of all these griefs; and, as the seat of the mind is in the head, he made them a crown of the proffered collar, which he put on the head of each one successively. At first, they were surprised at this novelty; they were pleased, however, when they saw the Father holding a little kettle, full of an excellent beverage, of which he

d'vn excellent breuuage, & que pour troifiéme
prefent il leur en fit boire à tous; afin d'extirper la
douleur, & [58] appliquer le remede iufqu'au fond du
cœur, & des entraille: ce qui fut accompagné d'vn
beau collier.   Et pour effuier le fang, & femer la
ioye par tout & ne laiffer aucun veftige de trifteffe
en quelque endroit que ce fuft, le Pere fit quatre
prefents aux quatre Nations Iroquoifes, c'eftoient
quatre peaux de Caftor, vne pour chaque Nation.

Le 9. prefent les toucha encor beaucoup.   Le Pere
fit paroiftre vn petit arbre, dont les branches d'en-
haut portoient les noms de leurs Capitaines defunts,
& ces branches eftoient coupées, pour fignifier leur
mort; mais l'arbre auoit quantité d'autres branches
fortes & bien vertes, qui reprefentoient leurs enfans,
par le moyen defquels, on faifoit reuiure ces Heros
decedez, en la perfonne de leurs neveux.   Ils regardoient bien plus attentiuement ce bois, que la
pourcelaine, qui eftoit iointe à ce prefent.

Les deux fuiuants eftoient pour les affeurer, que
Annenraj & Tehaïonhacoua, deux fameux Capitaines
tuez à la guerre, dont le premier auoit iuré [59]
ferment de fidelité entre les mains du Gouuerneur
de Montreal; & le fecond eftoit mort inuoquant le
Ciel, pour les affeurer, dy-je, que ces deux braues,
n'étoient pas morts; & qu'ils demeuroient auffi
fortement vnis auec les François, que les colliers
qu'on prefentoit pour eux, eftoient infeparablement
attachez par enfemble.

Ce qui leur agrea dauantage, fut l'onziéme prefent: car le Pere ayant tiré fon mouchoir, il leur fit
paroiftre dedans, d'vn cofté des cendres d'vn certain
Teotegouifen enterré aux trois Riuieres: & de l'autre,

made them all drink, as a third present — in order to
dispel their grief and [58] apply the remedy to their
very hearts and bowels. This was accompanied by
a beautiful collar. And, in order to wipe away the
blood, and implant joy in every breast, leaving no
trace of sadness anywhere, the Father presented four
Beaver-skins to the four Iroquois Nations, one for
each.

The 9th present affected them even more. He
brought forward a small tree, whose upper branches
bore the names of their deceased Captains, and were
lopped off to signify their death; but the tree had
many other branches, strong and in full leaf, representing their children, through whom these departed
Heroes would be restored to life in the persons of
their descendants. This tree attracted much more
attention than the beads accompanying it.

The two following gifts were to assure them that
Annenrai and Tehaionhacoua, two famous Captains
killed in war,— the former of whom had taken [59]
an oath of fidelity before the Governor of Montreal, and the latter had died invoking Heaven,— to
give assurance, I say, that these two brave men were
not dead, but continued as firmly united with the
French as the collars, presented in their name, were
inseparably attached to each other.

The eleventh present pleased them still more; for
the Father, drawing out his handkerchief, showed
them therein, on the one side the ashes of a certain
Teotegouisen, buried at three Rivers, and on the
other those of the French; and, mixing them
together, he declared that the Iroquois and the
French were but one, both before and after death.

des cendres des François, & les meſlant enſemble,
leur declaroit qu'eux & les François n'eſtoient tous
qu'vn, & auant & apres la mort. Il ioignit vn ſecond
collier à celuy qui accompagnoit ces cendres, pour
faire reuiure cét homme. Les approbations furent
icy fort grandes, & les eſprits bien diſpoſez pour
entendre, & pour voir ce qui ſuiuoit; c'eſtoit le plus
beau collier de tous, que le Pere fit paroiſtre, en
diſant, que tout ce qu'il auoit fait iuſqu'alors, n'eſtoit
qu'vn lenitif, & vn petit ſoulagement à [60] leurs
maux: Qu'il ne pouuoit pas les empeſcher d'eſtre
malades, ny de mourir; qu'il auoit pourtant vn
remede bien ſouuerain, pour toutes ſortes de maux;
que c'eſtoit proprement ce qui l'amenoit en leur païs:
& qu'ils auoient bien fait paroiſtre qu'ils auoient de
l'eſprit, en le venant chercher & demander iuſqu'à
Kebec: que ce grand remede eſtoit la Foy, qu'il leur
venoit annoncer, laquelle ſans doute, ils receuroient
auſſi fauorablement qu'ils l'auoient ſagement demandée. Le Pere pour lors preſcha proprement à
l'Italienne: il auoit vne eſpace raiſonnable pour ſe
pourmener, & pour publier auec pompe la parole de
Dieu. Et il me ſemble qu'on peut dire apres cela,
qu'elle a eſté annoncée à tous les Peuples de ces païs.
Quand il n'auroit pour recompenſe de tous ces trauaux, que la conſolation d'auoir preſché Ieſus-Chriſt
en vn ſi bel auditoire, il auroit ſujet de ſe tenir
plainement ſatisfait. Quoy qu'il en ſoit, ſon Sermon
fut fort bien écouté, pendant lequel, de temps en
temps, ſe faiſoient des cris d'approbation.

Il fallut adioûter vn autre preſent, pour [61]
purger la Foy, des calomnies qu'auoient fait courir
contre elle les ſuppoſts du demon. Et pour leur

He added a second collar to the one accompanying
these ashes, to restore that man to life.   Here the
applause was very great, and they were eager to see
and hear what would follow.   The most beautiful
collar of all was produced by the Father, when he
said that all he had thus far offered was but a lenitive
and slight alleviation for [60] their woes; he could
not prevent them from being ill, or from dying, but
he had a very sovereign remedy for all sorts of afflictions.   That was properly what brought him to their
country, and they had given excellent proof of their
good sense in going down to Kebec in quest of him.
This great remedy was the Faith, which he came to
proclaim to them, and which they would doubtless
receive with a favor equal to their wisdom in asking
for it.   The Father then preached in what was really
the Italian style, having a sufficient space for walking about and for proclaiming with pomp the word
of God.   After that, it can, I think, be said to have
been announced to all the Peoples of those countries.
Though he should have, as recompense for all these
labors, only the consolation of having preached Jesus
Christ before so fine an audience, he would have
reason to be fully satisfied.   At any rate, his Sermon
was attentively followed, cries of approval being
heard from time to time.

The addition of another present was necessary, to
[61] exonerate the Faith from the calumnies circulated
against it by the devil's agents.   In order to impress
his meaning upon their minds, he showed them a
fair sheet of white paper, symbolizing the integrity,
innocence, and purity of the Faith; and another, all
soiled and blackened, whereon were written the

faire entrer dans l'efprit ce qu'il leur difoit, il leur
fit paroître vne belle feüille de papier blanc, qui leur
reprefentoit l'integrité, l'innocence, & la pureté de
la Foy; & vne autre toute gaftée & charbonnée, où
eftoient écrites les calomnies qui fe debitoient contre
elle; Celle-cy fut lacerée & brûlée à mefure qu'on
répondoit & qu'on refutoit ces menfonges; mais auec
tant de zele & d'ardeur, accompagné d'vn torrent de
paroles fi puiffantes, que tous paroiffoient eftre bien
viuement touchez.

Pour donner vn relief à tout cela, fuiuoit le prefent des Meres Vrfulines de Kebec, qui s'offroient
de grand cœur à receuoir chez elles les petites filles
du païs, pour les éleuer dans la pieté, & dans la
crainte de Dieu; & puis celles des Meres Hofpita-
lieres, qui auoient bafti tout de nouueau vn grand
& fplendide Hofpital, pour receuoir auec foin &
guerir auec charité les malades de leur Nation qui
fe trouueroient à Kebec.

[62] Par le dix-feptieme prefent, nous demandions
qu'on nous erigeaft au pluftoft vne Chapelle, pour y
faire nos fonctions auec liberté, & auec bien-feance.
Et par le dix-huictiéme, qu'on pourueuft à ce qui
nous feroit neceffaire, pendant que nous trauaillerions
chez eux tout l'Hyuer.

Les quatre fuiuants, eftoient pour les affeurer qu'au
Printemps prochain la ieuneffe Françoife viendroit;
qu'alors il faudra mettre de bonne heure le canot à
l'eau pour les aller prendre; qu'eftant arriuée, ils
feroient vne paliffade pour la defenfe publique. Et
qu'il eftoit bon dés maintenant, de faire parer la
Natte pour receuoir les Algonquins & les Hurons
qui fuiuront les François. A cette nouuelle fe fit vn

calumnies uttered against it. The latter sheet was torn and burnt according as these lies were answered and refuted. The Father proceeded with so much zeal and ardor, and with such a torrent of forcible words, that all appeared very deeply moved.

As a relief to all this, there followed the present of the Ursuline Mothers of Kebec, who made a cordial offer to receive into their house the little girls of the country, for education in piety and in the fear of God. Then came the present of the Hospital Mothers, who had quite recently built a large and splendid Hospital, for the careful reception and charitable nursing of any sick persons of their Nation who might be at Kebec.

[62] With the seventeenth present we asked that a Chapel be erected as soon as possible, in which we might perform our functions with freedom and propriety; and, with the eighteenth, that the supplies be provided necessary for us during our Winter's labors among them.

The four following were a pledge that, in the following Spring, some young Frenchmen would come, and they must then launch their canoes early and go to receive them; and that these, upon their arrival, would erect a palisade for the public defense. They were also advised to prepare at the same time the Mat for receiving the Algonquins and Hurons who would follow the French. At this news, a shout, louder than usual, was given in expression of their sentiments.

To please the Onnontagueronnons, the next two presents were an invitation to the two other Nations to move their Villages nearer, in order the better to share the advantage of the vicinity of the French.

cry extraordinairement haut, par lequel ils decla-
rerent leurs fentiments.

Les deux autres prefents, eftoient pour complaire
aux Onnontagueronnõs, en inuitant les deux autres
Nations d'aprocher leurs Bourgs, pour pouuoir mieux
participer à l'aduantage du voifinage des François.
Il fallut adioufter vn prefent [63] pour les exhorter
d'arrefter la hache de l'Annieronnon, & vn autre pour
r'allier leurs efprits, afin de n'en auoir plus qu'vn.

Le premier des quatre fuiuants qui fe faifoient
pour les Algonquins, les affeuroit, que ces Peuples
viendroient le Printemps prochain en ambaffade.
Le deuxiéme, que quand les François & les Hurons
feroient établis, les Algonquins pourront bien les
fuiure. Le troifiéme, qu'ils voudroient bien reuoir
quelqu'vn de leurs neveux captifs. Et le quatriéme,
les fit reffouuenir des prefents que firent les Ondata-
ouaouat, lors qu'ils élargirent treize prifonniers entre
les mains des François de Montreal.

Nous nous trouuafmes obligez de faire encore vn
prefent bien confiderable, pour vn ieune François,
nommé Charles Garmant, qui eft parmy les Oneioutchronnons depuis quelques années; le Pere
s'adreffant au Chef de cette Nation, luy dit, qu'il
auoit trop d'efprit pour ne pas voir ce qui eftoit à
faire fur cette matiere, qu'il ne vouloit pas luy
reprefenter le plaifir qu'il feroit à Onnontio, & à
tous les [64] François de leur rendre leur frere, qu'il
voyoit affez la ioye que receuroient fes parens de fon
retour, & qu'il laiffoit tout cela à fa prudence.

Par le penultiéme le Pere s'applaniffoit le chemin,
pour marcher tefte leuée, par toutes les Bourgades
Iroquoifes, & leur donnoit la mefme liberté, pour
aller par tout le païs des François.

We were obliged to add a present [63] exhorting them to stay the Annieronnon's hatchet; and another to unite their minds, that henceforth they might be as one.

The first of the four following, which were offered in behalf of the Algonquins, was a pledge that the latter would send an embassy the coming Spring; the second, that, when the French and Hurons should have become settled, the Algonquins would probably follow them; the third, that they would like to see again some one of their captive nephews; while the fourth was to remind them of the presents given by the Ondataouaouats, upon delivering thirteen prisoners to the French of Montreal.

We felt obliged to make one more present, of considerable value, for a young Frenchman named Charles Garmant, who has been for some years among the Oneioutchronnons.[5] The Chief of that Nation was addressed by the Father, and told that he had too much sense not to see what course to pursue in the matter; that he, the Father, would not picture to him the pleasure he would afford Onnontio and all the [64] French, by restoring their brother to them; that he saw well enough what joy his relatives would feel at his return; and, therefore, all that was left to his discretion.

With the present next to the last, the Father cleared his path for walking, with head erect, through all the Iroquois Villages, and gave them like liberty to traverse the entire country of the French.

Finally, the last present was given in order to recapitulate all that had been said, and to impress it so firmly on their minds, that their ears should never

Enfin le dernier prefent fut vne recapitulation de
tout ce qui auoit efté dit, & pour l'inculquer fi fortement, & fi auant dans leur efprit, que iamais plus
leurs oreilles ne vinffent à s'ouurir aux calomnies,
que les ennemis du repos public pourroient inuenter.

Le Confeil finit par les applaudiffemens reïterez de
part & d'autre, auec vne réponfe qui difoit en deux
mots, que le lendemain on répondroit plus ample-
ment.

Il n'eft pas croyable combien le difcours du Pere
& fes belles façons d'agir rauirent ces peuples. Quant
il eut parlé iufqu'au foir, difoient quelques-vns, nos
oreilles n'auroient iamais efté pleines, & nos cœurs
fuffent encor reftez affamez [65] de fes paroles.
D'autres adiouftoient, que les Hollandois n'auoient
ny efprit, ny langue; qu'ils ne leur auoient iamais
entendu parler du Paradis, ny de l'Enfer: au contraire, qu'ils eftoient les premiers à les porter au mal.
Les autres declaroient leurs penfées d'vne autre
façon, mais tous difoient vnanimement en leur
langue, *Nunquam fic loquutus eft homo.* Ce qui parut
bien en fuite; car le premier des deputez d'Oïogoen
fut dire au Pere, à l'iffuë du Confeil, qu'il auoit
paffion de le prendre pour fon frere, qui eft vne
marque de la haute confiance parmy ces Peuples.

L'aprés-midy, le Pere s'eftant écarté dans vn
bois prochain, pour y faire en repos fes prieres:
quatre femmes Iroquoifes le furent chercher, pour
fe faire inftruire; & auant le foir il y en eut neuf
qui firent le mefme, parmy lefquelles eftoit la fœur
du premier de tous les Capitaines. Quoy qu'il y ait
defia des hommes qui faffent profeffion publique de
prier, ils font pourtant plus honteux, comme ils

again open to any calumnies invented by the enemies
of the public peace.

The Council closed with repeated applause on
both sides, and a brief reply that on the following
day a fuller response would be rendered.

It is past belief how the Father's speech and his
engaging ways charmed these people. " Though he
had spoken till evening," said some, " our ears
would never have been full, and our hearts would
still have been hungry [65] for his words." Others
added that the Dutch had neither sense nor tongues;
they had never heard them mention Paradise or Hell;
on the contrary, they were the first to incite them to
wrong-doing. The rest expressed themselves in
some other way, but all were unanimous in saying,
in their own tongue, *Nunquam sic loquutus est homo* —
which appeared plainly in the issue; for the chief
of the deputies from Oiogoen came to the Father,
after the Council, to say that he wished to adopt him
as his brother — a mark of great confidence with
these Peoples.

In the afternoon, when the Father had retired to
a neighboring wood, in order to say his prayers in
quiet, four Iroquois women went in quest of him for
the purpose of being instructed; and, before evening, nine of them did the same, among whom was
the sister of the chief of all the Captains. Although
some of the men already make public profession of
prayer, yet they are more bashful, — as they admitted
on that very evening, when, coming in great number [66] to our cabin, and hearing the Father speak
for two hours without wearying them, they confessed
that they indeed believed at heart, but dared not yet
declare themselves. They added that what made

aduoüerent le foir mefme, lorfqu'eftants venus en
bon nombre [66] chez nous, & ayant entendu parler
le Pere deux heures durant fans s'ennuyer, ils con-
fefferent à la verité qu'ils croyoient dans le cœur:
mais qu'ils n'ofoient pas encore fe declarer. Qu'au
refte ce qui les portoit à croire, eftoit en partie la
derniere victoire qu'ils auoient remportée fur la
Nation de Chat, leurs ennemis, n'eftant que douze
cent contre trois à quatre mille hommes; & qu'ayants promis deuant le combat, d'embraffer la Foy
s'ils retournoient victorieux, ils ne pouuoient à prefent s'en dedire, apres auoir fi heureufement triom-
phé. En fuite de ce difcours, le Pere les fit tous
prier Dieu: & vn des Deputez fe fit par plufieurs
fois repeter la priere, pour pouuoir l'apprendre par
cœur.

them believe was partly their last victory over the
Cat Nation, their enemies, when they were only
twelve hundred against three or four thousand; and,
as they had promised, before the battle, to embrace
the Faith if they returned victorious, they could not
now retract after so successful a triumph. This
speech ended, the Father made them all pray to
God; and one of the Deputies had the prayer repeated
to him several times, that he might learn it by heart.

[67] CHAPITRE VII.

RÉPONCE AUX PRESENTS DES PERES.

L E feiziême iour fut encor plus heureux que les
precedents, eſtant deſtiné pour receuoir réponce
à nos preſents; mais la plus fauorable, que les
plus zelés amateurs de noſtre Foy, pourroient ſou-
haiter. Dés le matin, pendant qu'vn de nous Baptize
vn enfant malade dans vne cabanne; l'autre apres
auoir celebré la ſainĉte Meſſe en noſtre petit Oratoire, y Baptize deux ieunes filles, aportées pour cela
par leurs parens. La premiere eut le nom de Marie
Magdeleine; en conſideration de Madame de la Pelterie, qui porte ce nom, & qui a fait la premiere
aumoſne pour cette Miſſion, dés auant meſme qu'elle
fuſt commencée. L'autre, eſt la fille de cette Teo-
tanharaſon, dont nous auons deſia parlé, & parlerons
encor, & dont la cabanne nous ſert de Chapelle.
Voila [68] proprement les deux premieres Baptizées
auec quelques Ceremonies de l'Egliſe. Apres cette
ſainĉte aĉtion, vers le midy, tous les notables du
Bourg s'étants trouuez dans noſtre Cabanne, auec
les Deputez des autres Nations, & tout ce qu'elle
pouuoit contenir de monde: ils commencerent leur
remerciement par ſix airs, ou ſix chants, qui n'auoient
rien de ſauuage, & qui exprimoient tres-naïfuement,
par la diuerſité des tons, les diuerſes paſſions qu'ils
vouloient repreſenter. Le premier chant diſoit ainſi.
O la belle terre! la belle terre! qui doit eſtre habitée par
les François. Agochiendagueſé commençoit ſeul en

[67] CHAPTER VII.

REPLY TO THE FATHERS' PRESENTS.

THE sixteenth day was still more successful than those preceding, being appointed for receiving a reply to our presents; and this reply was as favorable as could be desired by the most zealous adherents of our Faith. Early in the morning, while one of us Baptized a sick child in a cabin, the other, after saying holy Mass in our little Oratory, Baptized two young girls, brought thither for the purpose by their parents. The first received the name of Marie Magdeleine, in honor of Madame de la Pelterie, who bears that name, and who gave the first alms for this Mission, even before it was started. The other is the daughter of that Teotanharason, of whom we have already spoken and shall speak again, whose cabin serves us as a Chapel. Those are [68] properly the first two Baptized with some Ceremonies of the Church. After that sacred rite had been performed, toward noon all the notables of the Village assembled in our Cabin, with the Deputies of the other Nations, and all the people that it could hold. They began their acknowledgments with six airs, or chants, which savored nothing of the savage; and expressed very naïvely, by the variation of tones, the different passions which they sought to portray. The first chant was composed of these words: *Oh, the beautiful land, the beautiful land, that the French are to occupy!* Agochiendaguesé,

la perſonne d'vn Ancien qui tenoit ſa place; mais
touſiours de la meſme façon, comme ſi luy-meſme
euſt parlé, puis tous les autres repetoient, & ſa note
& ſa lettre, s'accordant merueilleuſement bien.

Au ſecond chant, le Chef entonnoit ces paroles,
Bonnes nouuelles, tres-bonnes nouuelles. Les autres les
repetoient à meſme ton.   Puis le Chef reprenoit,
C'eſt tout de bon, mon frere: c'eſt tout de bon que [69]
nous parlons enſemble, c'eſt tout de bon que nous auons vne
parole celeſte.

La troiſiéme chanſon auoit vn agreément par vn
refrain fort melodieux; & diſoit, *Mon frere ie te ſaluë;*
mon frere ſois le bien venu.   Aï, aï, aï, hî: O la belle
voix! ô la belle voix que tu as! aï, aï, aï, hi: O la belle
voix, ô la belle voix que i'ay, aï, aï, aï, hi.

Le quatriéme chant auoit vn autre agreément, par
la cadence que gardoient ces Muſiciens, en frappant
des pieds, des mains, & de leurs petunoirs contre
leur natte, mais auec vn ſi bon accord, que ce bruit
ſi bien reglé, mélé auec leurs voix, rendoit vne har-
monie douce à entendre; en voicy les paroles.   *Mon*
frere ie te ſaluë; encore vn coup ie te ſaluë: c'eſt tout de
bon: c'eſt ſans feintiſe que i'accepte le Ciel que tu m'as
fait voir; ouy ie l'agrée, ie l'accepte.

Ils chanterent pour la cinquiéme fois, diſants,
Adieu la guerre, adieu la hache; iuſqu'à preſent nous
auons eſté fous, mais deſormais nous ſerons freres: oüy
nous ſeron[s] veritablement freres.

Le dernier chant portoit ces mots, [70] *C'eſt auiour-*
d'hüy que la grande paix ſe fait.   Adieu la guerre, Adieu
les armes: car l'affaire tout de ſon long eſt belle; tu
ſouſtiens nos Cabannes, quand tu viens auec nous.

Ces chanſons furent ſuiuies de quatre beaux preſents.   Par le premier, Agochiendagueſé ayant fait

represented by an Elder, who continued just as if the chief himself had been speaking, began alone; then all the rest repeated his exact words and tones, harmonizing remarkably well.

In the second chant, the Chief intoned the words, *Good news, very good news;* and the others repeated them in the same tone. Then he resumed: *In very truth, my brother, in very truth,* [69] *we are speaking together; in very truth, we have a message from heaven.*

The third chant had an ornament, in the form of a very musical refrain, and was as follows: *My brother, I salute thee; my brother, be welcome. Aï, aï, aï, hî. O the beautiful voice, O the beautiful voice that thou hast! Aï, aï, aï, hi. O the beautiful voice, O the beautiful voice that I have! Aï, aï, aï, hi.*

The fourth chant had another ornament; the Musicians, namely, beat time by striking their feet, hands, and pipes against their mats. This they did in such perfect accord that the sound, so regular, blended with their voices and became a harmony pleasing to the ear. The words were as follows: *My brother, I salute thee; again I salute thee. In all sincerity, and without simulation, I accept the Heaven that thou hast shown me; yes, I approve it, I accept it.*

The fifth time, they sang as follows: *Farewell, war; farewell, hatchet! We have been fools till now, but in future we will be brothers; yes, we will really be brothers.*

The final song was composed of these words: [70] *To-day the great peace is made. Farewell, war; Farewell, arms! For the affair is entirely beautiful. Thou upholdest our Cabins, when thou comest among us.*

These songs were followed by four beautiful presents. With the first, Agochiendaguesé, after a long speech testifying his gratitude that he and

vn grand difcours, pour témoigner le reffentiment
qu'il auoit de n'eftre plus qu'vn auec Onnontio, dit,
que puis que les Hurons & les Algonquins eftoient
les enfans d'Onnontio, ils deuoient eftre auffi les
fiens; c'eft pourquoy il les adoptoit par les deux
premiers prefents qu'il iettoit aux pieds du Pere.

Le troifiéme & le plus beau de tous ceux qui ont
paru icy, eftoit vn collier compofé de fept mille
grains, qui n'étoit rien pourtant en comparaifon de
fes paroles, C'eft le prefent de la Foy, dit-il, c'eft
pour te dire que tout de bon ie fuis Croyant; c'eft
pour t'exhorter à ne te point laffer de nous inftruire:
continuë de courir par les Cabannes: prends patience,
voyant noftre peu d'efprit pour aprendre la Priere:
En vn mot mets nous-la bien auant dans la tefte &
dans [71] le cœur.   Là-deffus, voulant par vne ceremonie extraordinaire, faire éclater fon ardeur, il
prend le Pere par la main, le fait leuer, le mene au
milieu de toute l'affiftance, fe iette à fon colle, l'em-
braffe, le ferre, & tenant en main le beau collier, luy
en fait vne ceinture, proteftant à la face du Ciel &
de la terre, qu'il vouloit embraffer la Foy comme il
embraffoit le Pere, prenant tous les fpectateurs à
témoins, que cette ceinture, dont il ferroit fi étroitement le Pere, eftoit la marque de l'vnion étroite qu'il
auroit deformais auec les Croyants.   Il adioufte proteftations fur proteftations, & ferments fur ferments,
de la verité de fa parole.

Le Pere fait redoubler les cris d'aprobation autant
de fois que ce Chef promettoit vouloir croire. N'eftoit
ce pas là vn fpectacle capable de tirer les larmes aux
plus endurcis, de voir le premier d'vne Nation
infidelle, faire profeffion publique de la Foy, & tout
fon Peuple luy applaudir dans cette action? Ie prie

Onnontio were now but one, said that, since the Hurons and Algonquins were Onnontio's children, they
must be his also; he therefore adopted them by
offering the first two presents, which he cast at the
Father's feet.

The third and most beautiful of all the presents
offered was a collar of seven thousand beads, which,
however, was as nothing compared with his words.
" It is the present of the Faith," said he; " it is to
tell thee that I am really a Believer, and to exhort
thee not to weary in teaching us. Continue to visit
our Cabins, and have patience with our dullness in
learning the Prayer. In a word, impress it well
upon our minds [71] and hearts."   Thereupon,
wishing to make a striking display of his ardor, he
took the Father by the hand, raised him and led him
out before all the company, and threw himself on
his neck in a close embrace. Then, holding the
beautiful collar in his hand, he made for him a belt
with it,—declaring before Heaven and earth his
determination to embrace the Faith as he embraced
the Father, and calling all the spectators to witness
that this girdle, with which he encircled the Father
so closely, symbolized his own future close union
with the Believers. He protested and swore again
and again that he was sincere in his words.

The Father made the hearers redouble their shouts
of approval, as often as this Chief promised to become
a believer. Was not that a sight to draw tears from
the eyes of the most hardened — to see the head of
an infidel Nation making public profession of the
Faith, and all his People applauding his action? I
pray all who shall read this to lift up their hearts to
God in behalf of these poor Barbarians.

tous ceux qui liront cecy d'éleuer leur cœur à Dieu
pour ces pauures Barbares.

[72] Le quatriéme & dernier prefent, eftoit peu à
comparaifon du precedent; auffi n'eftoit-il que pour
affeurer le Pere que la chaudiere de guerre contre la
Nation de Chat eftoit fur le feu; qu'on iroit à cette
expedition vers le Printemps, & que le lendemain on
congedieroit les Ambaffadeurs Hurons, leur donnant
pour efcorte quinze des plus apparents du Païs.

Apres que ce Capitaine eût acheué de parler, le
Chef des Deputez d'Oiogoen fe leue, & prend la
parole, faifant vn remerciement d'vne bonne demy-
heure, auec grande eloquence, & bien de l'efprit.
Le fuiet de fon compliment, fut que luy & toute fa
Nation, fe tenoient extremément obligez à Onnontio,
de ce qu'il leur auoit fait l'honneur de fon adoption;
qu'ils ne derogeroient iamais à cette belle qualité, &
ne degenereroient pas d'vne fi illuftre adoption.
Qu'au refte toute éclatante qu'elle fuft, elle luy eftoit
honorable, puis que ny luy ny les fiens, n'auoient
iamais efté adoptez que par des gens d'apparence;
mais qu'Onnontio mettoit le comble à toute [73] la
gloire qu'ils tiroient de fes autres parents & alliez.
Et pour faire paroiftre la ioye que receuoit le Deputé
de cette gloire, il éleua vn chant auffi agreable que
nouueau. Tous les affiftans chantoient auec luy, mais
d'vn ton different, & plus pefant, frappant leur natte
en cadence, pendant quoy cét homme danfoit au
milieu de tous, fe demenant d'vne étrange façon, &
n'épargnant aucune partie de fon corps, de forte
qu'il faifoit des geftes des pieds, des mains, de la
tefte, des yeux, de la bouche, s'accordant fi bien, &
auec fon chant & auec celuy des autres, que cela
paroiffoit admirable. Voicy ce qu'il chantoit, *A, a,*

[72] The fourth and last present was little in com-
parison with the preceding, its purpose being merely
to inform the Father that the kettle of the war
against the Cat Nation was over the fire; that hostili-
ties would be opened toward Spring; and that the
Huron Ambassadors would be dismissed the next
day, with an escort of fifteen of the Country's leading men.

After this Captain had finished speaking, the Chief
Deputy from Oiogoen arose and made a speech of
thanks, of much wit and eloquence, which lasted a good
half-hour.   The pith of his polite address was, that he
and all his Nation deemed themselves greatly obliged
to Onnontio for the honor of adoption by him; that
they would never become unworthy of that high dis-
tinction, or fail to do honor to so illustrious a connection; and that, furthermore, brilliant as it was, it did
honor to Onnontio, since neither the speaker nor his
people had ever been adopted except by people of rank;
yet that this adoption of them by Onnontio crowned
all [73] the glory which they derived from all their
previous ties and alliances.   To show his joy over
this glory, the Deputy began a song, which was as
pleasing as it was new.   All present sang with him,
but in a different and a heavier tone, beating time
on their mats; while the man himself danced in the
midst of them all, performing strange antics,—keep-
ing his whole body in motion; making gestures with
his hands, feet, head, eyes, and mouth,—and all this
so exactly to the time of both his own singing and
that of the others, that the result was admirable.
He sang these words, *A, a, ha, Gaianderé, gaianderé;*
that is, translated into Latin, *Io, io triumphe.*   And
then, *E, e, he, Gaianderé, gaianderé; O, o, ho, Gaian-*

ha, Gaïanderé gaïanderé, c'eſt à dire proprement en
langue Latine, *Io, io triumphe.* Et en ſuite, *E, e, he,
Gaïanderé, gaïanderé, O, o, ho, Gaïanderé, gaïanderé.*
Il expliqua ce qu'il vouloit dire par ſon *Gaïanderé,*
qui ſignifie chez eux choſe tres-excellente. Il dit
donc que ce que nous autres nous appellons la Foy, ſe
deuoit nommer chez eux *Gaïanderé:* & pour mieux
ſignifier cela, il fit le premier preſent de pourcelaine.

[74] Le ſecond eſtoit de la partie de l'Onneioutch-
ronnon, pource qu'eſtans eux deux freres iumeaux,
il ſe croyoit eſtre obligé de faire auſſi à Onnontio des
remerciments de la part de ſon frere, qui auoit eu
pareillement le bon-heur de ſon adoption.

Par le troiſiéme, il aſſeuroit que le preſent que
nous auions fait le iour precedent, pour r'allier les
eſprits des Anniehronnons auec les quatre autres
Nations, auroit ſon effet.

Le quatriéme nous fut bien agreable, par lequel il
faiſoit proteſtation, que non ſeulement le Pere; mais
encore ſes deux enfants, ſeroient tous de bons Croyants, il vouloit dire, & que l'Onnontagueronnon, qui
eſt le pere, & Oïogoen, & Onneiout, qui ſont ſes
enfants, embraſſeroient la Foy.

Par le cinquiéme, il prenoit pour ſes freres, les
Hurons & les Algonquins. Et par le ſixiéme, il
aſſeuroit que les trois Nations ſe ioindroient enſemble, pour aller querir les François, & les Sauuages
qui voudront venir en leur Païs au Printemps
prochain.

[75] Il fallut répondre à tout cela : comme le Pere
fit en deux mots, & deux preſents ; dont l'vn eſtoit
pour reparer les brefches qui auoient eſté faites en
nôtre Cabanne, par l'affluence du peuple, qui la

deré, gaianderé. He explained what he meant by his
Gaianderé, which signifies, among the natives,
" something very excellent."   He said that, what
we call the Faith, would be called by them *Gaianderé;* and, to explain it better, he offered his first
present of porcelain.

[74] He offered the second in behalf of the Onnei-
outchronnon, because, as they both were twin brothers, he thought that he, too, ought to thank Onnontio,
since he shared the happiness of being adopted by
him.

The third was an assurance that the present
offered by us the day before, to unite the minds of
the Anniehronnons with those of the four other
Nations, would be effectual.

The fourth pleased us greatly, being given in
declaration that not only the Father, but also his two
children, would all become sincere Believers,— meaning, that both the Onnontagueronnon, who is the
father, and the Oiogoen and Onneiout, who are his
children, would embrace the Faith.

With the fifth, he adopted the Hurons and Algonquins as his brothers; and, with the sixth, promised
that the three Nations should unite, and go, in the
following Spring, to bring the French and the Savages who should desire to come into their Country.

[75] It was necessary to make a reply to all this,
which the Father did in two words, each accompanied by a present.   One was to repair the rents
made in our Cabin by the people who crowded it
every day, and who could not see their fill of us;
and the other was to clean the mat on which future
Councils between their Country and the French and
their Allies were to be held.

rempliſſant tout le iour, ne ſe pouuoient faouler de
nous voir. L'autre pour nettoyer la natte ſur laquelle ſe tiendront deformais les Conſeils de leur Païs
auec les François & leurs Alliez.

Cette belle iournée fut terminée par l'inſtruction
d'vne vingtaine de perſonnes de ce Bourg, qui ſe
preſenterent de nouueau pour prier.

Le dix-ſeptiéme, apres que nous euſmes celebré la
ſaincte Meſſe, on nous mena pour prendre les me-
ſures d'vne Chapelle. Elle fut baſtie le lendemain,
& par bon preſage, ce fut le iour de la Dedicace de
l'Egliſe ſaint Pierre & ſaint Paul. Il eſt vray que
pour tout marbre & pour tous metaux pretieux, on
n'employa que de l'écorce. Si-toſt qu'elle fut con-
ſtruite, elle fut ſanctifiée par le Bapteſme de trois
enfans, à qui le chemin du Ciel fut auſſi bien ouuert
ſous ces écorces, qu'à ceux qui ſont ſouſtenus [76]
ſur les fonds dont les voûtes ſont d'or & d'argent.

This beautiful day closed with the teaching of a score of people of the Village, who presented themselves anew in order to pray.

On the seventeenth, after celebrating holy Mass, we were taken out to make measurements for a Chapel. It was erected on the following day, which, by good omen, was the day of the Dedication of the Church of saint Peter and saint Paul. It is true that all our marble and precious metals were only bark. Upon its completion, it was consecrated by the Baptism of three children, to whom the way to Heaven was opened under that bark roof just as well as it is to those who are held [76] over fonts whose arches are of gold and silver.

CHAPITRE VIII.

LES PREMIERS FRUICTS RECUEILLIS EN CETTE MISSION.

L E vingt-troifiéme du mefme mois de Nouembre, le Pere parcourant les Cabannes, rencontra vne Ame, qui a bien des marques de fa prede- ftination; c'eft la fœur d'vn des principaux Capitaines d'icy; laquelle n'eût pas pluftoft entendu parler de noftre Foy, qu'elle voulut mettre toute fa famille en eftat de falut, priant le Pere de Baptizer fur l'heure fa petite fille, & d'aller au pluftoft à quelques ca- bannes champeftres, qui font de fa famille, pour y Baptizer fes autres enfants. Le Pere promit d'exe- cuter le tout dans peu de temps.

Le vingt-quatriéme, le Pere fut fort follicité de la mefme grace, pour la grande [77] mere de Teoton- harafon; c'eft la plus aagée de tout le Païs; Les plus vieux difent, que lors qu'ils eftoient enfants, celle-cy eftoit defia vieille, & auffi ridée qu'elle paroift; de forte qu'elle paffe de beaucoup cent ans. Dieu fans doute luy a conferué vne fi longue vie, pour la mettre en poffeffion de celle qui ne finit point. Le Pere luy ayant fait voir l'Image de noftre Seigneur, elle en fut fi rauie, qu'apres l'auoir bien confiderée, elle dit tout bonnement à celuy que l'Image reprefentoit: Prends courage, ne m'abandonne pas, & donne-moy ton Paradis apres ma mort: prends courage, ne nous quittons point. Nous verrons fon Baptefme dans peu de iours.

CHAPTER VIII.

THE FIRST-FRUITS GATHERED IN THIS MISSION.

ON the twenty-third of the same month of November, the Father, in going about among the Cabins, met a Soul which bore evident signs of its predestination. It was the sister of one of the chief Captains of the place. She had no sooner heard of our Faith, than she wished to prepare her whole family for salvation, begging the Father to Baptize her little daughter at once, and to go as soon as possible to some outlying cabins belonging to her family, there to Baptize her other children. The Father promised to do all this in a short time.

On the twenty-fourth, he was strongly pressed to grant the same favor to [77] Teotonharason's grandmother, the oldest woman in all the Country. The most aged people say that, when they were children, she was already old, and as wrinkled as she appears now; so that she is thought to be well over a hundred years old. God has, doubtless, preserved to her so long a life, to endow her with that which never ends. Upon the Father's showing her the Image of our Lord, she was so delighted with it that, after considering it well, she said in all simplicity to the one represented by the Image: " Courage! Do not forsake me; give me thy Paradise after my death. Courage! Let us never separate." We shall witness her Baptism in a few days.

Nous ne pûfmes refufer vne charité que nous fifmes
le vingt-cinquiéme, à vne petite orpheline captiue,
& morte peu apres auoir receu ce grand Benefice,
c'eftoit pluftoft pour condefcendre au defir de fes
parents, qui quoy qu'infidelles, demanderent inftam-
ment que nous allaffions prier Dieu fur fon corps.
On ne croiroit pas combien de confolation ils receurent de nous voir à genoux [78] aupres du corps
mort, & d'entendre qu'eftant Baptizée, elle menoit
vne vie bien-heureufe dans le Ciel.

Le vingt-huictiéme, premier Dimanche de l'Aduent, fe fit le premier Catechifme folemnel dans vne
des plus apparentes Cabannes d'Onontagué, nôtre
Chapelle eftant trop petite. On le commença par
les Prieres, que l'affiftance fit tout haut; puis le Pere
expliqua quelques points de noftre Creance; en fuite
il fit paroiftre quelques Images, pour aider à l'imagination, & faire entrer au cœur la deuotion par les
yeux. Il interroge les vns & les autres fur ce qui a
efté dit, & recompenfe ceux qui reüffiffent: & pour
conclure, on chante quelques motets fpirituels. Vne
petite poche eftant iointe, & s'accordant bien auec la
voix des Sauuages, laiffa dans tous les efprits vn grand
defir de fe trouuer encor à de femblables inftructions.

Nous ne pûfmes mieux celebrer la Fefte de fainct
François Xauier, qui a fait tant de Baptefmes, qu'en
le conferant la veille à deux des plus anciens du
Bourg, & le iour mefme à deux enfants, [79] & à
d'autres pendant toute l'Octaue, en Baptizant iufqu'à
quatre par iour; de forte qu'il femble que ce grand
Apoftre veuille à prefent faire en ce bout du monde,
ce qu'il faifoit autrefois fi abondamment en l'autre.

Le fecond Dimanche de l'Aduent fe continua la
Doctrine Chreftienne, comme le premier, auec cette

We could not refuse the charity which we granted, on the twenty-fifth, to a little orphan girl, a captive, who died soon after receiving this great Blessing. It was rather to yield to the wish of her relatives who, although unbelievers, begged us urgently to go and pray to God over her body. It is incredible how much comfort they received from seeing us kneeling [78] beside the dead body, and hearing that, as she was Baptized, she was leading a blessed life in Heaven.

On the twenty-eighth, the first Sunday in Advent, the first formal Catechism was held in one of the chief Cabins of Onontagué, our Chapel being too small. We began with Prayers, recited aloud by those present. Then the Father explained some points of our Belief, and next showed some Images, to aid the imagination, and impress the heart with devotion through the medium of the eyes. Questioning them, one by one, on what had been said, he gave rewards to those who answered correctly. In conclusion, some sacred motets were sung, accompanied by a little violin which harmonized well with the Savages' voices, and left in the minds of all a great desire to attend such lessons again.

We could not better celebrate the Feast of saint Francis Xavier, who performed so many Baptisms, than by conferring this sacrament, the evening before, upon two of the oldest people of the Village, upon two children on the day itself, [79] and upon others during the entire Octave, Baptizing as many as four in one day; so that this great Apostle appears to wish now, at this end of the world, to repeat what of old he so abundantly accomplished, at the other.

difference, qu'à la fin, le Baptefme fut donné publiquement à la grand'mere de Teotonharafon.

Le feptiéme de Decembre, mourut la premiere
Baptizée de tout le Bourg, c'eſtoit vne fille d'enuiron
vingt ans, qui languiſſoit depuis long-temps d'vne
fiévre ethique quand nous arriuaſmes; Dieu la fceut
ſi bien difpofer par le moyen des charitez du Pere,
qui luy fit prendre quelques remedes, & qui luy portoit fouuent de petits raffraifchiſſements, qu'enfin
elle demanda le Baptefme, du commencement dans
l'efperance de fa guerifon; mais elle changea bien
de penfée, quand le Pere luy porta nouuelle qu'elle
deuoit fe preparer pour aller au Ciel, elle le fit
comme ſi toute fa [80] vie elle euſt vefcu dans le
Chriſtianifme, iufques-là qu'elle n'auoit de ioye dans
fon mal, qu'en voyant le Pere, qui la confoloit auſſi
de tout fon poſſible; prenant la natte de cette pauure
malade pour cabinet, où il fe retiroit pour reciter
paiſiblement fon Office & y faire vne partie de fes
autres deuotions; à quoy la malade prenoit vn fingulier plaiſir.   Elle expira doucement pour aller, comme
nous prefumons, fe ioindre à ceux de fa Nation, qui
l'ont deuancée dans le Ciel, quoy qu'elle les euſt
preuenuë par le Baptefme.

Le troiſiéme & quatriéme Dimanche de l'Aduent,
fe fit pareillement le Catechifme; mais auec plus
d'affluence de peuple qu'auparauant.   Leur humeur
n'eſt pas ſi barbare qu'elle ne s'apriuoife, & ne prenne
plaiſir aux induſtries dont on fe fert pour leur faire
goufter nos Myſteres.   Vne bonne femme Huronne
entendant expliquer les ioyes que Dieu prepare au
Ciel à fes Elûs; rauie de tant de biens, s'écria, Ah,
mon frere, tu me perces le cœur; voila vn coup de
glaiue bien penetrant que tu me donnes; le [81] Pere

On the second Sunday in Advent, the Christian Doctrine was continued, as on the first,— with this difference, that, at the close, Baptism was conferred publicly upon Teotonharason's grandmother.

On the seventh of December, the first person Baptized in all that Village died. It was a girl of about twenty years, who, when we came, had long been ill of a consumptive fever. God knew so well how to prepare her through the kindness of the Father — who made her take some remedies, and who often brought her little delicacies — that at last she asked for Baptism. She did so, at first, in the hope of recovery; but she changed her views entirely, when the Father told her that she must prepare to go to Heaven, which she did as if [80] she had lived all her life a Christian,— so much so, that she found no other pleasure during her illness than seeing the Father, who on his part did his utmost to comfort her. He used that poor patient's mat as a closet, to which he retired to recite his Office in quiet, and to perform a part of his other devotions, in all of which the sick girl took a singular pleasure. She expired peacefully, to join, as we think, those of her Nation who had gone before her to Heaven, although her Baptism preceded theirs.

The Catechism was likewise held on the third and fourth Sundays in Advent, but with a larger attendance than before. Their nature is not so barbarous that it cannot be tamed, and made to take pleasure in our ingenious devices for making them enjoy our Mysteries. A good Huron woman, upon hearing explained the joys which God prepares in Heaven for his Elect, in her delight exclaimed: " Ah, my brother, thou piercest my heart; behold the sharp

furpris de cette exclamation, luy demande ce qu'elle
a.   Ce que i'ay, dit-elle, ne le vois-tu pas bien? i'ay
à me plaindre de toy, de ce que iufqu'à prefent tu
ne m'auois pas fait conceuoir ce que c'eft que du
Paradis; c'eft ce qui m'afflige maintenant, de ce que
i'ay ignoré fi long-temps l'excez du bon-heur que
i'efpere, & l'excez de la bonté de celuy qui me le
promet. Vne autre bonne vieille fit paroiftre de
femblables tendreffes; mais d'vne façon differente.
Le Pere la trouua fans la chercher, ou pluftoft Dieu
conduifit fes pas vers elle, lors qu'il penfoit aller à
vn autre; c'eftoit vn fruict tout meur pour le Ciel,
qui ne demandoit plus que d'eftre cueilly; auffi
eftoit-elle bien malade, quand le Pere la rencontra.
Il luy dit, entre autres chofes, qu'il ne regretoit pas
tant, de ce qu'il eftoit venu trop tard pour dõner
remede à fon corps, que pour le falut de fon ame, &
qu'ayant vefcu fi long-temps, elle n'auoit pas encore
pû reconnoiftre l'Autheur de la vie.   Là-deffus, il
luy explique quelques points de la Foy, luy fait voir
l'Image de Iefus-Chrift.   La voila defia Chreftienne.
[82] Il la fait prier; elle prie, mais d'vne façon qui
faifoit paroiftre fon cœur fur fa langue: car au lieu
que les autres repetent les Prieres apres le Pere, de
mefme ton & de mefme voix; elle voulut chanter à
chaque mot qu'elle prononçoit, & le fit fi doucement,
qu'on eftoit raui d'entendre ce Cygne, qui auoit
l'ame fur le bord des lévres pour l'enuoyer au Ciel.
Auffi mourut elle peu apres fon Baptefme.   Quelle
Prouidence!
     La veille de Noël, le Pere prit occafion de faire
feftin aux principaux du Bourg, pour leur faire
entendre ce grand Myftere.   Ils l'écouterent fort
attentiuement, & vn des fruits du Sermon, fut qu'vn

sword-thrust which thou givest me." The [81]
Father, surprised at this exclamation, asked her what
ailed her. " Dost thou not see plainly what ails
me?" she returned. " I must complain of thee,
because thou hast not told me before what Paradise
is. I grieve now at having been so long ignorant of
the great happiness that I hope for, and of the great
goodness of him who promises it to me." Another
good old woman showed similar feeling, but in a
different way. The Father found her without seeking her,— or, rather, God guided his steps to her
when he thought to visit another. She was fruit all
ripe for Heaven, only requiring to be plucked. She
was also very ill when the Father met her. He told
her, among other things, that he did not so much
regret that he came too late to apply a remedy to
her body, as he deplored the loss of her soul and her
inability, after so long a life, to acknowledge the
Author of her being. Thereupon, he explained to
her some points of our Faith, and showed her the
Image of Jesus Christ. She became a Christian immediately. [82] He taught her to pray; and she did
so in a way which made it evident that her heart was
on her lips; for, while others say their Prayers after
the Father and in the same tone of voice, she was
bent on singing at each word she uttered. She sang
so sweetly, that she charmed those who listened to
this Swan, whose soul was on her very lips, ready to
fly away to Heaven. Thus she died, soon after her
Baptism. What a Providence!

On Christmas eve, the Father took occasion to give
a feast to the Village chiefs, in order to make them
understand that great Mystery. They heard him
very attentively, and one of the fruits of the Sermon

de ces Capitaines vint le lendemain de grand matin
à la porte de noſtre Chapelle, & là exhortoit ceux
qui entroient à bien prier; puis eſtant entré luy-
meſme, les inuita de nouueau à ſe bien comporter en
cette action, & de bien écouter ce que le Pere diſoit.
Il ne ſe preſenta pas pourtant pour prier, & luy & la
pluſpart des anciens font la ſourde-oreille à la parole
de Dieu.   Ils inuitent bien le Pere de continuer à
inſtruire la ieuneſſe: [83] mais le reſpect humain, &
la prudence de la chair, les tient encore au maillot
tout âgez qu'ils ſont.

    Les ſonges ſont l'vn des grands empeſchements
qu'ils ayent à leur Conuerſion.   Il ſont tellement
attachez à ces réueries, qu'ils leur attribuent tous les
grands ſuccez qu'ils ont eu iuſqu'à preſent, & à là
guerre & à la chaſſe.   Or ſçachant bien que la creance
aux ſonges eſt incompatible auec la Foy, cela les
rend plus opiniaſtres; veu meſmement qu'ils ſe
perſuadent que dés lors que les Hurons ont receu la
Foy, & qu'ils ont quitté leurs ſonges, ils ont commencé à ſe perdre: & tout leur Païs a touſiours depuis
eſté en decadence, iuſqu'à ſa ruïne totale.   Le diable
ſuſcite encore de faux bruits, par le moyen de quelques Hurons captifs & renegats, qui publient que les
robes noires feront icy comme chez eux: que nous
prenons par eſcrit les noms des enfants que nous les
enuoyons en France; & que là on leur fait des rayes
ſur le corps auec du charbon, & à meſure que ces
rayes s'effacent, les perſonnes qui les portent, ſont
affligées de maladies iuſqu'à la mort.   [84] Quoy
que cette calomnie ſoit bien groſſiere, & bien ridicule, le diable ne laiſſe pas de s'en ſeruir, pour
commencer à nous diſputer la conqueſte que nous

was, that one of these Captains came early next morning to our Chapel door, and there exhorted those who entered to pray well; then, entering himself, he bade them anew to conduct themselves properly during the service, and to heed well the Father's words.   But he did not offer to pray himself, both he and most of the elders turning a deaf ear to God's word.   They invite the Father, indeed, to continue his instruction of the young people; [83] but fear of the world and regard for the flesh hold them still in swaddling-clothes, old as they are.

Dreams form one of the chief hindrances to their Conversion; and to these they are so attached that they attribute to them all their past great successes, both in war and in hunting.   Now, as they well know that the belief in dreams is incompatible with the Faith, they become even more obstinate; especially, as they are aware of the fact that, the moment the Hurons received the Faith and abandoned their dreams, their ruin began, and their whole Country has ever since been declining to its final total destruction.   The devil still circulates false reports, through certain Huron prisoners and renegades, who proclaim that the black gowns will pursue the same course here as with them; that we write down the names of children; that we send them to France, where their bodies are marked with charcoal; and that, in the same ratio as these marks gradually become defaced, the persons bearing them are afflicted with ailments, until at last they die.   [84] Gross and ridiculous though this calumny is, the devil does not fail to use it, to dispute with us the advantage which we are gaining over him.   But he has not yet succeeded in preventing the large attendance at Prayers

faifons fur luy. Mais il n'a pû encore empefcher
le concours qui fe fait aux Prieres tous les matins:
& malgré luy, pour mieux folemnifer la Fefte de
Noël, nous auons donné le nom de cette Fefte à vne
bonne Iroquoife, qui a demandé le Baptefme auec
inftance; & celuy de Ieanne à vne autre bien malade,
qui fe traina pourtant iufqu'à la Chapelle le iour de
S. iean l'Euangelifte.

Le Pere fut aduerti, mais trop tard, pour l'aller
conferer à vne pauure fille captiue de la Nation de
Chat, qui fut cruellement maffacrée par le comman-
dement de fa Maiftreffe, à laquelle elle ne plaifoit
pas, à caufe qu'elle eftoit de temps en temps opiniaftre.   Ce fut le vingt-feptiéme de Decembre, que fa
Maiftreffe fe mit en l'efprit de s'en defaire; c'eft
pourquoy fans beaucoup deliberer, elle donna commiffion à vn ieune homme de la tuër; Il prend fa
hache, fuit cette pauure victime, lors qu'elle alloit
au bois; [85] mais il fe rauife, & vient faire fon coup
à la veuë de tout le monde; il la laiffe donc retourner,
& lors qu'elle eftoit à la porte du Bourg, il luy
décharge vn coup de fa hache fur la tefte, & la iette
par terre comme morte: elle n'eftoit pas pourtant
bleffée à mort, fi bien qu'elle fut portée dans vne
Cabanne prochaine, pour eftre penfée: mais comme
on eut reproché au meutrier, qu'il ne fçauoit ce que
c'eftoit de caffer des teftes: il retourne, arrache la
proye d'entre les mains de ceux qui la tenoiët, la
traine, & luy décharge d'autres coups, qui luy ofterent
la vie.   Ce meutre n'eftonna point les enfants qui fe
recreoient là auprés, & ne les diuertit point de leur
ieu: tant ils font defia accoutumez à voir le fang
des pauures captifs. Sur le foir, le meutrier, ou

every morning; and, in spite of him, in order the
better to solemnize the Christmas Festival, we gave
its name to a good Iroquois woman, who urgently
asked for Baptism; and that of Jeanne to another
woman, who, though very sick, dragged herself as
far as the Chapel on the day of St. John the Evan-
gelist.

The Father was sent for, but too late, to confer
this sacrament upon a poor captive girl of the Cat
Nation, who was cruelly murdered by order of her
Mistress, whom she displeased by her occasional
obstinacy. On the twenty-seventh of December, her
Mistress took a notion to get rid of her; therefore,
without much deliberation, she commissioned a young
man to kill her. Taking his hatchet, he followed
this poor victim on her way to the woods; [85] but
he changed his mind, and came back to do the deed
in the sight of all. Accordingly, he allowed her to
return, and, when she was at the entrance to the
Village, struck her on the head with his hatchet,
felling her to the ground, apparently dead. Yet,
she was not mortally wounded, and was therefore
carried into a neighboring Cabin to have her wound
dressed. When, however, the murderer was taunted
with his want of skill in head-splitting, he returned,
snatched his prey from those who held her, dragged
her away, and gave her more blows which killed
her. This murder did not startle the children play-
ing near by, or even divert them from their game,
so accustomed are they to the sight of these poor
captives' blood. Toward evening, the murderer,
or some one else, went crying aloud through the
streets and cabins, that such and such a person had
been put to death; whereupon all began to make a

quelqu'autre, fut crier tout haut par les ruës, & par
les cabannes, qu'vne telle perfonne auoit efté mife à
mort.   Alors chacun fe mit à faire du bruit des pieds
& des mains: quelques-vns auec des baftons frap-
poient fur les écorces des cabãnes, pour épouuenter
l'ame de la defunᵈte, & la chaffer bien loin.   Les
Predicateurs de l'Euangile font [86] tous les iours
dans les mefmes dangers, parmy ces Peuples.

Vne bonne Catechumene Iroquoife, abhorrant cette
cruauté, donna quafi à mefme temps au Pere des
marques de l'amour qu'elle a pour la Foy: car eftant
recherchée par vn des confiderables du Païs, homme
bon guerrier & bon chaffeur, deux qualitez qui font
icy les bons partis; elle luy declara d'abord, que
voulant eftre Chreftienne, elle ne prendroit point de
Mary, qui n'euft le mefme defir.   Il promet de fe
faire inftruire: & comme il auoit grande paffion pour
cette femme, il fut trouuer le Pere pour cela; voila
de beaux commencements: la Catechumene eftoit
bien-aife, en gagnant cét homme à Dieu, de l'épou-
fer: mais le Pere luy ayant dit, qu'elle ne pouuoit
contraᵈter auec luy, pource qu'il auoit defia vne autre
femme, elle luy declara genereufement, qu'elle ne
le prendroit point, puis que cela eftoit contre les Loix
de la Religion qu'elle vouloit embraffer.

Vn autre en fuitte fe prefente auec les mefmes
auantages, & le mefme empefchement: [87] elle le
rebutte courageufement; c'eftoient là deux rudes
attaques pour vne Catechumene.   On luy dit qu'elle
ne doit donc pas efperer de fe marier, puis qu'il n'y
a perfonne dans le Bourg fans femme: qu'elle ne doit
plus s'attendre à de fi bons rencontres, & qu'elle
fe va décrier par tout; elle tient ferme, perfiftant

noise with their feet and hands, while some beat
with sticks the bark of their cabins, to frighten the
soul of the departed and drive it far away. The
Preachers of the Gospel are [86] daily exposed to
like dangers among these Peoples.

A good Iroquois woman, a Catechumen, who
abhorred such cruelty, gave the Father, at about
this time, evidence of her attachment to the Faith.
Being sought in marriage by one of the leading men
of the Country, a brave warrior and a good hunter,—
two qualities which here mark a desirable suitor,—
she told him at once that, intending to become a good
Christian, she would take no Husband who had not
the same desire. He promised to seek instruction;
and, as he had a strong passion for her, went to find
the Father for that purpose. These were fine begin-
nings. The Catechumen was very glad to win this
man to God and to marry him; but, being told by
the Father that she could not be united to him, as he
already had a wife, she nobly declared that she would
not take him, as it was against the Laws of the
Religion which she wished to embrace.

Then another man offered himself, with the same
advantages and the same disqualification, [87] and
she bravely rejected him. Those were two severe
assaults for a Catechumen. She was told that now
she must not hope to marry, as there was no unmar-
ried man in the Village; that she must not expect
any more such good offers; and that she would be
universally censured. But she held firm, bravely
clinging to her first resolution; and what she did a
month later well shows the spirit with which she
embraced Christianity. One of the chief Captains of
the Village, a man of proud and arrogant bearing,

courageufement dans fon premier deffein. Ce qu'elle fit vn mois apres, montre bien de quel cœur elle embraffoit le Chriftianifme. Vn des principaux Capitaines du Bourg, homme fier & fuperbe en apparence, la va trouuer vn foir en fa cabanne, pour la folliciter au mal. Cette façon d'agir eft fi commune parmy ces Iroquois, qu'elle fe fait quafi publiquement & fans honte. Cette pauure femme n'eut point d'égard à la condition de ce méchant homme; elle l'éconduit au commencement auec douceur. Il perfifte; elle le rebute. Il prie, il menace, il fe met en colere: la pauure femme le voyant en fougue, s'échappe & s'enfuit dans vne cabanne où eftoit le Pere, luy raconte le tout, & fait vne nouuelle proteftation de mourir [88] pluftoft que de faire chofe aucune contre fa promeffe. Refifter au peché, combattre pour la vertu, c'eft la marque d'vne Foy veritable. Cette action luy acquit de l'honneur: chacun difoit qu'elle meritoit d'eftre Chreftienne, & qu'elle auoit toufiours mené vne vie fort innocente.

La premiere Baptizée de cette année 1656. eut des affauts auffi rudes, mais d'vne autre façon. C'eft cette Teotonharafon, qui a fi bien commencé, comme nous auons dit, & qui a prefché la Foy des premiers dans fon Païs, & qui l'a plantée dans fa cabanne, où les Prieres fe font reglement tous les iours, auec grande confolation du Pere. Si elle euft prefté l'oreille aux faux bruits que quelques Hurons ont femé contre la Foy, il y a long-temps qu'elle auroit tout abandonné. Dieu a permis pour l'éprouuer, que les chofes que les Payens luy ont predites, luy foient arriuées. Auffi-toft que tu feras du nombre des Croyans, luy difoient-ils, tu feras attaquée de maladie;

sought her one evening in her cabin, for the purpose of seducing her to evil — something so common
among these Iroquois that it is done almost openly
and without shame.   The poor woman heeded not
the rank of that wicked man; she refused him, gently
at first; and, when he persisted, she repulsed him.
He begged, threatened, flew into a passion; and the
poor woman, seeing him carried away with wrath,
escaped, fled into a cabin where the Father was, told
him all, and made a fresh vow to die [88] rather
than break her promise.   To resist sin, to fight for
virtue,— those are the acts which distinguish a true
Faith.   The deed brought her honor, all agreeing
that she deserved to become a Christian, and that
she had always led a very innocent life.

The first person Baptized this year, 1656, was
assaulted just as severely, but in another way.   I
allude to that Teotonharason, who made so good a
beginning, as we have related, and who was one of
the first to preach the Faith in her Country and plant
it in her cabin, where Prayers are held regularly
every day, to the Father's great gratification.   Had
she listened to the false reports circulated against
the Faith by certain Hurons, she would long ago
have abandoned the whole matter.   In order to try
her, God suffered the Pagans' predictions to be veri-
fied in her case.   " As soon as thou hast joined the
Believers," they said to her, " thou wilt be attacked
with illness, and all thy family will be visited with
misfortunes and calamities."   Strange to relate, [89]
at the height of her devotion, while we were using
her cabin as a Chapel and as a place for holding
Catechisms, she was seized with a malignant disease,
and, at the same time, received word that her mother,

toute ta famille fe remplira de mal-heurs & de
miferes.   Chofe eftonnante, [89] au fort de fes deuotions, lors que nous nous feruions de fa cabanne pour
Chapelle, & pour y faire les Catechifmes, elle fut
prife d'vne méchante maladie, & à mefme temps, on
luy apporta nouuelle que fa mere, bonne Catechumene, s'étoit rompu la iambe, la veille mefme que
fa grand'mere venoit d'eftre Baptizée.   Et pour .
comble de fes mal-heurs, ou de fes benedictions, vn
fien petit fils de dix à douze ans, qui n'a rien de
fauuage, ny dans fon humeur, ny dans fa façon
exterieure, qui prie Dieu à merueille, & qui fçait
tres-parfaitement tout le Catechifme, fut faifi d'vne
fiévre lente, qui le confommoit à veuë d'œil.   Tout
cela n'ébranle point l'efprit de Teotonharafon: les
Prieres fe continuent dans fa cabanne: elle les fait,
quoy que gifante fur fa natte: le pauure enfant tout
décharné & tout foible qu'il eft, s'aproche toufiours
du Pere, quand il faut prier Dieu, & répondre aux
demandes de fon Catechifme: Enfin cette pauure
femme fe fit Baptizer le 23. de Ianuier, pour ne pas
perdre le fruit de fes fouffrances.

a good Catechumen, had broken her leg — all this, on the very eve of her grandmother's Baptism.   To crown her misfortunes, or her blessings, a little boy of hers, between ten and twelve years old, — who had nothing of the savage either in disposition or appearance, who had a wonderful gift of prayer, and who knew the whole Catechism perfectly, — was taken with a slow fever, from which he wasted away before our eyes.   Through all this, Teotonharason remained firm; Prayers were continued in her cabin, in which she joined, though lying on her mat; the poor child, weak and wasted though he was, always drew near to the Father to pray and to answer his Catechism; and, finally, the poor woman, not to lose the reward of her sufferings, received Baptism on the 23rd of January.

[90] CHAPITRE IX.

QUELQUES GUERISONS REMARQUABLES.   LE PERE CON-
TINUË SES INSTRUCTIONS.   LES SAUUAGES
OBEÏSSENT À LEURS SONGES.

CEUX qui auoient predit des afflictions à la
famille, dont nous venons de parler, ſi elle
receuoit la Doctrine de Ieſus-Chriſt, croyoient
auoir vn grand argument contre la Foy, quand ils
virent ces pauures gens à deux doigts de la mort:
mais ils ne connoiſſoient pas la puiſſance de celuy,
qui deducit ad inferos & reducit, qui conduit les perſonnes iuſques à l'ouuerture du tombeau, & puis les
ramene quand il luy plaiſt.   Dieu enuoye quelquefois des maladies purement pour faire paroiſtre ſa
gloire.   Celle de Theotonharaſon eſtoit de cette
nature.   Tout le monde la iugeoit incurable.   Elle-
meſme s'attendoit à la mort.   Auſſi-toſt qu'elle eut
[91] receu le Bapteſme, ſon corps receut ſes forces,
& fit paroiſtre que ce Sacrement luy auoit rendu la
vie du corps auſſi bien que de l'ame.   La gueriſon
de ſon fils fut encore plus miraculeuſe.   Ce pauure
enfant s'en alloit mourant, il ne faiſoit que languir,
vne fiévre etique le minoit iuſques aux os; il nous
faiſoit grande compaſſion, ce n'eſtoit plus qu'vn
ſquelette; & il ſe trouuoit pourtant aux Prieres tous
les iours, auec vne affection & vne deuotion, qui
paroiſſoit ſur ſon viſage & en ſa parole.   Au fort
de ſon mal, le Pere luy donne le ſainct Bapteſme,
de peur qu'il ne meure ſans ce benefice.   Choſe

[90] CHAPTER IX.

SOME REMARKABLE CURES.   THE FATHER CONTINUES
HIS TEACHINGS.   THE SAVAGES OBEY
THEIR DREAMS.

THOSE who had prophesied misfortunes for the
family of which we have just spoken, if it
received the Doctrine of Jesus Christ, thought
they had a strong argument against the Faith when
they saw those poor people within two finger-breadths
of death; but they knew not the power of him, *qui
deducit ad inferos et reducit* — who leads men to the
mouth of the tomb, and brings them back again,
when he chooses.   God sometimes sends disease
simply to make his glory manifest.   Theotonharason's illness was of this nature.   Every one thought
her incurable, and she herself expected to die; but,
as soon as she was [91] Baptized, her strength
returned, showing that this Sacrament had imparted
life to body as well as to soul.   Her son's cure was
still more miraculous.   The poor child was wasting
and dying away; a consumptive fever left him
naught but bones; we were filled with compassion,
seeing him reduced to a mere skeleton; and yet he
attended Prayers every day, with a love and devotion
that was apparent in face and speech.   At the height
of his illness, the Father gave him holy Baptism,
fearing lest he should die without that sacrament.
Marvelous to relate, no sooner had he received it,
than the fever, as if in fear of those sacred Waters,

prodigieufe! il ne l'eut pas pluftoft receu, que
comme fi la fiévre eut eu peur de ces Eauës facrées,
elle le quitta fur l'heure, pour ne plus retourner.   Le
voila donc guery, fans reffentir depuis aucun mal:
bref, il fe porte mieux qu'aucun de fes compagnons.

Nous auons veu encore quelque chofe de plus
grand.   Cette Theotonharafon auoit deux Tantes,
dont l'vne eftoit fur le point de mourir; & l'autre
languiffoit [92] d'vne fiévre opiniaftre, fans qu'on y
pût remedier.   Noftre Neophyte leur dit que le vray
remede à leurs maux, eftoit le Baptefme: qu'elle &
fon fils, auoient efté gueris par ce remede.   Ces
pauures malades font venir le Pere, luy expofent leur
defir: Le Pere les inftruit; elles écoutent, *fides ex
auditu*, la Foy entre par leurs oreilles; & leur donne
des penfées plus fortes de l'Eternité, que de la fanté.
Eftant bien difpofées, le Pere les Baptize, & le
Baptefme les guerit foudainement toutes deux, auec
l'eftonnement de tout le monde.   Auffi-toft qu'elles
furent affranchies des maladies de l'ame & du corps,
elles publierent par tout les merueilles de Dieu,
combattant ceux qui attaquent noftre Creance, & qui
l'accufent de tous les maux qui arriuent en leur Païs.

Le diable nous oppofe encore deux autres ennemis; fçauoir eft, les fonges; comme nous auons defia
remarqué, & l'indiffolubilité du Mariage.   On dit
aux hommes qu'ils feront mal-heureux s'ils méprifent
leurs fonges: & aux femmes qu'il n'y a plus de
mariages pour elles, fi [93] elles fe font Chreftiennes,
pource qu'en quittant vn mechant mary, elles n'en
pourront pas prendre vn autre.   Dieu fçaura bien
triompher, quand il luy plaira, de tous ces obftacles.

Le neufiéme de Ianuier, fur le foir, nous fufmes
fpectateurs de la plus r'affinée forcellerie du Païs:

left him on the instant, never to return.   He is per-
manently cured, and, in short, enjoys better health
than any of his comrades.

We have witnessed something still more wonderful.   This Theotonharason had two Aunts, one of
whom was at death's door, while the other was ill
[92] with an obstinate fever which defied every remedy.   Our Neophyte told them that the true remedy
for their ailments was Baptism, which had cured
both herself and her son.   The poor invalids sum-
moned the Father and declared to him their wish.
He instructed them; they listened; *fides ex auditu* —
"the Faith entered by their ears," and made them
think more of Eternity than of health.   Being well
prepared, they were Baptized by the Father, and the
Baptism immediately cured them both, to the aston-
ishment of all.   As soon as they were delivered from
their diseases of body and of soul, they proclaimed
God's marvels everywhere, combating those who
attack our Belief and accuse it of all the ills that
occur in their Country.

The devil still opposes us with two other enemies,—
namely, dreams, as already noted, and the indissolu-
bility of Marriage.   Men are told that they will
have ill luck if they disregard their dreams; and
women, that there will be no more marriages for
them if [93] they become Christians, because then
they cannot take another husband when they have
left a bad one.   God will know well how to overcome all these obstacles when he sees fit.

Toward evening of the ninth of January, we were
spectators of the most subtle sorcery of the Country,
employed for the cure of a sick woman of our cabin
who had long been ailing.   The Sorcerer entered

c'eſtoit pour guerir vne malade de noſtre cabanne,
qui trainoit depuis long-temps; le Sorcier entre auec
vne écaille de Tortuë en ſa main, à demy pleine de
petits cailloux; c'eſt dequoy ils ſe ſeruent pour faire
leurs inuentions. Il prend place au milieu d'vne
douzaine de femmes, qui doiuent l'aider à chaſſer le
mal; le voiſinage s'aſſemble pour voir cette ſuperſti-
tion, qui n'eſt autre, ſinon que le Magicien frappant
de ſa Tortuë ſur vne natte, & entonnant quelques
chanſons, les femmes dancent autour de luy à la
cadence de ſon chant & du bruit qu'il fait auec ſa
Tortuë: vous les voyez remuër pieds, bras, teſte &
tout le corps, auec tant de violence, qu'elles en ſuent
à groſſes gouttes, en peu de temps. Au premier
branſle le mal ne fut pas encore [94] chaſſé, non plus
qu'au ſecond, ny au troiſiéme. Ce qui fit prolonger
la dance bien auant dans la nuit, pendant laquelle la
malade ne laiſſa pas d'eſtre autant incommodée
qu'auparauant.

Le quinziéme, apres auoir Baptizé en noſtre
Chapelle vn ieune Huron, nous paſſaſmes vne bonne
partie de la matinée à celebrer le ſainꝗ iour du
Dimanche, faiſant prier & enſeignant ceux qui
venoient, en telle quantité, que noſtre Chapelle fut
remplie par ſept fois. Comme nous leur expliquons
nos Myſteres, auſſi nous racontent-ils par fois leurs
fables. Ils ont vne plaiſante réuerie touchant la
producꝗion des hommes ſur la terre. Ils diſent qu'vn
iour le Maiſtre du Ciel arrachant vn gros arbre, fit
vn trou qui repond du Ciel en terre: & qu'vn homme
de ce Païs là, s'eſtant mis en colere contre ſa femme,
la ietta dans ce trou, & la precipita du Ciel en terre,
ſans la bleſſer, quoy qu'elle fut enceinte de deux
enfants, garçon & fille. Or c'eſt de ces deux Iumeaux

with a Tortoise-shell in his hand, half full of small pebbles,— such are their instruments of magic. He took a seat in the midst of a dozen women who were to help him in banishing the disease, and the neighbors gathered about to see this superstitious ceremony. All it consists in is, that the Magician strikes the Tortoise-shell against a mat, and intones a song, while the women dance about him, in time with his singing and with the noise of the Tortoise-shell. You see them move their feet, arms, head, and entire body, with such violence that great drops of perspiration soon cover their bodies. At the first trial, the disease was not [94] expelled, or at the second, or at the third; this caused the dance to be prolonged far into the night, while the patient's illness abated not a particle.

On the fifteenth, after Baptizing a young Huron in our Chapel, we spent a good part of the morning in observing the holy Sabbath day, teaching, and directing the prayers of our visitors, who came in such numbers as to fill our Chapel seven times over. As we explain our Mysteries to them, so they at times relate their legends to us. They have an amusing myth touching the creation of mankind on earth. They say that one day the Master of Heaven, plucking up a large tree, made a hole leading from Heaven to earth; and a man of that Country, becoming angry with his wife, threw her into this hole, and so made her fall from Heaven to earth. She was not hurt, however, though she was pregnant with two children, a boy and a girl. Now, by these Twins the earth was peopled.[6] How dark is man's mind when it walks without the torch of the Faith!

que la terre a efté peuplée.   Que l'efprit de l'homme
eft tenebreux, quand il marche fans le flambeau de
la Foy.

[95] La calomnie que font courir quelques mauuais
Hurons, eft bien plus dangereufe.   Ils difent que
pour nous venger des torts que nous auons receus
des Iroquois & des autres Sauuages, nous en voulons
mener au Ciel le plus que nous pourrons, pour les
brûler & les roftir auec plaifir : & que cette vengeance
eft la feule recompence que nous pretendons pour
toutes les peines, les foins, les miferes & les trauaux
que nous prenons à les conuertir.   O qu'il eft vray
que les hommes iugent des autres felon leur humeur,
& felon leurs difpofitions.

D'autres qui n'ont pas l'efprit fi mal fait que de
s'arrefter à ces fottifes, difent que la Foy eft bonne
pour les François, à qui le Ciel appartient ; mais que
pour eux ils n'ont pas de fi hautes pretentions, &
qu'ils fe contentent apres leur mort, de la demeure
de leurs Anceftres.   Il y en a qui ne font pas maris
d'entendre parler du Ciel, des plaifirs qu'on y promet
à ceux qui croyent ; mais ils ne veulent pas qu'on
leur parle de la mort, ny de l'Enfer, ny de méprifer
les fonges, qu'ils reconnoiffent pour le [96] grand
Demon & le grand Genie du Païs, à qui toutes les def-
ferences & tous les facrifices fe rendent, auec vne fidelité qui n'eft pas croyable, en voicy quelques marques.

Il n'y a pas long-temps qu'vn homme du Bourg
d'Oïogoen, vit vne nuit en dormant dix hommes, qui
fe plongeoient en la riuiere gelée, entrant par vn trou
fait à la glace, & fortants par l'autre ; à fon réueil, la
premiere chofe qu'il fait, c'eft de preparer vn grand
feftin, & d'y inuiter dix de fes amis : Ils y viennent
tous ; ce n'eft que ioye, & que réjouïffances.   On y

[95] The calumny circulated by some malicious Hurons is much more dangerous. They say that, in order to take revenge for injuries received from the Iroquois and other Savages, we wish to lead to Heaven as many of them as we can, in order to burn and roast them there at our pleasure; and that this revenge is the sole recompense that we expect in return for all the pains, troubles, hardships, and labors that we undergo in converting them. Oh, how true it is that men judge others according to their own nature and character!

Others, who are not so dull as to be caught by these stupidities, say that the Faith is good for the French, to whom Heaven belongs; but, as for themselves, they have no such high pretensions, and are content, after death, with the abode of their Ancestors. There are some who are not displeased to hear about Heaven, and the pleasures promised to believers; yet they are unwilling to be told of death and Hell, or to be enjoined to set dreams at naught, which to them represent the [96] great Demon and Genius of the Country, to whom all homage is paid, and all sacrifices are rendered, with a fidelity that passes belief. This will be illustrated by what follows.

Not long ago, a man of the Village of Oiogoen saw one night, in his sleep, ten men plunge into the frozen river, entering through a hole made in the ice, and coming out through another. The first thing that he did on waking was to prepare a great feast, to which he invited ten of his friends. They all came; joy and gladness prevailed, with singing, dancing, and every accompaniment of a good feast. "This is well," said the Master of the feast, "you

chante, on y dance, & on y fait toutes les ceremonies
d'vn bon banquet. Voila qui va bien, dit le Maiſtre du
feſtin, vous me faites plaiſir, mes freres, de témoigner par cette ioye, que vous agreez mon feſtin; mais
ce n'eſt pas tout, il faut me faire paroiſtre ſi vous
m'aimez. Là-deſſus, il leur raconte ſon ſonge, qui
ne les eſtonna pas pourtant: car ſur l'heure meſme,
ils ſe preſenterent tous dix à l'executer: On va donc
à la riuiere, on perce la glace, & on y fait deux trous
éloignez l'vn de [97] l'autre de quinze pas. Les
Plongeurs ſe dépoüillent: le premier fraye le chemin
aux autres, ſautant dans vn des trous, il ſort heureuſement par l'autre: le ſecond en fait de meſme, &
ainſi des autres iuſqu'au dixiéme, qui paya pour tous:
car il ne pût s'en tirer, & mourut miſerablement ſous
la glace.

Dans le meſme Bourg d'Oïogoen, il ſe fit l'an paſſé
vne choſe qui mit bien en peine tous ſes habitans.
Vn d'eux auoit ſongé qu'il faiſoit feſtin d'vn homme,
il inuite tous les principaux du Païs, pour venir chez
luy entendre vne choſe d'importance. Eſtans aſſemblez, il leur dit que c'eſtoit fait de luy, puis qu'il
auoit eu vn ſonge, qu'on n'executeroit pas; mais
que ſa perte cauſeroit celle de toute la Nation; qu'il
falloit s'attendre à vn renuerſement, & à vn debris
vniuerſel de la terre. Il s'étend bien au long ſur
cette matiere, & puis donne à deuiner ſon ſonge;
perſonne n'en approchoit. Il n'y en eut qu'vn, qui
ſe doutant bien de la choſe, luy dit, Tu veux faire
feſtin d'vn homme, tiens, prend mon frere que voila,
ie le met entre tes mains [98] pour eſtre preſentement
couppé en morceaux, & mis dans la chaudiere. La
frayeur ſaiſit tous les aſſiſtans, excepté celuy qui
auoit ſongé: qui repliqua que ſon ſonge demandoit

give me pleasure, my brothers, showing by your joy
that you like my entertainment. But it is not all;
you must show me whether you love me." Thereupon, he told them his dream, which, however, did
not confound them; for, instantly, all ten offered to
fulfill it. Accordingly, they went to the river, and
pierced the ice, making two holes, [97] fifteen paces
apart. The Divers stripped. The first one prepared
the way for the others, plunging into one of the
holes and coming out successfully at the other.
The second did the same, and likewise the rest, until
the tenth man's turn came, who paid the penalty for
all; he could not find his way out, and perished
miserably under the ice.

In the same Village of Oiogoen, there occurred last
year an event which caused all the inhabitants much
anxiety. One of them, having dreamed that he gave
a feast of human flesh, invited all the chief men of
the Country to his cabin to hear a matter of importance. When they had assembled, he told them that
he was ruined, as he had had a dream impossible of
fulfillment; that his ruin would entail that of the
whole Nation; and that a universal overthrow and
destruction of the earth was to be expected. He
enlarged at great length on the subject, and then
asked them to guess his dream. All struck wide of
the mark, until one man, suspecting the truth, said
to him: " Thou wishest to give a feast of human
flesh. Here, take my brother; I place him in thy
hands [98] to be cut up on the spot, and put into the
kettle." All present were seized with fright, except
the dreamer, who replied that his dream required a
woman. Superstition went so far, that they adorned
a girl with all the riches of the Country,— with

vne femme. La fuperſtition fut iuſques-là, qu'on
para vne fille de toutes les richeſſes du Païs, de
braſſelets, de colliers, de couronnes, & de tous les
ornements ordinaires aux femmes; comme autresfois
on paroit les viⅽtimes qui deuoient eſtre immolées:
& de vray cette pauure innocente, qui ne ſçauoit pas
pour quoy on la faiſoit ſi iolie, fut menée au lieu
deſtinée pour le ſacrifice. Tout le peuple s'y trouue
pour voir ce ſpeⅽtacle ſi eſtrange. Les conuiez prennent leur place; l'on fait paroiſtre au milieu du cercle
cette viⅽtime publique. On la met entre les mains
du Sacrificateur, qui eſtoit celuy-là meſme pour qui
ſe deuoit faire le ſacrifice. Il la prend: on le regard
faire: on porte compaſſion à cette innocente: & lors
qu'on penſoit qu'il luy alloit décharger le coup de la
mort. Il s'écrie; ie ſuis content, mon ſonge n'en
veut pas dauantage. N'eſt-ce pas vne grande charité,
[99] d'ouurir les yeux à vn peuple ſi groſſierement
abuſé.

Non ſeulement ils croient à leurs ſonges, mais ils
font vne feſte particuliere du Demon des ſonges.
Cette feſte ſe pourroit appeller la feſte des fous, ou
le Carnaual des mauuais Chreſtiens: car le diable y fait
quaſi faire la meſme choſe, & à meſme temps. Ils
nomment cette feſte HONNONOVARORIA. Les Anciens
la vont proclamer par les ruës du Bourg. Nous en
viſmes la ceremonie le vingt-deuxiéme de Février
de cette année 1656. Auſſi-toſt que cette feſte fut
intimée par ces cris publics, on ne voyoit que des
hommes, des femmes & des enfants, courir comme des
fous, par les ruës & par les cabannes, mais bien d'vne
autre façon que ne font les Maſquarades en Europe;
la pluſpart ſont preſque tous nuds, & ſemblent eſtre
infenſibles au froid, qui eſt preſque inſupportable à

bracelets, collars, crowns, and all the ornaments used by women,—just as victims of old were decked for immolation; and that poor innocent, not knowing why she was made to look so pretty, was actually led to the place appointed for the sacrifice. All the people attended to witness so strange a spectacle. The guests took their places, and the public victim was led into the middle of the circle. She was delivered to the Sacrificer, who was the very one for whom the sacrifice was to be made. He took her; they watched his actions, and pitied that innocent girl; but, when they thought him about to deal her the death-blow, he cried out: " I am satisfied; my dream requires nothing further." Is it not a great charity [99] to open the eyes of a people so grossly in error?

Not only do they believe in their dreams, but they also hold a special festival to the Demon of dreams. This festival might be called the festival of fools, or the Carnival of wicked Christians; for, in both, the devil plays almost the same part, and at the same season. They call this celebration HONNONOUARORIA, and the Elders announce it through the Village streets. We witnessed the ceremony on the twenty-second of February, of this year, 1656. Immediately upon the announcement of the festival by these public cries, nothing was seen but men, women, and children, running like maniacs through the streets and cabins,— this, however, in a far different manner from that of Masqueraders in Europe, the greater number being nearly naked, and apparently insensible to the cold, which is well-nigh unbearable to those who are most warmly clothed. Some, indeed, give no farther evidence of their folly, than to run

ceux qui font les mieux couuerts. Il eſt vray que
quelques-vns ne donnêt point d'autre marque de leur
folie, que de courir auſſi demy-nuds par toutes les
cabannes; mais d'autres font malins: les [100] vns
portent de l'eau, ou quelque choſe de pire, & le
iettent fur ceux qu'ils rencontrent.   D'autres prennent les tifons du foyer, les charbons & les cendres,
& les éparpillent ça & là, fans conſiderer fur qui tout
cela peut tomber.   D'autres briſent les chaudieres &
les plats, & tout le petit meſnage qu'ils trouuent en
leur chemin.   Il y en a qui vont armez d'eſpées, de
bajonnetes, de couſteaux, de haches, de baſtons, &
font ſemblant d'en vouloir décharger fur les premiers
venus, & tout cela fe fait iuſques à ce qu'on ait trouué
& executé leur ſonge, en quoy il y a deux choſes
bien remarquables.

La premiere eſt, qu'il arriue quelquefois, qu'on
n'eſt pas aſſez bon deuin pour rencontrer leurs penſées: car ils ne les propoſent pas clairement; mais
par enigmes, par mots couuerts, en chantant, & quel-
ques-fois par geſtes ſeulement; ſi bien qu'on ne
trouue pas toujours de bons Oedipes.   Et neantmoins
ils ne partent point du lieu, qu'on n'ait rencontré
leur penſée; & ſi l'on tarde trop, ſi on ne la veut pas
deuiner, ou ſi [101] l'on ne peut pas, ils menacent de
reduire tout à feu & à cendres: ce qui n'arriue que
trop ſouuent, & nous l'auons quaſi experimenté à nos
deſpens.   Vn de ces infenſez s'eſtant gliſſé en noſtre
cabanne, vouloit à toute force qu'on deuinât ſon
ſonge, & qu'on y ſatisfiſt.   Or iaçoit que nous euſſions
declaré au commencemêt, que nous n'eſtions pas
pour obeïr à ces refueries: il perſiſta neantmoins
pendant vne longue eſpace de temps à crier, à tem-
peſter & faire le furieux; mais en noſtre abſence:

thus half naked through all the cabins; but others are mischievous. [100] Some carry water, or something worse, and throw it at those whom they meet; others take the firebrands, coals, and ashes from the fire, and scatter them in all directions, without heeding on whom they fall; others break the kettles, dishes, and all the little domestic outfit that they find in their path. Some go about armed with javelins, bayonets, knives, hatchets, and sticks, threatening to strike the first one they meet; and all this continues until each has attained his object and fulfilled his dream. In this connection, two things are worthy of note.

First, it sometimes happens that one is not bright enough to guess their thoughts; for they are not clearly put forth, but are expressed in riddles, phrases of covert meaning, songs, and occasionally in gestures alone. Consequently, a good Œdipus is not always to be found. Yet, they will not leave a place until their thought is divined; and, if they meet with delay, or a disinclination or [101] inability to guess it, they threaten to burn up everything,—a menace which is only too often executed, as we very nearly learned to our own cost. One of these maniacs stole into our cabin, determined that we should guess his dream and satisfy it. Now, we had declared at the outset, that we would not comply with these dreams; yet he persisted for a long time in shouting, storming, and raving—in our absence, however, for we retired to an outlying cabin to avoid the riot. One of our hosts, annoyed by these cries, came to him to learn what he wanted. The madman answered, "I kill a Frenchman; that is my dream, which must be fulfilled at any cost." Our host

car nous nous retirafmes dans vne cabanne cham-
peftre pour éuiter tous ces defordres. Vn de nos
hoftes ennuyé de ces cris, fe prefente à luy pour
fçauoir ce qu'il pretendoit. Ce furieux repart. Ie
tuë vn François: voila mon fonge, qui doit eftre
executé, quoy qu'il en coufte. Noftre hofte luy iette
vn habit à la Françoife, comme les dépoüilles d'vn
homme mort: & à mefme temps fe mettant luy-
mefme en furie, dit qu'il veut vanger la mort du
François; que fa perte fera fuiuie de celle de tout le
Bourg, qu'il va reduire en cendre, commençant par
fa propre cabanne. [102] Là-deffus il en chaffe &
parens & amis, & domeftiques, & tout plein de
monde, qui s'eftoit amaffé pour voir l'iffuë de ce
tintamarre. Eftant demeuré feul, il ferme les portes,
& met le feu par tout. Dans ce mefme inftant que
le monde s'attendoit de voir toute cette cabanne en
flamme; Le Pere Chaumonot venant de faire vne
action de charité, arriue. Il voit fortir vne horrible
fumée de fa maifon d'écorce; on luy dit ce que c'eft.
Il enfonce vne porte: il fe iette au milieu du feu &
de la fumée, retire les tifons, eteint le feu, fait
doucement fortir fon hofte, contre l'attente de toute la
populace, qui iamais ne refifte à la fureur du Demon
des fonges. Cét homme continuë dans fa fureur.
Il courre les ruës & les cabannes, crie tant qu'il peut
qu'il va mettre tout en feu, pour vanger la mort du
François. On luy prefente vn chien, pour eftre la
victime de fa colere, & du Demon de fa paffion. Ce
n'eft pas affez, dit-il, pour effacer la honte & l'affront
qu'on me fait, de vouloir tuër vn François logé en
ma maifon. On luy en prefente vn fecond. Il
s'appaife tout [103] à coup, & s'en retourne chez foy
auffi froidement, comme fi rien ne fe fuft paffé.

threw him a French coat, pretending that it had been stripped from a dead man; at the same time, working himself into a frenzy, he declared his determination to avenge the Frenchman's death, saying that his destruction should be followed by that of the whole Village, which he was going to reduce to ashes, beginning with his own cabin. [102] Thereupon, he drove out relatives and friends and servants, and all the crowd which had gathered to witness the outcome of this hubbub. Left alone, he shut the doors, and set the whole place on fire. At the moment when all were expecting to see the entire cabin burst into flames, Father Chaumonot, returning from an errand of charity, arrived on the scene. He saw a fearful smoke issuing from his bark house, and was told the reason. Breaking in a door, he rushed into the midst of the fire and smoke, removed the firebrands, extinguished the fire, and gently forced his host to withdraw,—to the surprise of the entire populace, who never thwart the fury of the Demon of dreams. The man's frenzy, however, did not abate; he ran through the streets and cabins, crying at the top of his voice that he would set everything on fire, in order to avenge the Frenchman's death. A dog was offered him, to become the victim of his wrath and of the Demon of his passion. " That is not enough," he said, " to wipe out the shame and indignity done me in wishing to kill a Frenchman lodged in my house." A second dog was offered him, and he became pacified [103] at once, returning to his cabin as calmly as if nothing had occurred.

Note, if you please, by the way, that, just as he who has captured a prisoner in war, often takes only

Remarquez, s'il vous plaiſt, en paſſant, que comme
en leurs guerres, celuy qui a pris vn priſonnier, n'en
a ſouuent que les dépoüilles & non pas la vie: De
meſme celuy qui a ſongé qu'il doit tuër quelqu'vn,
ſe contente bien ſouuent de ſes habits, ſans attenter
à ſa perſonne.   C'eſt pour cela qu'on donna vn habit
de François au ſongeur.   Paſſons outre.

Le frere de noſtre hoſte voulut iouër ſon perſon-
nage, auſſi bien que les autres.   Il s'habilla quaſi en
Satyre, ſe couurant de paille de bled d'Inde depuis
les pieds iuſques à la teſte.   Il fait accommoder deux
femmes en vrayes Megeres: elles auoient les cheueux épars, la face noire comme du charbon, le corps
couuert de deux peaux de Loups, elles eſtoient armées
chacune d'vn leuier, ou d'vn gros pieu.   Le Satyre
les voyāt bien equippées, ſe pourmene par noſtre
cabanne, chantant & heurlant à pleine teſte.   Il
monte en ſuite ſur le toict, il y fait mille tours,
criant comme ſi tout [104] eut eſté perdu.   Cela fait,
il deſcend, s'en va grauement par tout le Bourg, les
deux Megeres le precedent, & fracaſſent tout ce
qu'elles rencontrent, auec leurs pieux.   S'il eſt vray
de dire que tous les hommes ont quelque grain de
folie, puis que *Stultorüm infinitus eſt numerus*; il faut
confeſſer que ces peuples en ont chacun plus de
demie once.   Ce n'eſt pas encore tout.

A peine noſtre Satyre & nos Megeres, s'eſtoient
dérobez à nos yeux; que voila vne femme qui ſe iette
dans noſtre cabane.   Elle eſtoit armée d'vne arque-
buſe, qu'elle auoit obtenuë par ſon ſonge.   Elle
crioit, hurloit, chantoit, diſant qu'elle s'en alloit à la
guerre contre la Nation de Chat, qu'elle les com-
battroit, & qu'elle rameneroit des priſonniers.   Se

his apparel, and not his life, so he who has dreamed
that he is to kill some one, very often contents himself with his clothes, without assailing his person.
For that reason, the dreamer was given a Frenchman's coat.   Let us proceed.

Our host's brother, like all the rest, wished to
play his part.   Dressing himself somewhat like a
Satyr, and decking his person from top to toe with
the husks of Indian corn,— he had two women disguise themselves as veritable Megeras,— their hair
flying, their faces coal-black, their persons clothed
with a couple of Wolfskins, and each armed with a
handspike or large stake.   The Satyr, seeing them
well fitted out, marched about our cabin, singing
and howling at the top of his voice.   Then, climbing
to the roof, he went through a thousand antics, with
an outcry as if [104] the day of destruction had come.
After that, he came down, and proceeded solemnly
through the entire Village, the two Megeras walking
before him, and striking with their stakes whatever
chanced to come under their hands.   If it be true
that every one has some grain of folly,— since *Stulto-*
rum infinitus est numerus,— then these people must
be acknowledged to possess more than half an ounce
apiece.   But this is not all.

Scarcely had our Satyr and Megeras passed out of
our sight, when a woman, armed with an arquebus
which she had obtained through her dream, rushed
into our cabin.   She was shouting, howling, and
singing, saying that she was going to war against the
Cat Nation, that she would fight them, and bring
back some prisoners — with a thousand imprecations
and curses on herself, if what she had dreamed
should not take place.

donnant mille imprecations, & mille maledictions fi
la chofe n'arriuoit comme elle l'auoit fongé.

Vn guerrier fuiuit cette Amazone. Il entra l'arc
& les fléches en la main, auec vne baionnette. Il
dance, il chante, il crie, il menace: puis tout à coup
fe iette fur vne femme, qui eftoit entrée pour [105]
voir cette comedie: il luy prefente la baionnette à la
gorge: la prend par les cheueux, fe contente d'en
couper quelques-vns, & puis il fe retire, pour faire
place à vn Deuin, qui auoit fongé qu'il deuineroit
tout ce qu'on auroit caché.   Il eftoit habillé ridicule-
ment, tenant en main vne façon de caducée, dont il
fe feruoit pour montrer l'endroit où eftoit la chofe
cachée.   Il falloit neantmoins que fon compagnon,
qui portoit vne vafe remply de ie ne fçay quelle
liqueur, en remplift fa bouche, & la iettaft en
foufflant, fur la tefte & fur le vifage, fur les mains
& fur le caducée du Deuin, qui ne manquoit point
apres cela, de trouuer ce dont il eftoit queftion.   Ie
m'en rapporte.

Vne femme furuient, auec vne natte qu'elle tend,
& qu'elle prepare, comme fi elle vouloit prendre du
poiffon.   C'eftoit à dire qu'on luy en deuoit donner,
parce qu'elle l'auoit fongé.

Vne autre met feulement à terre vn hoyau.   On
deuine qu'elle veut qu'on luy donne vn champ, ou
vne piece de terre.   C'eft iuftement ce qu'elle penfoit,   [106] Elle fe contenta de cinq foffes à planter
du bled d'Inde.

On vint apres cela mettre deuant nos yeux vn petit
marmoufet; nous le rejettons: on le place deuant
d'autres perfonnes, & apres qu'on euft marmotté
quelques paroles, on l'emporta fans autre ceremonie.

This Amazon was followed by a warrior, who came in carrying his bow and arrows and a bayonet. He danced and sang, shouted, and threatened; and then suddenly rushed at a woman who had entered to [105] view this comedy. He leveled the bayonet at her throat, then seized her by the hair, but was satisfied with cutting off a few locks; after this, he retired, to give place to a Diviner, who had dreamed that he could guess the location of any concealed article. He was ridiculously attired, and bore in his hand a sort of divining-rod, which he used for pointing out the place of concealment. Still, his companion, who carried a vase filled with some kind of liquor, was obliged to take a mouthful and blow it out upon the head, face, hands, and wand of the Diviner, before the latter could find the object in question. I leave the solution of the mystery to the reader.

A woman came in with a mat,[7] which she spread out, and arranged as if she wished to catch some fish; she thus indicated that some must be given her, to satisfy her dream.

Another simply laid a mattock on the ground. It was guessed that she wanted a field or a piece of ground, which was exactly her desire. [106] She was content with five furrows for planting Indian corn.

After that, a little grotesque figure was put in front of us. We rejected it, and it was placed before other persons; after the mumbling of some words, it was carried off without further ceremony.

One of the Village chiefs appeared in wretched attire, and all covered with ashes. Because his dream, which called for two human hearts, was not

Vn des principaux du Bourg parut en tres-pauure
équipage. Il eſtoit tout couuert de cendres; & parce
qu'on ne deuinoit pas ſon ſonge, qui demandoit deux
cœurs humains, il fit prolonger d'vn iour la ceremonie, & ne ceſſa pendant ce temps-là de faire ſes folies.
Il entra dans noſtre cabanne, où il y a pluſieurs foyers,
ſe met aupres du premier, iette en l'air, & cendres &
charbons. Il fait le meſme au deuxiéme & au troiſiéme foyer; mais il ne fit rien au noſtre, par reſpect.

Il y en a qui viennent tout armez, & comme s'ils
eſtoient aux priſes auec l'ennemy; ils font les poſtures,
les cris, & les chamaillis qui ſe pratiquent entre deux
armées qui ſont aux mains.

D'autres marchent en bandes, & font [107] des
dances auec des contorſions de corps, qui approchent
de celles des poſſedez.   Enfin ce ne ſeroit iamais fait,
ſi on vouloit rapporter tout ce qu'ils font pendant
trois iours & trois nuits que dure cette folie, auec vn
tel tintamarre, qu'on ne peut preſque trouuer vn
moment pour eſtre en repos.   Ce qui n'empeſcha pas
pourtant, que les Prieres ne ſe fiſſent à l'ordinaire en
noſtre Chapelle, & que Dieu ne fiſt paroiſtre ſon
Amour enuers ces pauures peuples, par quelques
gueriſons miraculeuſes, accordées en vertu du ſainct
Bapteſme, dont nous ne parlons pas icy.   Acheuons
le diſcours commencé, de l'obeïſſance qu'ils rendent
à leurs réueries.

Ce ſeroit vne cruauté, & vne eſpece de meurtre, de
ne pas donner à vn homme ce qu'il a ſongé: car ce
refus ſeroit capable de le faire mourir: de-là vient
qu'il y en a qui ſe voyent dépoüiller de tout ce qu'ils
ont, ſans eſpoir d'aucune retribution: Car, quoy que
ce ſoit qu'ils donnent, on ne leur rendra iamais rien,

guessed, he caused the ceremony to be protracted
one day, never ceasing his foolish actions during that
time. Entering our cabin, in which there are
several fireplaces, he went to the first, and tossed
ashes and coals into the air; he repeated the per-
formance at the second and third, but did nothing at
ours, out of respect.

Some come entirely armed, and behave as if they
were engaging the enemy. They assume the atti-
tudes, shout the battle-cries, and join in the scramble
of two armies in action.

Others march about in companies, and perform
[107] dances with contortions of body that resemble
those of men possessed. In short, one would never
end if he tried to relate all that is done during the
three days and three nights in which this nonsense
lasts, such a din prevailing the while that scarcely a
moment's quiet is to be had. Yet this did not prevent us from holding Prayers as usual in our Chapel,
or hinder God from manifesting his Love toward
these poor peoples in certain miraculous cures,
granted by virtue of holy Baptism. Of them, however, we shall not speak here. Let us finish the
account already begun of their obedience to their
dreams.

It would be cruelty, nay, murder, not to give a
man the subject of his dream; for such a refusal
might cause his death. Hence, some see themselves
stripped of their 'all, without any hope of retribution; for, whatever they thus give away will never
be restored to them, unless they themselves dream,
or pretend to dream, of the same thing. But they
are, [108] in general, too scrupulous to employ simulation, which would, in their opinion, cause all sorts

s'ils ne fongent eux-mefmes, ou s'ils ne feignent auoir fongé. Mais ils font, [108] pour la plufpart, trop fcrupuleux, pour vfer de feintife, qui feroit caufe, à leur auis, de toutes fortes de mal-heurs. Il s'en trouue pourtant qui paffent par deffus le fcrupule, & qui s'enrichiffent par vne belle fiction.

Le Satyre dont nous auons parlé cy-deffus, voyant qu'on auoit enleué de chez luy quantité de chofes à noftre occafion, parce que les grands & les petits fongeoient aux François: & comme nous ne voulions pas les écouter, luy nous aimant, leur fatisfaifoit: mais enfin fe voulant recompenfer, il fe mit en l'équipage que nous auons décrit, contrefaifant non feulement le Satyre; mais encore le phantofme, qu'il feignoit luy eftre apparu la nuit, & luy auoir commandé d'amaffer quarante peaux de Caftors. Ce qu'il fit en cette forte. Il fe mit à crier par les ruës, qu'il n'eftoit plus homme, qu'il eftoit deuenu befte brute. Là-deffus les Anciens tinrent confeil, pour faire retourner en fon premier eftre vn de leurs Chefs. Ce qui fut fait auffi-toft qu'on luy euft donné ce qu'il defiroit, & qu'il feignoit auoir fongé.

[109] Vne pauure femme ne fut pas fi heureufe dans fon fonge. Elle courrut iour & nuit, & n'atrapa qu'vne maladie. On la veut guerir par les remedes les plus ordinaires du Païs; ce font des vomitoires faits de certaines racines infufées dans de l'eau. On luy en fit tant boire, qu'elle creua fur l'heure, fon ventre s'eftant fendu pour donner paffage à deux chaudronnées d'eau qu'on luy auoit fait prendre.

Vn ieune homme de noftre cabanne, en fut quitte pour eftre bien pouldré. Il fonge qu'il eft enfoüy

of misfortunes. Yet there are some who overcome
their scruples, and enrich themselves by a shrewd
piece of deception.

The Satyr mentioned above found his cabin
stripped of many articles, for which we were indirectly
responsible; because great and small dreamed of the
French, and as we would not listen to their demands,
he, being fond of us, satisfied them. But, at length,
wishing to reimburse himself, he assumed the garb
already described, and impersonated not only a
Satyr, but also the phantom which he feigned had
appeared to him in the night with an order to collect
forty Beaver-skins. This he accomplished in the
following manner. He began to shout through the
streets that he was no longer a man, but a brute
beast; whereupon the Elders held a council for the
restoration of one of their Chiefs to his original
form. This was effected as soon as he had been
given what he wished and pretended to have dreamed
about.

[109] A poor woman was less fortunate in her
dream, running about day and night, and catching
only an illness. They wished to cure her with the
commonest remedies of the Country, which are
emetics compounded of certain roots steeped in
water; but they gave her such a quantity that she
died immediately, her stomach bursting to let out
two kettlefuls of water that she had been made to
take.

A young man of our cabin came off with a good
powdering. He dreamed that he was buried in
ashes, and, on awaking, was bent on making the
illusion a reality. He invited ten of his Friends to
a feast for the purpose of fulfilling his dream, and

dans de la cendre. A fon réueil, il veut que le men-
fonge foit vne verité. Il inuite au feftin dix de fes
Amis pour executer fon fonge. Ils s'acquittent
excellemment bien de cette commiffion. Ils le cou-
urent de cendres depuis les pieds iufques à la tefte:
ils luy en fourent dedans le nez, & dans les oreilles,
& par tout. Nous auions auerfion d'vne ceremonie
fi ridicule: & tous les autres la regardoient auec
filence & auec admiration, comme vn grand myftere.
Ces pauures gens ne font-ils pas dignes de com-
paffion? Ie voy bien qu'il [110] faudra que quelques-
vns de nous autres meurent pour des fonges. Ie me
trompe, ce fera pour Iefus-Chrift. Laiffons ces
badineries, qui feroient vn gros volume, fi on vouloit
tout dire.

Le vingtiéme de ce mois de Ianuier, les Anciens
en plein Confeil, firent prefent au Pere d'vn collier
de deux mille grains, pour répondre à celuy que nous
auions fait touchant la deliurance du ieune François,
qui eft entre les mains des Oïogoenhronnons; c'eft
pour dire qu'ils fongent ferieufement à la liberté, &
qu'ils efperent que bien-toft ils parleroient autrement
qu'en pourcelaine.

they acquitted themselves most excellently of the commission, covering him with ashes from head to foot, and rubbing them into his nose, ears, and all parts of his body. We were disgusted with such a ridiculous ceremony, which all the rest viewed with silent admiration, as some great mystery. Do not these poor people deserve pity? I see clearly that [110] some of us will have to die for these dreams,— no, I am wrong, for Jesus Christ. Let us drop these buffooneries, which would fill a large volume if one described them all.

On the twentieth of this month of January, the Elders, in full Council, presented the Father with a collar of two thousand beads, in return for one that we had given, requesting the deliverance of the young Frenchman in the hands of the Oiogoenhron-nons. Their present indicated a serious intention to liberate him, and their hope that soon they would speak otherwise than through porcelain.

CHAPITRE X.

CEREMONIES POUR LA GUERRE.   ET QUELQUES COM-
BATS.

NOUS vifmes fur la fin du mois de Ianuier, la
Ceremonie qui fe fait tous les Hyuers, & qui
fert de preparatifs pour la guerre; à laquelle
ils s'exhortent [111] les vns les autres en deux façons.

Premierement la chaudiere de guerre, comme ils
l'appellent, eft fur le feu dés l'Automne, afin que
tous les Alliez y puiffent mettre quelque bon mor-
ceau, qui cuife tout l'Hyuer: c'eft à dire, afin qu'ils
contribuënt à l'entreprife qu'ils premeditent.   La
chaudiere ayant bien boüilly iufques au mois de
Février, grand nombre de Chaffeurs de Sonnontouan
& d'Oïogoen, s'eftans icy trouuez, firent le feftin de
guerre, qui dura plufieurs nuits.   Ils chantent, ils
danfent, ils font mille grimaces, qui feruent de
proteftation publique de ne reculer iamais dans le
combat, & de mourir pluftoft dans toutes fortes de
tourments, que de lacher le pied.   A mefme temps
qu'ils font cette proteftation, ils s'entrejettent des
charbons ardens, & de la cendre chaude.   Ils s'entre-
frappent rudement.   Ils fe brûlent les vns les autres,
pour voir fi quelqu'vn aura peur des feux de l'ennemy.
Il faut pour lors tenir bon, & fe voir roftir par fes
meilleurs amis, fans faire paroiftre aucun figne de
[112] douleur, autrement on fe feroit décrier & on
pafferoit pour vn lâche.

CHAPTER X.

CEREMONIES PREPARATORY TO WAR.   SOME ENGAGE-
MENTS.

TOWARD the end of the month of January, we
witnessed the Ceremony performed every Winter in preparation for war, to which they incite
[111] one another in two ways.

First, the war-kettle, as they call it, is hung over
the fire in Autumn, that each of the Allies may put
therein some choice bit to cook all Winter; that is,
that they may participate in the intended enterprise.
When the kettle had boiled until the month of February, many Hunters being present from Sonnontouan
and Oiogoen, they held the war-feast, which lasted
several nights.   They sang, danced, and made
countless grimaces, as a public announcement of their
determination never to draw back in this fight, and
to die in all sorts of torment rather than yield.   With
this declaration, they threw live coals and hot ashes
at one another, exchanged heavy blows, and burned
one another, to see if any were likely to fear the
enemy's fires.   One must bear it all, on this occasion,
and submit to be roasted by his best friends, without
showing a sign of [112] pain; otherwise, he would
be disgraced and branded as a coward.

The Father was invited to put something into the
kettle to make it better, and he told them that he
intended to do so; then, adapting himself to their

Le Pere fut inuité de mettre quelque chofe dans la chaudiere, pour la rendre meilleure.   Il leur dit que c'eftoit bien fon deffein, & s'accommodant à leur façon d'agir; Il les affeura que les François mettroient de la poudre fous cette chaudiere.   Ce qui leur pleut fort.

La feconde chofe qu'ils font tous les Hyuers, pour s'animer au combat, regarde les drogues neceffaires pour penfer les bleffez.   Et pour cela tous les Sorciers, ou Iongleurs du Bourg, qui font les Medecins du Païs, s'affemblent pour donner vne energie à leurs drogues, & pour leur infpirer par cette ceremonie, toute vne autre force qu'elles n'en tirent de la terre:

Le principal des Sorciers fe tient au milieu des autres, entourez d'vn grand peuple.   Puis éleuant fa voix, il dit qu'il va communiquer aux drogues, ou aux racines, qu'il tient dans vn fac, la force de guerir toutes fortes de playes: & là-dëffus, [113] il fe met à chanter à gorge déployée, & les autres Sorciers répondent, & repetent la mefme chanfon, iufques à tant que la vertu s'infufe dans ces racines: & pour les éprouuer, il fait deux chofes.   La premiere, il fe fcarifie les lévres, & en fait fortir du fang, qu'il laiffe écouler fur fon menton: puis appliquant à la veuë de tout le monde fa drogue fur fes lévres, il fucce adroitement le fang qui coule: & le peuple voyant ce fang arrefté, fait vne grande acclamation, comme fi veritablement la drogue auoit foudainement guery la playe.

Et pour montrer que fes remedes ne rendent pas feulement la fanté aux malades, mais qu'ils rendent auffi la vie aux morts.   Il fait fortir de fon fac vn petit Efcurieux mort, qu'il tient fecretement attaché par le bout de la queuë.   Il le met fur fon bras, chacun le voyant mort, il luy applique fes drogues, puis

ways, he said that the French would put some gun-
powder under it, which pleased them greatly.

The other ceremony that they perform every Winter, to gain courage for fighting, regards the drugs
used in dressing wounds. For this, all the Village
Sorcerers or Jugglers, the Physicians of the Country,
assemble, to give strength to their drugs, and, by
the ceremony performed, to impart to them a virtue
entirely distinct from that derived from the soil.

The chief Sorcerer takes his place in the middle
of the group, surrounded by a great crowd. Then,
raising his voice, he says that he is about to impart
to the drugs or roots in his pouch the power of curing
all kinds of wounds. Thereupon, [113] he begins to
sing at the top of his voice, the other Sorcerers
responding and repeating the same song, until the
desired virtue has been infused into the roots. To
prove this, he does two things. First, he bites his
lips, drawing blood and letting it run down his chin;
then, in plain sight of all, he applies his drug to his
lips, adroitly sucking up the flowing blood; and
the people, seeing the bleeding checked, applaud
loudly, as if the drug had indeed quickly cured the
wound.

And, to show that his remedies not only restore
the sick to health, but also raise the dead to life, he
causes to come out of his pouch a little dead Squirrel,
which he holds by a cunning attachment to the
end of the tail. He places it on his arm; all see that
it is dead; then he applies his drugs, and, pulling
the string as slyly as possible, he makes it return to
his pouch, apparently revived before the spectators'
eyes. Producing it again, he makes it move, as the
Jugglers of France move their puppets. [114] In

tirant la corde le plus fubtilement qu'il peut, il le
fait r'entrer dans fon fac, & paroiftre reffufcité aux
yeux des fpectateurs. Il le produit encore, le fait
remuer, comme les Iongleurs de France leurs marion-
nettes. [114] Il n'y a quafi perfonne dans cette
grande affemblée qui ne leue les épaules, & n'admire
la vertu des herbes, qui font vn fi grand miracle. Et
en fuitte de ce grand prodige, le Maiftre Sorcier s'en
va par toutes les ruës, fuiui d'vne groffe foule de
monde, chantant à gorge déployée, faifant parade de
fes drogues. Or tout cela fe fait pour ofter aux
ieunes guerriers la crainte d'eftre bleffez en guerre:
puis qu'ils trouueront vn remede fi fouuerain. Ce
n'eft pas dans l'Amerique feulement, mais encore en
Europe, que les hommes femblent prendre plaifir
d'eftre trompez.

Si ces iongleries ne font impreffion fur les efprits,
du moins firent-elles paroiftre l'an paffé, vn courage
admirable dans le combat qu'ils liurerent à ceux de
la Nation de Chat. Voicy la caufe de cette nouuelle
guerre.

that large assembly, there is scarcely a person who
does not show his admiration for the virtue of the
herbs which work so mighty a miracle.   After this
great prodigy, the Master Sorcerer parades through
all the streets, followed by a great crowd, singing at
the top of his voice, and showing off his simples.
Now, all this is done to make the young warriors
fearless of wounds in battle, since they possess so
sovereign a remedy.   It is not in America alone that
people seem to take pleasure in being deceived, but
in Europe also.

If these juggleries do not produce an impression
upon the mind, they at least caused an admirable
display of courage last year, in the engagement which
occurred with the Cat Nation.   The reason for that
new war follows.

[115] CHAPITRE XI.

L'OCCASION DE LA GUERRE CONTRE LA NATION DE CHAT.

LA Nation de Chat auoit enuoyé trente Ambaſſadeurs à Sonnontouan, pour confirmer la paix,
qui eſtoit entre eux; mais il arriua qu'vn Sonnontouahronnon fut tué par vn de la Nation de Chat,
par quelque rencontre inopinée. Ce meutre choqua
tellement les Sonnontouahronnons, qu'ils mirent à
mort les Ambaſſadeurs, qui eſtoient entre leurs
mains, excepté cinq qui s'éuaderent. Voila donc la
guerre allumée entre ces deux Nations; c'eſtoit à
qui feroit plus de priſonniers les vns ſur les autres,
pour les brûler. Entr'autres il y eut deux Onnontagehronnons, qui furent pris par ceux de la Nation de
Chat, l'vn s'enfuit, & l'autre, homme de conſideration, eſtant mené au païs pour paſſer par le feu,
plaida ſi bien ſa cauſe, qu'il fut donné à la [116] ſœur
d'vn des trente Ambaſſadeurs mis à mort. Elle
n'eſtoit pas pour lors dans le Bourg, on ne laiſſa pas
pourtant de couurir cét homme de beaux habits; ce
ne ſont que feſtins, & que bonne chere; on l'aſſeure
quaſi qu'il ſera r'enuoyé en ſon Païs. Quand celle,
à qui il auoit eſté donné, fut de retour, on luy porte
nouuelle que ſon frere deffunct va reuiure, & qu'elle
ſe prepare à le bien regaler, & à le congedier de bonne
grace. Elle tout au contraire, ſe met à pleurer, elle
proteſte qu'elle n'eſſuyera iamais ſes larmes, que la
mort de ſon frere ne ſoit vangée. Les Anciens luy

[115] CHAPTER XI.

THE CAUSE OF THE WAR AGAINST THE CAT NATION.

THE Cat Nation had sent thirty Ambassadors to Sonnontouan, to confirm the peace between them; but it happened, by some unexpected accident, that a Sonnontouahronnon was killed by a man of the Cat Nation. This murder so incensed the Sonnontouahronnons, that they put to death the Ambassadors in their hands, except five who escaped. Hence, war was kindled between these two Nations, and each strove to capture and burn more prisoners than its opponent. Two Onnontagehronnons, among others, were captured by the men of the Cat Nation; one of them escaped, and the other, a man of rank, was taken home by the enemy to be burnt. But he pleaded his cause so well, that he was given to the [116] sister of one of the thirty Ambassadors who had been put to death. She was absent from the Village at the time; but the prisoner was nevertheless clothed in fine garments, and feasting and good cheer prevailed, the man being all but assured that he would be sent back to his own Country. When she to whom he had been given returned, she was told that her dead brother was to be restored to life, that she must prepare to regale him well, and then to give him a gracious dismissal. She, however, began to weep, and declared that she would never dry her tears until her brother's death was avenged. The Elders showed her the gravity of the

reprefentent l'importance de cette affaire: que c'eſt
pour attirer ſur leurs bras vne nouuelle guerre: elle
ne defiſte point pour cela.   Enfin on fut contraint de
luy liurer ce miſerable, pour en faire à ſa volonté.
Il eſtoit encore dans la réjouïſſance du banquet,
quand tout cela ſe paſſoit.   On le tire du feſtin, &
on le mene dans la cabanne de cette cruelle, ſans luy
rien dire.   A ſon entrée il fut ſurpris, quand on luy
enleua ſes habits.   Alors il vit bien que c'eſtoit fait
de ſa vie.   Il s'écria deuant que de mourir, qu'on
alloit [117] brûler tout vn peuple en ſa perſonne, &
qu'on vangeroit cruellement ſa mort.   Ce qui fut
vray: car les nouuelles n'en furent pas pluſtoſt portées à Onnontagué, que douze cens hommes bien
déterminez ſe mettent promptement en chemin, pour
aller prendre raiſon de cét affront.

Nous auons deſia remarqué que la Nation de Chat
porte ce nom, pource qu'il ſe trouue en leur Païs,
vne grande quantité de Chats ſauuages, fort gros &
fort beaux.   Cette Contrée eſt fort temperée: on
n'y voit pendant l'Hyuer, ny glace, ny neige: &
pendant l'Eſté, on y recueille, à ce qu'on dit icy,
des bleds & des fruits en abondance, & d'vne groſſeur
& bonté extraordinaire.

Nos Guerriers furent pluſtot rendus en ce Païs-là,
quoy que fort éloigné d'Onnontagué, qu'ils ne furent
apperceus.   Ce qui ietta par tout vne ſi grande
alarme, qu'on abandonne & Bourgs, & maiſons; à la
mercy du Cônquerant: qui apres auoir tout brûlé, ſe
met à pourſuiure les fuyarts.   Ils eſtoient deux à
trois mille combatans, ſans les femmes & les enfants:
qui ſe voyants [118] pourſuiuis de prés, ſe reſolurent,
apres cinq iours de fuite, de faire vn fort de bois, &

situation, which was likely to involve them in a new
war; but she would not yield. Finally, they were
compelled to give up the wretched man to her, to do
with him as she pleased. All this occurred while
he was still joyfully feasting. Without a word, he
was taken from the feast and conducted to this cruel
woman's cabin. Upon entering, he was surprised at
being stripped of his clothes. Then he saw that his
life was lost, and he cried out, before dying, that
[117] an entire people would be burned in his person,
and that his death would be cruelly avenged. His
words proved true; for, no sooner had the news
reached Onnontagué, than twelve hundred determined men started forth to exact satisfaction for this
affront.

We have already observed that the Cat Nation is
so called from the large number of Wildcats, of great
size and beauty, in their Country.[8] The Climate is
temperate, neither ice nor snow being seen in the
Winter; while in Summer it is said that grain and
fruit are harvested in abundance, and are of unusual
size and excellence.

Our Warriors entered that Country, remote though
it was from Onnontagué, before they were perceived.
Their arrival spread such a panic, that Villages and
dwellings were abandoned to the mercy of the Con-
queror,—who, after burning everything, started in
pursuit of the fugitives. The latter numbered from
two to three thousand combatants, besides women
and children. Finding themselves [118] closely followed, they resolved, after five days' flight, to build
a fort of wood and there await the enemy, who
numbered only twelve hundred. Accordingly, they
intrenched themselves as well as they could. The

là attendre leurs ennemis, qui n'eſtoient que douze
cent. Ils ſe retrancherent donc le mieux qu'ils
peurent. L'ennemy fait ſes approches, les deux
Chefs les plus conſiderables, veſtus à la Françoiſe, ſe
font voir pour les épouuenter, par la nouueauté de
cét habit, vn d'eux Baptizé par le Pere le Moine: &
fort bien inſtruit, ſollicita doucement les aſſiegez de
capituler, autrement que c'eſt fait d'eux s'ils ſouffrent
l'attaque. Le Maiſtre de la vie combat pour nous,
diſoit-il, vous eſtes perdus ſi vous luy reſiſtez. Quel
eſt ce Maiſtre de nos vies, répondent ſuperbement
les Aſſiegez? Nous n'en reconnoiſſons point d'autres
que nos bras & nos haches. Là-deſſus l'aſſaut ſe
donne, on attaque de tous coſtez la palliſſade, qui eſt
auſſi bien defenduë qu'attaquée; le combat dure
long-temps, & auec grand courage de part & d'autre.
Les Aſſiegeants font tous leurs efforts pour enleuer
la place par force; mais c'eſt en vain: on en tuë
autant qu'il s'en preſente. Ils s'auiſerent de ſe
ſeruir de leurs canots, [119] comme de boucliers: ils
les portent deuant eux, & à la faueur de cét abry, les
voila au pied du retranchement. Mais il faut franchir les grands pieux, ou les arbres dont il eſt baſty.
Ils dreſſent leurs meſmes canots, & s'en ſeruent
comme d'échelles, pour monter par deſſus cette groſſe
paliſſade. Cette hardieſſe eſtonna ſi fort les Aſſiegez,
qu'eſtans deſia au bout de leurs munitions de guerre,
dont ils n'eſtoient pas bien pourueûs, notamment de
poudre, ils ſongerent à la fuite: ce qui cauſa leur
ruïne: car les premiers fuyarts ayants eſté tuez pour
la pluſpart, le reſte fut inueſty par les Onnontaguehronnons, qui entrerent dans le fort, & y firent vn
tel carnage de femmes & d'enfants, qu'on auoit du

enemy drew near, the two head Chiefs showing themselves in French costume, in order to frighten their opponents by the novelty of this attire.   One of the two, who had been Baptized by Father le Moine and was very well instructed, gently urged the besieged to capitulate, telling them that they would be destroyed if they allowed an assault. '' The Master of life fights for us,'' said he; '' you will be ruined if you resist him.''   '' Who is this Master of our lives?'' was the haughty reply of the Besieged. '' We acknowledge none but our arms and hatchets.'' Thereupon, the assault was made and the palisade attacked on all sides; but the defense was as spirited as the attack, and the combat was a long one, great courage being displayed on both sides.   The Besieging party made every effort to carry the place by storm, but in vain; they were killed as fast as they advanced.   They hit on the plan of using their canoes [119] as shields; and, bearing these before them as protection, they reached the foot of the intrenchment.   But it remained to scale the large stakes, or tree-trunks, of which it was built.   Again they resorted to their canoes, using them as ladders for surmounting that stanch palisade.   Their boldness so astonished the Besieged that, being already at the end of their munitions of war,— with which, especially with powder, they had been but poorly provided,— they resolved to flee.   This was their ruin; for, after most of the first fugitives had been killed, the others were surrounded by the Onnontaguehronnons, who entered the fort and there wrought such carnage among the women and children, that blood was knee-deep in certain places.   Those who had escaped, wishing to retrieve their honor, after

ſang iuſqu'au genoüil en certains endroits. Ceux
qui s'étoient ſauuez, voulants reparer leur honneur:
apres auoir vn peu repris leurs eſprits, retournerent
ſur leurs pas au nombre de trois cent, à deſſein de
ſurprendre l'ennemy à l'impourueu, lors qu'il ſeroit
moins ſur ſes gardes dans ſa retraite. C'étoit vn
bon conſeil; mais il fut mal conduit: car s'eſtans
effrayez au premier cry [120] que firent les Onnontaguehronnons, ils furent entierement deffaits. Le
Vainqueur ne laiſſa pas de perdre vn bon nombre de
ſes gens: en ſorte qu'il fut obligé de s'arreſter deux
mois dans le païs des ennemis, pour enſeuelir ſes
morts & penſer ſes bleſſez.

recovering their courage a little, returned, to the number of three hundred, to take the enemy by surprise while he was retiring and off his guard. The plan was good, but it was ill executed; for, frightened at the first cry [120] of the Onnontaguehronnons, they were entirely defeated. The Victors did not escape heavy losses,— so great, indeed, that they were forced to remain two months in the enemy's country, burying their dead and caring for their wounded.

CHAPITRE XII.

CONSEILS TENUS ENTRE CES PEUPLES. RENCONTRE
DE HURONS. EXECUTION D'V[N] PRISON-
NIER. VISION D'VN SAUUAGE.

L E cinquiéme de Février arriuent à Onnontagué
grand nombre de Chaffeurs de Sonnontouan,
& d'Oïogoen. Le Pere les falüa par deux prefents de mille grains à chaque Nation: leur difant
qu'ils n'entroient pas feulement dans le païs des
Onnontaguehronnons: mais auffi dans le Païs des
François, puis que ce n'eftoit plus qu'vn Peuple: que
la ioye de leur arriuée eftoit cõmune: [121] & qu'il
fouhaitoit qu'Onnontio pût voir de fi beaux enfants
qu'il auoit en ce Pays-là: qu'il en reffentiroit vn
contentement tout particulier: qu'au refte il effuyoit
par le prefent qu'il faifoit en fon nom, le fang qui
reftoit encore fur leurs corps, du dernier combat
rendu contre la Nation de Chat. Ils refpondirent
par deux femblables prefents: apres quoy, ils fe
difpoferent à leur feftin de guerre. Nous nous
retirafmes, pour les laiffer faire en liberté toute la
ceremonie dont nous auons parlé cy-deffus.

Le feptiéme, les Anciens du Bourg, firent vn prefent à ces nouueaux hoftes, pour les prier de nous
refpecter, & de ne fe point choquer de nos façons de
faire: de ne point trouuer à redire à nos prieres: &
de fe comporter enuers nous, comme font obligez de
bons enfants enuers leurs Peres.

CHAPTER XII.

COUNCILS HELD BY THESE TRIBES.   MEETING WITH
HURONS.   EXECUTION OF A PRISONER.
A SAVAGE'S VISION.

O N the fifth of February, there came to Onnontagué many Hunters from Sonnontouan and
Oiogoen, whom the Father greeted with two
presents of a thousand beads to each Nation; telling
them that they entered not only the country of the
Onnontaguehronnons, but also that of the French,
since the two formed but one People.   He added
that the joy at their coming was general; [121] and
he wished that Onnontio could have seen what fine
children he had in that Country, for he would be
especially pleased with them.   He also, with the
present offered in his name, wiped away the blood
still remaining on their persons from their latest
engagement with the Cat Nation.   They responded
with two similar presents, after which they prepared
for their war-feast.   We withdrew, to leave them at
liberty to carry out fully the ceremony already
mentioned.

On the seventh, the Village Elders made a present
to these new guests, asking them to pay us respect,
and not to take offense at our ways or find fault
with our prayers, but to behave toward us as
good children are obliged to behave toward their
Fathers.

Among these Hunters were many Christian Hu-

Parmy ces Chaffeurs, il fe trouua bon nombre de
Hurons Chreftiens, qui donnerent bien de la confolation au Pere, luy faifants paroiftre comme la mifere
n'auoit pas éteint la Foy dans leur cœur, [122] & luy
aprenant plufieurs particularitez des reftes de cette
pauure Eglife Hurõne.   Vne bonne femme nommée
Gandigoura, eftant interrogée fi pendant les fix ans
de fa captiuité, parmy les perfecuteurs de la Foy,
elle l'auoit conferuée: répondit, qu'elle n'auoit garde
d'oublier vne chofe qu'elle tenoit plus pretieufe que
fa vie.   Et fe fouuenant que depuis fon Baptefme,
elle auoit eu le bien de Communier huiẟt fois: cette
penfée eftoit affez forte, pour l'empefcher de tomber
dans fes premieres erreurs, & pour luy conferuer
iufqu'au dernier foûpir, la memoire de fa Religion.

Vne autre, nommée Gannendio, difoit, qu'ayant
veu maffacrer fes enfants, & ayant receu neuf coups
de coufteau, par ordre de ceux à qui elle auoit efté
donnée; elle fe confoloit dans la penfée du Ciel, où
elle penfoit aller auec fes petits innocens: mais que
Dieu luy auoit rendu la vie d'vne façon merueilleufe.

René Tfondihouannen, difoit-elle, qui fut tué à la
prife de Rigué, prioit Dieu foir & matin, pendant
fon efclauage: [123] & tous les Samedys, il aduer-
tiffoit ceux qu'il pouuoit du iour de Dimanche, afin
qu'ils le gardaffent.   Il auoit luy-mefme Baptizé
deux enfants gemeaux de fa fille Aatio.

Cette mefme Aatio montra bien que la Foy eftoit
profondement grauée dans fon cœur, puis qu'elle ne
chancela iamais au milieu des plus grandes trauerfes,
qui la pouuoient ébranler.   Au contraire, quoy que
chaque iour luy fuft vn iour funefte, elle ne laiffoit
pas de le confacrer à Dieu par fes prieres, qu'elle

rons, who greatly cheered the Father by showing
him that disaster had not extinguished the Faith in
their hearts, [122] and by giving him some account
of the remains of that poor Huron Church.   A good
woman named Gandigoura, when asked whether,
during her six years' captivity among the persecutors
of the Faith, she had kept her religion, answered that
she was careful not to forget a thing which she held
dearer than life.   The consciousness that, since her
Baptism, she had eight times enjoyed the privilege
of receiving Communion, was sufficient to keep her
from falling into her former sins, and to preserve
her, to the last moment, in the remembrance of her
Religion.

Another woman, named Gannendio, said that,
after seeing her children slain, and herself receiving
nine knife-wounds, by order of those to whom she
had been given, she consoled herself with thoughts
of Heaven, whither she expected to go with her
little innocents; but that God had miraculously
restored her to life.

René Tsondihouannen, she said, who was killed
at the taking of Rigué, prayed to God morning and
evening during his captivity, [123] and every Saturday reminded those whom he could of the approaching Sunday, in order that they might observe the
day.   He himself had Baptized his sister Aatio's twin
children.

This same Aatio showed that the Faith was deeply
graven on her heart, as she never wavered amid the
severest trials that could assail her.   On the contrary, although each day was for her a fatal day, she
failed not to consecrate it to God by her prayers, in
which she always persevered with a constancy worthy

continua toufiours auec vne conftance d'vne Macha-
bée vrayement Chreftienne.   Son fils nommé Tehannonrakouan, ayant efté tué par les Andaftogue-
ronnons, il ne luy reftoit que fes deux gemeaux dans
fa captiuité; qu'elle porta long-temps fur fon dos,
fuiuant les Vainqueurs, fe confolant auec cette pretieufe charge, qui eftoit les feules reliques du debris
de fa grande famille.   Mais comme ce doux fardeau
l'empefchoit de marcher auffi vifte que fes con-
ducteurs defiroient; ils maffacrerent ces deux pauures
innocens à la veuë de leur [124] mere, qui ne laiffoit
pas de prendre patience, & de fe preparer à dauã-
tage.   De vray, vn mal de genoüil luy eftant furuenu,
le fit enfler fi fort, qu'à peine pouuoit-elle fe trainer.
Ces cruels Barbares ne voulurent pas luy faire la
grace de la deliurer de ce monde par vn coup de
hache: mais ils la firent paffer par le feu.

L'onziéme de Février, arriua vn Deputé de la part
d'Onneiout, pour traiter des affaires communes du
païs.   Il dit au Pere entr'autres chofes, que la paix
entre les François & les Anniehronnons eftoit ftable,
& fi bien cimentée, qu'il n'y auoit rien à craindre
de part ny d'autre.   Mais ie ne voudrois pas m'y
beaucoup fier.

Il fit tenir confeil, & les Deputez des autres Nations s'eftant affemblez auec les Anciens du Bourg,
le Pere fut inuité de venir prendre place, pour fçauoir
quelle eftoit la commiffion de ce Deputé.   Il y va, &
s'adreffant à ceux qui venoiët de la part d'Onneïout,
& d Oïogoen, Il leur dit qu'il eftoit bien-aife de les
voir, & qu'il les exhortoit à l'vnion & à ne point
prefter l'oreille aux médifances [125] des enuieux.
La conclufion du difcours, fut vn prefent de mille
grains à chaque Nation.

of a Christian Maccabee. Her son, Tehannonrakouan, having been killed by the Andastogueronnons, there remained to her in her captivity only her twins, whom she carried on her back a long time, following the Victors and cheering herself with this precious burden, the sole relics left from the destruction of her large family.   But, as this dear burden prevented her from making such rapid progress as her conductors desired, they murdered the two poor innocents before their mother's eyes.   [124] She never lost patience, but prepared herself for further misfortune. And indeed, her knee becoming diseased, and so badly swollen that she could scarcely drag herself along, those cruel Barbarians, unwilling to grant her a speedy deliverance from the pains of this world by a hatchet-stroke, caused her to be burned to death.

On the eleventh of February, a Deputy from Onneiout came to treat of the general affairs of the country.   He told the Father, among other things, that the peace between the French and the Anniehronnons was a permanent one, and so well compacted that there was nothing to fear on either side.   But I would not place much confidence in it.

He caused a council to be held, and, when the Deputies of the other Nations had assembled, with the Elders of the Village, the Father was invited to attend, for the sake of learning this Deputy's errand. He went, and, addressing the representatives of Onneiout and Oiogoen, he told them that he was glad to see them, enjoined union upon them, and begged them not to give ear to the slanders [125] of the envious.   His speech ended with a present of a thousand beads to each Nation.

Le Deputé d'Onnejout s'eftant leué, parut auec vn
beau collier à la main, de deux mille grains, qu'il
prefenta au Pere, pour effuyer le fang refpandu par
les Anniehronnons, depuis le premier pourparler de
paix: Il en donna vn autre femblable, pour le remercier de ce qu'il les auoit pris pour enfants, & pour
compatriotes; l'exhortãt d'eftre vray Pere, non feulement de parole; mais d'effet, comme on s'y attendoit
bien.   Le troifiéme prefent fut pour encourager le
Pere dans l'entreprife que luy & Agochiendaguefé
auoient fi heureufement commencé, & prefqu'acheué.
En fuite pour témoigner fa ioye d'eftre adopté par
Onnontio; il chanta, & fit chanter fes compagnons.
La chanfon finie, il parla vne grande demy-heure,
declarant fes fentiments fur fon adoption, nommant
tous les parents qu'il auoit, & à Kebec, & aux trois
Riuieres, & à Montreal.   Iamais Farceur ne fit mieux
fon perfonnage que cét homme, fur tout quand il fe
[126] mit à entretenir la compagnie pendant plus de
deux heures, fur les proüeffes de ceux de fa Nation,
reprefentant par geftes & par paroles, les combats,
les attaques, les faits, les victoires, les déroutes, les
morts, les viuants, plus agreablement & plus naïfue-
ment, qu'on ne peut s'imaginer.

Sur le foir du mefme iour, arriuerent trois Soldats
de ce Bourg, qui portoient trois cheuelures, prifes fur
quelques peuples d'autre langue que celle de ces
Contrées, & d'vn païs fort eloigné d'icy.   Ils ame-
noient auffi deux ieunes hommes de la Nation de
Chat; bien faits, bien couuerts, puiffants, & de l'aage
de vingt à trente ans.   Soit que les Onnontaguehronnons ne les euffent pas pris de bonne guerre: foit qu'ils
fe fuffent eux-mefme rendus dans le defefpoir de

The Deputy from Onneiout rose, and brought forward a handsome collar of two thousand beads, which
he presented to the Father, to wipe away the blood
shed by the Anniehronnons since the first negotiations for peace. He gave him another, a similar one,
to thank him for adopting them as his children and
compatriots, exhorting him to be a veritable Father,
not only in word, but also in reality, as indeed he
was expected to be.   The third present was to
encourage him in the enterprise, which he and Agochiendaguesé had so happily begun and nearly
completed.   Then, to attest his joy at being adopted
by Onnontio, he sang, and made his companions
sing. That done, he spoke for a full half-hour,
declaring his sentiments upon his adoption, and
naming all the relatives he had at Kebec, at three
Rivers, and at Montreal.   Never Actor played his
part better than this man did, especially when he
[126] undertook to entertain the company for more
than two hours with his Countrymen's deeds of
prowess, portraying, by voice and gesture, battles,
assaults, exploits, victories, defeats, the dead, the
living,—and all with a grace and simplicity beyond
conception.

Toward evening of the same day, three Soldiers
of this Village arrived with three scalps, taken from
some people of another language than that of these
Regions, and of a country far distant from here.
They also brought home two young men of the Cat
Nation, well formed, well dressed, strong, and
between twenty and thirty years of age.   Whether
because the Onnontaguehronnons had not taken them
in regular warfare, or because they, in despair of
escaping, had given themselves up voluntarily, they

pouuoir éuader, Ils ne croyoient pas deuoir eftre
traitez en captifs: & de vray, eftant arriuez, on les
place dans deux familles des plus honorables, pour
tenir la place de deux deffunéts.   Le plus ieune & le
mieux fait, Neveu de l'autre, fut donné au plus grand
guerrier du Pays, nommé [127] Aharihon; Capitaine
fameux pour fes exploits de guerre: mais auffi
fuperbe, & fanguinaire que genereux, comme il va
faire paroiftre.

Vn de fes freres ayant efté tué depuis peu par la
Nation de Chat, on le remplaça par ce nouueau
adopté.   Ce cruel faifoit tant d'eftat de fon frere,
qu'il luy auoit defia facrifié quarante hommes, qu'il
auoit fait paffer par le feu, ne croyant pas qu'il y euft
perfonne qui pût dignement tenir fa place.   Ce ieune
homme luy ayant donc efté donné pour ce mefme
fuiet: il luy donne quatre chiens, pour en faire le
feftin de fon adoption.   Au milieu du banquet, lors
qu'il eftoit en ioye, & qu'il chantoit pour diuertiffe-
ment des conuiez, Aharihon fe leue, & dit à la
compagnie, qu'il faut que celuy-là expie encore la
mort de fon frere.   Ce pauure garçon eft bien eftonné
à cette parole: il regarde du cofté de la porte pour
éuader; mais il eft arrefté par deux hommes, qui ont
commiffion de le brûler.   Le quatorziéme iour de
Février, ils commencerent le foir par les pieds, qu'on
deuoit roftir [128] à petit feu iufqu'à la ceinture, pendant la plufpart de la nuit: & apres minuit, on luy
deuoit laiffer reprendre fes forces, & vn peu de repos
iufqu'au point du iour, qu'on deuoit acheuer cette
funefte tragedie.   Ce pauure homme eftant dans les
tourmens, faifoit retentir fes cris & fes gemiffements
par tout le Bourg: c'étoit vne chofe épouuentable, de

thought that they ought not to be treated as captives; and, indeed, upon their arrival, they were assigned to two of the most honorable families, to take the place of two deceased members. The younger and handsomer one, a Nephew of the other, was given to the greatest warrior of the Country, named [127] Aharihon, a Captain famous for his warlike exploits, but as arrogant and bloodthirsty as he is brave, as will presently appear.

One of his brothers having been recently killed by the Cat Nation, he was replaced by this newly-adopted man. The cruel Captain held his brother in such high esteem that he had already made him a sacrifice of forty men,—causing them to be burned, since he did not believe that there was any one worthy to occupy his place. When, accordingly, this young man was given him as a substitute for the deceased, he presented to him four dogs, upon which to hold his feast of adoption. In the middle of the feast, while he was rejoicing and singing to entertain the guests, Aharihon arose, and told the company that this man too must die in atonement for his brother's death. The poor lad was astounded at this, and turned toward the door to make his escape, but was stopped by two men who had orders to burn him. On the fourteenth of February, in the evening, they began with his feet, intending to roast him, [128] at a slow fire, as far up as the waist, during the greater part of the night. After midnight, they were to let him rally his strength and sleep a little until daybreak, when they were to finish this fatal tragedy. In his torture, the poor man made the whole Village resound with his cries and groans. It was fearful to hear him shrieking in the dead of

l'entendre hurler pendant l'horreur de la nuit: il
iettoit de groſſes larmes, contre la couſtume des
autres, qui font gloire de ſe voir brûler membre
apres membre, & ſans parler que pour chanter: mais
comme cettuy-cy ne s'attendoit pas à la mort, il
pleuroit & crioit d'vne façon, qui touchoit meſme ces
Barbares: ce qui fit que l'vn des parents d'Aharihon,
emû de compaſſion, fut pour mettre fin à ſes tourmens, en luy donnant vn coup de couſteau dans le
ſein.   C'euſt eſté vn coup de grace, s'il eut eſté
mortel: cela fut pourtant cauſe, qu'on continua de le
brûler ſans s'arreſter, en ſorte qu'il finit ſes peines
auec ſa vie auant le iour.

Le dix-ſeptiéme, trois mille grains de pourcelaine,
ayants eſté perdus, on [129] conſulte le Deuin, qui ſe
maſque le viſage, & ſe cache les yeux, pour voir plus
clair, à ce qu'on dit.   Il court par les ruës ſuiuy de
la populace: & apres auoir bien couru, il va droit au
pied d'vn arbre, où il trouue deux mille grains; il
retint le troiſiéme millier pour ſe payer de ſes peines;
Ce ne ſont là-deſſus qu'acclamations: c'eſt à qui luy
propoſera plus d'enigmes pendant qu'il eſt en chaleur.

Le vingt-quatriéme, lors qu'on celebroit l'Honnaouaroria, dont nous auons parlé cy-deſſus à propos
des ſonges, arriuerent trois Soldats, qui retournoient
de la guerre contre la Nation de Chat: pour laquelle
ils eſtoient partis il y auoit plus d'vn an.   Vn d'eux
dit à ſon arriuée qu'il auoit vne choſe de tres-grande
importance à communiquer aux Anciens.   Eſtant
aſſemblez, il leur raconte qu'étant à chercher l'ennemy, il fit rencontre d'vne Tortuë, d'vne groſſeur
incroyable; & quelque temps apres, il vit vn Demon
en forme d'vn petit Nain, qu'ils diſent s'eſtre deſia

night. He shed great tears, contrary to the usual
custom, the victim commonly glorying to be burned
limb by limb, and opening his lips only to sing;
but, as this one had not expected death, he wept and
cried in a way that touched even these Barbarians.
One of Aharihon's relatives was so moved with
pity, that he advised ending the sufferer's torments
by plunging a knife into his breast — which would
have been a deed of mercy, had the stab been mortal.
However, they were induced to continue the burning
without interruption, so that before day he ended
both his sufferings and his life.

On the seventeenth, three thousand porcelain
beads having been lost, [129] the Soothsayer was
consulted. Covering his face and blindfolding his
eyes,— in order to see more clearly, as was said,—
he ran about through the streets, the people following. After he had run for a considerable time, he
went straight to the foot of a tree, where he found
two thousand beads — the third thousand being
retained by him to pay for his trouble. Thereupon
followed great applause, and an emulous propound-
ing of riddles while he was in heat.

On the twenty-fourth, while the Honnaouaroria —
of which we spoke above, in connection with dreams —
was being held, there arrived three Warriors, returning, after more than a year's absence, from the war
against the Cat Nation. One of them announced, on
his arrival, that he had a matter of very great importance to communicate to the Elders. These having
assembled, he told them that, while seeking the
enemy, he met a Tortoise of incredible size; and,
some time after, he saw a Demon in the guise of a
little Dwarf, who is said to have already appeared to

apparu à quelques autres: ils l'appellent Taronhiaouagui, qui fignifie celuy qui tient le [130] Ciel.   Ce
Nain, ou ce Demon, parla en ces termes.   C'eft moy
qui tient le Ciel, & qui a foin de la terre; c'eft moy
qui conferue les hommes, & qui donne les victoires
aux combattans; c'eft moy qui vous ay rendus les
maiftres de la terre & les conquerants de tant de
Nations; c'eft moy qui vous ay fait eftre victorieux
des Hurons, de la Nation du Petun, des Ahondihronnons, des Atiraguenrek, des Atiaonrek, des Takoulguehronnons, des Gentaguetehronnons.   Enfin c'eft
moy qui vous ay fait ce que vous eftes; fi vous voulez
que ie vous continuë ma protection, écoutez ma
parole, & executez mes ordres.

Premierement, vous trouuerez trois François dans
voftre Bourg, lors quë vous y arriuerez.   Secondement, vous y entrerez lors qu'on fera l'Honnaouaroria.
Tiercement, apres voftre arriuée, qu'on me faffe vn
facrifice de dix chiens: de dix grains de pourcelaine
par chaque cabanne; d'vn collier large de dix rangs;
de quatre mefures de graine de tournefol, & autant
de febves; Et pour toy, qu'on te donne deux femmes
mariées, [131] qui feront à ta difpofition pendant cinq
iours.   Si tout cela ne s'execute de point en point,
ie mets ta Nation en proye à toutes fortes de mal-
heurs.   Et apres que tout fera fait, ie te declareray
mes ordres pour l'aduenir.   Cela dit, le Nain difpa-
rut.   Cét homme raconta auffi-toft fa vifion à fes
compagnons, qui en virent, à leur dire, vne preuue
dés le iour mefme: car vn Cerf s'eftant trouué à leur
rencontre, il l'appella de loin, & luy commanda de
venir à luy.   Le Cerf obeït, s'aproche, & vient receuoir le coup de la mort de noftre Vifionnaire.   Quoy

others.   They call him Taronhiaouagui, which
means "he who holds up the [130] Sky."⁹   This
Dwarf or Demon spoke as follows: "I am he who
holds up the Sky, and the guardian of the earth; I
preserve men, and give victories to warriors.   I have
made you masters of the earth and victors over so
many Nations; I made you conquer the Hurons,
the Tobacco Nation, the Ahondihronnons, Atiraguenrek, Atiaonrek, Takoulguehronnons, and
Gentaguetehronnons; in short, I have made you
what you are; and, if you wish me to continue my
protection over you, hear my words, and execute my
orders.

"First, you will find three Frenchmen in your
Village when you arrive there.   Secondly, you will
enter during the celebration of the Honnaouaroria.
Thirdly, after your arrival, let there be sacrificed to
me ten dogs, ten porcelain beads from each cabin, a
collar ten rows wide, four measures of sunflower
seed, and as many of beans.   And, as for thee, let
two married women be given thee, [131] to be at
thy disposal for five days.   If that be not executed
item by item I will make thy Nation a prey to all
sorts of disasters; and, after it is all done, I will
declare to thee my orders for the future."   So
saying, the Dwarf vanished.   This vision the man
immediately related to his companions, who witnessed, as they affirmed, its verification that very
day.   Seeing by chance a Stag, he called it from a
distance, and bade it come to him.   The Stag obeyed,
approaching and coming up to receive its death-
stroke from our Visionary.   Though the whole story
was probably only a fiction of these three Warriors,
who invented the dream to cover their shame at

que tout cela ne foit probablement qu'vne fiction de
ces trois Soldats, qui ont inuenté cette refuerie, pour
couurir leur honte, de retourner fi long-temps apres
leur depart, fans auoir rien fait: Il eft neantmoins
certain, que cét homme eft autant defait, pafle &
abatu, comme s'il auoit parlé au Diable: il crache le
fang, & il eft fi défiguré, qu'on n'oferoit quafi le regar-
der en face.   Les Anciens n'ont pas manqué de faire
le facrifice ordonné, tant ils font [132] prompts à
obeïr à tout ce qui approche du fonge.

returning empty-handed after so long an absence, still it is certain that the man was as wasted, pale, and depressed, as if he had spoken with the Devil. He spat blood, and was so disfigured that one scarcely dared to look him in the face. The Elders did not fail to offer the sacrifice as commanded, so [132] prompt are they to obey whatever resembles a dream.

CHAPITRE XIII.

DEPART DU PERE CLAUDE D'ABLON D'ONNONTAGUÉ, POUR RETOURNER À KEBEK.

NOUS eſtions bien en peine, comment nous pourrions faire ſçauoir à KebeK, l'eſtat où eſtoient icy les affaires, & combien paſſionnement ces peuples deſirent que noſtre établiſſement ſe faſſe au pluſtoſt. Ils le firent paroiſtre pour la derniere fois, en vn celebre Conſeil, tenu le vingt-neufiéme Février, où, entr'autres choſes, ils dirent au Pere, qu'il falloit ioüer de ſon reſte à ce coup; qu'il y auoit plus de trois ans qu'ils eſtoient ſur l'attente de la venuë des François; qu'on les remettoit toûjours d'année en année; qu'ils ſe laſſoient enfin de tant de remiſes, & que ſi la choſe ne ſe faiſoit à preſent, il n'y falloit [133] plus ſonger; qu'on vouloit rompre tout à fait, puis qu'on vſoit de tant de delay. Ils adiouſterent de plus, qu'ils ſçauoient bien, que ce n'eſtoit pas le commerce qui nous faiſoit venir chez eux; mais ſeulement la Foy, que nous leur voulions publier. Que ne venez-vous donc au pluſtoſt, diſoient-ils, puis que vous voyez tout noſtre Bourg l'embraſſer? On n'a point ceſſé tout cét Hyuer d'aller en foulle dans la Chapelle, pour prier & pour ſe faire inſtruire. Vous auez eſté tres-bien accueillis dans toutes les Cabannes, quand vous y auez eſté pour enſeigner: vous ne pouuez douter de nos volõtez, puis que nous vous auons fait vn preſent ſi ſolemnel, auec des proteſtations ſi publiques, que nous ſommes Croyants. Ils

CHAPTER XIII.

FATHER CLAUDE D'ABLON'S DEPARTURE FROM ON-NONTAGUÉ TO RETURN TO KEBEK.

WE were much perplexed how to inform those at Kebek of the state of affairs here, and of this people's passionate desire for our speedy settlement among them. They made their wishes known for the last time in a notable Council, held on the twenty-ninth of February,— when among other things, they told the Father that he must employ his last resources to this end. They said that they had been awaiting the coming of the French for more than three years, but had always been put off from year to year, until at last they were tired of so many postponements; and, if the affair were not settled now, it was needless [133] to think any more about it, for they would break with us entirely, in view of the continued delay. They added further that they knew well that it was not trade which brought us to their country, but solely the Faith, which we wished to make known to them. " Why do you not come at once," they asked, " since you see our whole Village embracing it? All this Winter the Chapel has been crowded, for prayers and instruction; you have been very well received in all the Cabins, when you visited them to teach the inmates; and you cannot doubt our wishes after receiving so solemn a present from us, with such public protestations that we are Believers." Much else they added,

adioufterent quantité d'autres chofes, pour declarer
leurs fentiments fur ce fujet: En quoy certes, la
Prouidence de Dieu eft tout à fait admirable, de
difpofer de la forte des Peuples à le rechercher, qui
eftoient il y a peu de temps les plus grands perfecuteurs de fon Eglife: Et ce qui paroift inconceuable, ces
bonnes gens qui font [134] tant d'inftance pour nous
auoir, ne fçauent pas comment cela fe fait, & d'où leur
vient ce grand defir quafi malgré eux.   Ils preffent
noftre établiffement en leur Païs, & fe plaignent les
vns des autres, de ce qu'ils nous font venir.   Les
Anciens difent qu'ils ne peuuent pas s'oppofer à la
ieuneffe, qui demande des François: La Ieuneffe dit,
que les Anciens veulent à cette fois ruïner tout leur
païs en nous y appellant: & auec tout cela, & ceux-cy
& ceux-là, ne ceffent de faire inftance fur inftance, &
de nous menacer d'eftre nos ennemis, fi nous ne
fommes au pluftoft leurs Compatriotes.

   C'eft ce qui nous faifoit rechercher toutes les voyes
poffibles, pour faire fçauoir leurs difpofitions à Kebek,
& pour hafter la venuë des François, de peur de
perdre vne fi belle occafion.   Perfonne apres tout,
ne vouloit entreprendre de remener quelqu'vn de
nous à Kebec; de peur de laiffer paffer la faifon de
fe fournir de Caftors, & les prouifions de toute leur
année: car nous eftions au temps, que toute la
Ieuneffe [135] partoit pour la chaffe.   Nous eftions
dans le defefpoir de pouuoir faire le voyage, quoy qu'il
fuft abfolument neceffaire pour noftre établiffement.
Il y auoit defia plus de deux mois, que nous vfions
de toutes fortes de machines pour en venir là; mais
en vain.   Enfin nous nous aduifafmes de faire vne
neufuaine à fainct Iean Baptifte, Patron de cette
Miffion, difants neuf Meffes, pour obtenir du iour en

to declare their sentiments in the matter,— wherein, in truth, God's Providence appears most wonderful, in causing himself to be sought by People who were but recently the bitterest persecutors of his Church. Moreover,— a thing apparently inconceivable,— these good people, who [134] so strongly urge us to come, know not the reason of this, or whence arises, almost in spite of themselves, this strong desire of theirs. They urge on our settlement in their Country, and reproach one another for not making us come.   The Elders say that they cannot resist the young men's desire for the French; the Young men say that the Elders are bent on ruining the whole country, this time, by calling us into it; and yet, neither the former nor the latter cease to press the matter vehemently, and to threaten us with their enmity unless we speedily become their Compatriots.

Therefore, fearing to lose so favorable an opportunity, we sought every possible way to send word to Kebek of their state of mind, and to hasten the coming of the French.   But no one would undertake to conduct one of us to Kebec, fearing to let slip the season for securing Beavers and a whole year's supplies; for just then all the Young men [135] were departing for the chase. We despaired of being able to make the journey, although it was absolutely necessary for our settlement.   For more than two months we had been using all sorts of expedients to gain our end, but in vain.   At last, it occurred to us to make a novena to saint John the Baptist, Patron of this Mission; and we said nine Masses, to gain light upon a matter in which we were beset with utter darkness.   And lo! contrary to our expectation and to all human probability, without knowing how

vne affaire où nous ne voyons goutte. Et voila, que
contre noſtre attente, & contre toute apparence
humaine, ſans ſçauoir comment cela s'eſt fait, ny par
qui; immediatement apres la neufiéme Meſſe; ie pars
d'Onnontagué, accompagné de deux ieunes hommes
des plus conſiderables du Bourg, & de quelques
autres: à qui, ſans doute, ſainⅽt Iean inſpira l'entrepriſe de ce voyage: auſſi le Chef de l'eſcorte ſe
nommoit Iean Baptiſte; c'eſt le premier Baptizé des
Iroquois en pleine ſanté.

Ce fut ſur les neuf heures du ſecond iour de Mars,
apres auoir celebré la ſainⅽte Meſſe, & dit mon adieu
au Pays, [136] par le Bapteſme d'vn enfant, à qui ie
le conferay, auant mon depart. Nous fiſmes cinq
lieuës pour cette premiere iournée, d'vn temps de
printemps pluſtoſt que d'hyuer, il ſe changea bien-
toſt, & la pluie nous obligea de paſſer vn iour & deux
nuits, au milieu d'vn bois, dans vne maiſon ſans
portes, ſans feneſtres & ſans murailles.

Le quatriéme de Mars, apres ſix petites lieuës,
nous giſtons au bord du lac, qui ſe termine à Tirhiroguen. Cette iournée fut rude, ayant preſque toujours
eu, ou la neige, ou l'eau iuſqu'au genoux. Nous
paſſons encore vn iour & deux nuits en ce ſecond
giſte: car le Lac que nous penſions trauerſer ſur la
glace, commençoit à ſe dégeler: mais nous reſſen-
tions bien, par le froid de la ſeconde nuit, que le
paſſage ſeroit libre, & le pont ſolide.

En effet, nous fiſmes ſur la glace vne grande lieuë
& demie; apres quoy, c'étoit vn plaiſir de marcher
mollement ſur la nege; il nous fallut pourtant mettre
bien auant dans l'eau, pour paſſer vne petite Riuiere,
qui auoit reſiſté à la violence du froid.

[137] Le ſeptieme de Mars, apres vn leger repos

or by whom it was effected, immediately after the ninth Mass I left Onnontagué, accompanied by two of the Village's leading young men and by several others,—whom saint John undoubtedly prompted to undertake this journey.   Moreover, the Leader of the escort was named Jean Baptiste, and was the first of the Iroquois Baptized in perfect health.

Toward nine o'clock on the second day of March, after celebrating holy Mass and bidding farewell to the Country [136] by attending to the Baptism of a child, upon whom I conferred this sacrament before departing, we started.   On the first day we advanced five leagues, in spring rather than winter weather; but it soon changed, and we were forced by rain to spend a day and two nights in the woods, in a house without doors, without windows, and without walls.

On the fourth of March, after proceeding six short leagues, we camped on the shore of the lake which ends at Tirhiroguen.   This was a hard day's journey, through almost uninterrupted snow or water up to our knees.   Again a day and two nights were passed in this second halting-place, as the Lake, which we purposed to cross on the ice, was beginning to thaw; but the cold of the second night convinced us that the passage would be free and the bridge firm.

We did, indeed, accomplish a long league and a half on the ice, after which it was a pleasure to walk over the soft snow; we were, however, forced to wade in deep water to cross a small River that had withstood the heavy frost.

[137] On the seventh of March, after a light meal, we started in the morning and walked until evening

[*sc.* repas], nous partons le matin, & marchant iuſqu'au ſoir ſans rien prendre: Nous ne peuſmes arriuer
à Oeiatonnehengué, que le lendemain vn peu auant
midy.   Nous eſperions nous pouuoir embarquer ſur
le grand Lac: mais quoy qu'il ne fuſt pas gelé, tous
les bords eſtoient tellement occupez de monceaux de
neges, & de gros glaçons, qu'il ne faiſoit pas bon s'en
approcher.   Nous fiſmes donc deux petites lieuës ſur
le beau ſable: & apres auoir donné la chaſſe à vn
nombre incroyable d'Outardes, qui font là leur
retraite pendant l'Hyuer, en vn petit mareſcage, nous
y faiſons la noſtre pour cette nuit.

Le neufiéme iour nous fut aſſez fâcheux.   Nous
marchâmes ſur vn Eſtang glacé; mais touſiours le
pied en l'eau, à cauſe que la pluye, qui eſtoit tombée
le matin, n'eſtoit pas encore gelée.   Nous vinſmes
enfin ſur vn beau ſable, ſur les riues du grand Lac:
mais nous fuſmes arreſtez par vne Riuiere profonde,
dont la glace n'eſtoit pas aſſez forte pour nous porter.
On cherche toutes ſortes [138] de moyens pour la
paſſer: & comme on n'en trouuoit point, mes gens
font alte pour deliberer de ce qu'on deuoit faire.   Ils
paſſent plus de trois heures à trembler de froid,
pluſtoſt qu'à conſulter.   Vous pouuez croire que i'en
auois auſſi ma part.   Le reſultat fut de retourner ſur
vne partie de nos pas, pour chercher vn endroit
propre pour paſſer la nuit.   Nous trauerſons donc vn
autre Lac, auec la meſme incommodité que le matin;
mais auec cette difference, que nous fuſmes accompagnez d'vne groſſe pluye, qui enfin nous contraignit
de nous cacher ſous des écorces.

Le iour d'apres, nous montons vne lieuë au deſſus
de l'embouchure de la Riuiere qui nous auoit arreſté.
Nous la trouuions aſſez fortement gelée pour la

without eating. We were unable to reach Oeiatonnehengué until nearly noon on the following day.
We hoped to be able to cross the great Lake in
canoes; but, though it was not frozen, its entire
shore was so encumbered with piles of snow and
great blocks of ice, that it was nearly inaccessible.
Accordingly, we made two short leagues along the
smooth sand; and, after hunting an incredible number of Bustards, which make their Winter retreat
there in a little swamp, we made ours in the same
place for that night.

The ninth was a hard day for us. We proceeded
over a frozen Pond, but with our feet always in the
water, as the rain that had fallen in the morning
was not yet frozen. At length, we reached a fine
sandy beach on the great Lake, but were stopped by
a deep River, the ice on which was too weak to bear
us. We sought all kinds [138] of expedients for
crossing, but, as we found none, my people called a
halt to deliberate on our future course. They spent
more than three hours trembling with cold, rather
than consulting; and you may believe that I had my
share in this. The result was, that we retraced a
part of our steps, seeking a suitable place for passing
the night. So we crossed another Lake, under the
same inconvenience as in the morning, but with the
addition of a heavy rain, which finally compelled us
to take refuge under a shelter of bark.

The next day, we ascended a league above the
mouth of the River which had stopped us, and there
found it frozen firmly enough for crossing. But oh,
how hard it was to resume our course! We were
forced to cross a vast prairie flooded with water, to
make our way over soft and half-melted snow,

trauerfer.   Mais, ô mon Dieu, que de peine, pour aller
reprendre noftre chemin.   Il fallut paffer au trauers
d'vne vafte prairie pleine d'eau, parmy des neges
molles & à demy fonduës, par des bois & par des
eftangs: & apres auoir franchy ces difficultez, il nous
fallut mettre trois fois à l'eau pour paffer les [139]
Riuieres qui fe rencõtroient.   Enfin ayãt cheminé
tout le iour, nous trouuafmes fur le foir, que nous
n'auions auancé que trois lieuës dans noftre route.
C'eft dans les fatigues que Dieu eft fort: & dans
l'amertume qu'on le trouue bien doux.

Nous marchons prefque tout l'onziéme iour fur la
glace du grand Lac, mais toufiours le pied à l'eau, à
caufe du degel, qui faifoit que noftre marche n'étoit
pas trop affeurée: car nous entendions quelquesfois
craquer la glace fous nous; & il falloit que quelques-
vns des plus hardis marchaffent deuant, pour fonder
le fort & le foible.   Nous ne laiffions pas pourtant de
nous écarter de deux & trois lieuës de la terre, pour
abreger le chemin qu'il nous euft fallu faire, fi nous
euffions cottoyé les bords du Lac.   Apres fept bonnes
lieuës, la pluye nous arrefte; elle ne ceffe ny la nuit,
ny le iour fuiuant, elle redouble fi fort la feconde
nuit, que nous eftans couchez fur la terre, nous nous
trouuafmes bien-toft eftendus dedans l'eau; noftre
petite cabanne eftoit deuenuë en peu de temps vn
grand eftang.   On fe leue: on cherche [140] à fe
placer à fec.   Les vns fe mettent fur de petites
buttes; mais ils s'expofent à l'eau qui tombe du Ciel
en abondance, voulant éuiter celle qui eftoit fur la
terre.   Quelques-vns vont chercher vn endroit plus
eminent, pour y faire du feu & baftïr vne cabanne;
mais la nuit, la neige & la pluye les en empefchent.
Les plus pareffeux demeurent iufqu'au iour en l'eftat

through woods and across ponds; and, after surmounting all these difficulties, we were thrice
compelled to wade through water, to cross the [139]
Rivers in our course.   Finally, after walking all day,
we found toward evening that we had advanced
only three leagues on our route.   In weariness God
is strong, and in bitterness we find him indeed
sweet.

On the eleventh, we walked nearly all day over
the frozen surface of the great Lake, but with our
feet constantly in the water, owing to the thaw which
made our steps none too secure; for we occasionally
heard the ice cracking under us, and some of the
bolder ones had to go ahead and test its strength.
Yet, we were not deterred from going out two and
three leagues from land, to find a shorter route than
that along the shore of the Lake.   After making
seven good leagues, we were stopped by rain, which
did not cease during the night or on the next day;
it so increased in violence during the second night,
that, lying as we were on the ground, we soon found
ourselves stretched in the water.   Our little cabin
had become, in a short time, a great pond.   We
rose, and tried [140] to find a dry place.   Some
took their station on little hills, but exposed themselves to the downpour of water from the Sky, while
seeking to avoid that which was on the earth.
Others went to look for higher ground, in order
to make a fire and build a cabin; but darkness,
snow, and rain prevented them.   The more indolent
remained till daylight as they were, fearing lest they
should fare worse.   Under such conditions, a night
would seem long indeed, did not God illumine the

où ils eſtoient, de peur de trouuer pis; vne nuit ſem-
bleroit bien longue en cét eſtat, ſi Dieu ne l'éclairoit.
Quoy qu'il en ſoit, celuy qui auoit plus de patience,
eſtoit le mieux couché.

Le iour venu, nous nous viſmes tous trempez, &
tous en deſordre.   Si fallut-il encore patienter: car
le vent, la neige, & la pluye, ſembloient conſpirer
enſemble, à nous arreſter en vn ſi mauuais poſte.

Nous le quittons apres deux iours & trois nuits: &
ayants fait ſept lieuës ſur la glace, & partie ſur la
neige, nous baſtiſſons noſtre hoſtellerie en vn lieu vn
peu plus raiſonnable.   Nos Sauuages ſe laſſants de
viure dans ces fatigues, auec vne nourriture moindre,
que ſi nous n'euſſions [141] eu que du pain ſimplement,
& de l'eau, ſe mirent à chaſſer.   Ils tuërent vn Cerf,
& quelques Chats ſauuages, qui rétablirent nos forces.

Nous partons le feiziéme auec vn tres-beau temps;
mais l'attrait de la proye eſt trop grand, pour des
perſonnes qui en font tout leur bon-heur.   Apres
deux lieuës de chemin, les vns ſe cabannent, pendant
que les autres courent le Cerf.   La iournée ne fut
pas difficile, puis qu'outre que nous fiſmes peu de
chemin, nous en fuſmes quittes pour nous mettre vne
fois à l'eau iuſqu'aux genoux.

Tout le dix-feptiéme ſe paſſa le pied à l'eau, dans
vn temps rude, & par vn chemin affreux; tantoſt il
faut grimper ſur des montagnes de neiges, auec les
pieds & les mains; tantoſt marcher ſur de gros glaçons; tantoſt paſſer des Marais, puis s'enfoncer dans
des broſſailles; abbattre des arbres pour faire des
ponts ſur des Riuieres, trauerſer des torrens; s'écha-
per des precipices; & au bout de la iournée, nous
n'auions fait que quatre bien petites lieuës.   Enfin
pour [142] reconfort, nous log[e]ons dans vne hoſtele-

gloom.   At any rate, the most patient were the best
bedded.

Day breaking, we found ourselves all soaked and
in disorder, yet were forced still to have patience;
for wind, snow, and rain seemed to conspire to detain
us in our wretched position.

We left it after two days and three nights, and,
advancing seven leagues over ice and snow, built
our inn on a site that was slightly more tolerable.   Our Savages, weary of bearing these hardships
on a diet more meager than one [141] of bread and
water only, we started out to hunt.   They killed
a Deer and some Wildcats, which restored our
vigor.

We left on the sixteenth, with very fine weather;
but the charms of the chase were too great for men
who find all their happiness therein.   After making
two leagues, some built themselves a cabin, while
the rest hunted Deer.   It was an easy day; for,
besides the shortness of our march, we had to wade
only once in water as high as our knees.

We passed all the seventeenth with feet in the
water, weather rough, and road frightful.   At times,
we had to climb with feet and hands over mountains
of snow; again, to walk over great ice-blocks; and
again, to pass over Marshes, plunge into thickets,
fell trees for bridging Rivers, cross streams, and
avoid precipices; while, at the day's end, we had
made barely four short leagues.   Finally, to [142]
comfort us, we lodged at an inn where there was
neither bread nor wine nor bed; but truly God was
wholly there.

On the eighteenth, we proceeded six leagues.

rie, où il n'y a pain, ny vin, ny lict; mais en verité,
Dieu y eſt tout entier.

Le dix-huictiéme, nous fiſmes ſix lieuës.

Le dix-neufiéme, iour de S. Ioſeph, comme nous
pourſuiuons noſtre route, marchant ſur la glace du
grand Lac, elle s'ouurit ſous l'vn de mes pieds. Ie
m'en tiray plus heureuſement qu'vn pauure Chaſſeur
Onnontaguehronnon, qui apres s'eſtre long-temps
debattu contre les glaces qui luy auoient manqué, fut
abyſmé & perdu dedans l'eau, ſans que iamais on le
pût ſecourir. Apres auoir éuité ces dangers, nous
entrons dans vn chemin extremément difficile. Ce
ſont des rochers hauts comme des tours, & tellement
eſcarpez, qu'on y marche autant des mains que des
pieds. Cela fait; il fallut courrir trois lieuës ſans
relaſche ſur d'autres glaces, de peur d'enfoncer; &
en ſuitte paſſer la nuit ſur vn rocher vis à vis d'Otondiata, qui eſt le paſſage & le chemin ordinaire pour
aller à la Chaſſe des Caſtors. Nous fiſmes vn canot
pour trauerſer le Lac. Comme nous [143] eſtions
vingt de compagnie, quelques-vns s'embarquerent
les premiers. Approchant de l'autre riue du Lac,
ils briſerent le deuant de leur batteau contre vne
glace: les voila tous à l'eau, les vns attrapant le
debris du canot, & les autres la glace qui l'auoit
rompu. Ils font ſi bien qu'ils ſe ſauuerent tous: &
apres auoir radoubbé ce Nauire d'écorces; ils nous
le renuoyent pour paſſer apres eux: ce que nous
fiſmes la nuit du vingt & vniéme de Mars. Nous
n'auions mangé à noſtre diſner, que fort peu de
racines boüillies dans l'eau claire: ſi fallut-il nous
coucher ſans ſoupper, & ſur des cailloux, à l'enſeigne
des Etoilles, abriez d'vn vent de biſe, qui nous
glaçoit. La nuit ſuiuante nous couchaſmes plus

On the nineteenth, St. Joseph's day, as we were pursuing our course over the ice of the great Lake, it opened under one of my feet. I came off better than a poor Onnontaguehronnon Hunter, who, after a long struggle with the ice, which had given way under him, was swallowed up and lost in the water beyond the possibility of rescue. Having escaped these dangers, we entered a road of extreme diffi- culty, beset with rocks as high as towers, and so steep that one makes his way over them with hands as well as with feet. After this, we were again forced to run three leagues over the ice, never stop- ping, for fear of breaking through; and then, to pass the night on a rock opposite Otondiata,[10] which is on the route commonly taken by Beaver-Hunters. We made a canoe for crossing the Lake; and, as we [143] were a company of twenty, a part went over first. On nearing the other shore, they struck their prow against an ice-floe; and there they were all in the water, some catching at the battered canoe, and others at the ice that had wrecked it. They all succeeded in saving themselves, and, after repairing this Boat of bark, sent it back to us, that we might follow them. We did so on the night of the twenty- first of March. We had eaten for dinner only a very few roots, boiled in clear water; yet we were forced to lie down supperless, on a bed of pebbles, at the sign of the Stars, and under shelter of an icy north wind. On the following night, we lay more softly, but not more comfortably, our bed being of snow; and, the day after, rain attended us on a frightful road, over rocks fearful to behold, both for their height and for their size, and as dangerous to descend as they are difficult to climb. In order to scale them,

mollement; mais non pas plus commodement, noftre
lict fut la neige, & le iour d'apres, la pluye nous fit
compagnie dans vn chemin horrible, par des rochers
épouuantables à voir, tant pour leur hauteur, que
pour leur groffeur; & auffi dangereux à defcendre,
que difficiles à monter: on s'entredonne la main les
vns aux autres pour les franchir; ils bordent le [144]
Lac, qui n'eftant pas encore tout deglacé, nous oblige
à ce trauail.

Vn Cerf, fur le matin du vint cinquiéme, nous
retarde iufqu'au midy.   Nous fifmes trois lieuës de
beau temps, d'affez beau chemin.   Nous trouuons
bien à propos à noftre gifte, vn canot, ou pluftoft vn
arbre entier creufé, que Dieu femble nous auoir mis
entre les mains, pour paffer le refte du Lac fans
craindre la glace.

Nous nous embarquons le lendemain fept perfonnes dans cét arbre, & arriuons le foir à l'embouchure du Lac, qui fe termine par vn fault & par des
rapides violents.   Dieu nous fit encore icy vne grace
bien particuliere, en quittant nôtre arbre, nous fifmes
rencontre d'vn affez bon canot d'ecorce, auec lequel
nous fifmes quarante lieuës en vn iour & demy: n'en
ayant pas fait dauantage à pied les trois femaines
precedentes, tant pour l'horreur du temps, que des
chemins.

Enfin le trentiéme de Mars nous arriuons à Montreal, eftant partis d'Onnontagué le fecond.   Noftre
cœur trouua icy la ioye que reffentent les Pelerins,
quand ils arriuent en leur païs.   Et Dieu nous [145]
ayant conferué d'vne façon fi particuliere, dans vn fi
dangereux voyage, nous fait voir qu'il veille plus
qu'on ne peut s'imaginer fur le falut des Iroquois.
Qu'il en foit beny à iamais.

we lent one another a hand.   They border the [144]
Lake; and, as it was not yet wholly free from ice,
we were forced to undergo this labor.

On the morning of the twenty-fifth, a Deer delayed
us until noon.   We made three leagues, in pleasant
weather, and over a tolerable road, finding very
seasonably, at our halting-place, a canoe, or rather a
whole tree-trunk hollowed out, which God seems to
have put into our hands for completing the passage
of the Lake without fear of the ice.

On the morrow, seven of us embarked in this
dugout, and in the evening reached the mouth of the
Lake, which ends in a waterfall and turbulent rapids.
Here, God showed us still another special favor; for,
on leaving our dugout, we found a fairly good bark
canoe, with which we accomplished forty leagues in
a day and a half, not having made more than that on
foot during the three preceding weeks, owing both to
the severe weather and to the bad roads.

Finally, on the thirtieth of March, we arrived at
Montreal, having left Onnontagué on the second.
Our hearts found here the joy felt by Pilgrims on
reaching their own country.   God's [145] preserva-
tion of us in so signal a manner, on so dangerous a
journey, shows us that he watches with unimagin-
able care over the salvation of the Iroquois — for
which may he be forever blessed.

*You will note, if you please, in passing, that letters
have recently been received from Kebec, by the latest vessel,
saying that Father Claude d'Ablon, whose Journal we have
just seen, has returned to Onnontagué with Father François
le Mercier, Superior of that Mission, Fathers René
Menard and Jacques Fremin, and Brothers Ambroise Broar*

Vous remarquez, s'il vous plaiſt en paſſant, qu'on a receu des lettres venuës nouuellement de Kebec, par le dernier vaiſſeau, qui portent, que le Pere Claude d'Ablon, dont nous venons de voir le Iournal, eſt retourné à Onnontagué auec le Pere François le Mercier, Superieur de cette Miſſion, le Pere René Menard, le Pere Iacques Fremin, le Frere Ambroiſe Broar, & le Frere Ioſeph Bourſier: qui vont tous ioindre le Pere Ioſeph Chaumonot, demeuré dans le Païs des Iroquois. Ils ſont eſcortez d'vne cinquantaine de braues François, qui ont deſia commencé vne bonne habitation au cenire de toutes ces Nations. Nous en verrons le ſuccez l'an prochain, Dieu aidant. Les Peres demandent des Ouuriers Euangeliques, & le ſecours des prieres de tous ceux qui aiment le ſalut de ces Peuples. Comme les dépenſes qu'il faut faire pour ſoûtenir vne telle entrepriſe, ſont tres-grandes, ſi ceux qui ſont profeſſion de contribuer à la Conuerſion [146] des Sauuages, vouloient ſouſtenir cette Miſſion, ils feroient vn grand ſeruice à Dieu. On a Baptizé en diuers endroits depuis quelque temps, plus de quatre cents cinquante Sauuages, petits & grands, nonobſtant les troubles & les obſtacles de la guerre. Si on peut maintenir les Predicateurs de l'Euangile, dans ces Contrées, que i'appellerois volontiers le Païs des Martyrs, on en Baptizera bien dauantage. Fiat, fiat.

and Joseph Boursier.   They are all going to join Father
Joseph Chaumonot, who remained in the Iroquois Country.
They are escorted by fifty valiant Frenchmen, who have
already begun a good settlement in the very center of these
Nations; and we shall, with God's help, see its success
next year.   The Fathers ask for Gospel Laborers, and the
aid of prayers from all who desire the salvation of those
Tribes.   As the expense of maintaining such an enterprise
is very great, if those who profess to contribute toward the
Conversion [146] of the Savages would support this Mission, they would render a great service to God.   Within a
recent period, there have been Baptized, in different places,
despite the disturbances and hindrances of war, more
than four hundred and fifty Savages, children and adults.
If the Preachers of the Gospel can be maintained in those
Regions,— which I would willingly call the Land of
Martyrs,— many more will be Baptized.   Fiat, fiat.

CHAPITRE XIV.

DE L'ARRIUÉE D'VNE TROUPPE D'ALGONQUINS, NOM-MEZ LES OUTAOUAK.

L E fixiéme iour du mois d'Aouſt de l'année 1654. deux ieunes François pleins de courage, ayant eu permiſſion de Monſ. le Gouuerneur du Païs, de s'embarquer auec quelques-vns de ces Peuples, qui eſtoient defcendus iufques à nos habitations Françoifes, firent vn voyage de plus de cinq cents lieuës, fous la conduitte de ces Argonautes; [147] portés, non dans de grands Gallions, ou dans de grandes Rambergues; mais dans de petites Gondoles d'écorce. Ces deux Pelerins penfoient bien retourner au Printemps de l'an 1655. mais ces Peuples ne les ont ramenez, que fur la fin du mois d'Aouſt de cette année 1656. Leur arriuée a caufé vne ioye vniuerfelle à tout le Païs. Car ils eſtoient accõpagnez de cinquante canots chargés de marchandifes, que les François vont chercher en ce bout du monde. Cette flotte marchoit grauement, & en bel ordre, pouſſée par cinq cents bras fur noſtre grand fleuue, & conduitte par autant d'yeux; dont la plufpart n'auoient iamais veu les grands canots de bois, ie veux dire les Nauires des François.

Ayant mis pied à terre, au bruit eſtonnant des Canons, & ayant baſty en vn moment leurs maifons volantes, les Capitaines monterent au Fort fainct Louys, pour aller faluer Monſ. noſtre Gouuerneur, portant leurs paroles en la main, c'eſtoient deux prefents,

CHAPTER XIV.

OF THE ARRIVAL OF A COMPANY OF ALGONQUINS CALLED THE OUTAOUAK.

ON the sixth day of August, 1654, two young Frenchmen, full of courage, having received permission from Monsieur the Governor of the Country to embark with some of the Peoples who had come down to our French settlements, began a journey of more than five hundred leagues under the guidance of these Argonauts,—[147] conveyed, not in great Galleons or large oared Barges, but in little Gondolas of bark. The two Pilgrims fully expected to return in the Spring of 1655, but those Peoples did not conduct them home until toward the end of August of this year, 1656. Their arrival caused the Country universal joy, for they were accompanied by fifty canoes, laden with goods which the French come to this end of the world to procure. The fleet rode in state and in fine order along our mighty river, propelled by five hundred arms, and guided by as many eyes, most of which had never seen the great wooden canoes of the French,—that is to say, their Ships.

Having landed, amid the stunning noise of Cannon, and having quickly built their temporary dwellings, the Captains ascended to Fort saint Louys to salute Monsieur our Governor, bearing their speeches in their hands. These were two presents, which represent words among these Peoples. One

qui paffent pour des paroles parmy ces Peuples.
L'vn de ces deux prefents, demandoit [148] des François pour aller paffer l'Hyuer en leur Païs: & l'autre
demandoit des Peres de noftre Compagnie, pour
enfeigner le chemin du Ciel à toutes les Nations de
ces grandes Contrées. On leur répondit à leur mode,
par des prefents, leur accordant tres-volontiers tout
ce qu'ils demandoient. Mais pendant que ceux qui
font deftinez pour cette grande entreprife, fe preparent, apprenons quelque chofe de nouueau des
deux Pelerins François, & de leurs hoftes.

Premierement, il eft bon de remarquer que la
langue Huronne s'eftend bien cinq cent lieuës du
cofté du Sud: & la langue Algonquine, plus de cinq
cents du cofté du Nord. Ie fçay bien qu'il y a quelque petite difference entre ces Nations; mais cela con-
fifte en quelques dialectes, qu'on a bien-toft apprifes,
& qui n'alterent point le fond de ces deux langues.

Secondement, il y a quantité de Lacs au quartier
du Nord, qui pafferoient bien pour des Mers douces,
& le grand Lac des Hurons, & vn autre qui luy eft
voifin, ne cedent point à la Mer Cafpie.

[149] En troifiéme lieu, on nous a marqué quantité
de Nations aux enuirons de la Nation de Mer, que
quelques-vns ont appellé les Puants, à caufe qu'ils ont
autrefois habité fur les riues de la Mer, qu'ils nomment *Ouinipeg*, c'eft à dire eau puante. Les *Liniouek*,
qui leur font voifins, font enuiron foixante Bourgades.
Les *Nadouefiouek*, en ont bien quarante. Les *Pouarak*,
en ont pour le moins trente. Les *Kiriftinons* paffent
tous ceux-là en eftenduë; ils vont iufques à la Mer du
Nord. Le Païs des Hurons, qui n'auoit que dix-fept
Bourgades dans l'eftenduë de dix-fept lieuës, ou
enuiron, nourriffoit bien trente mille perfonnes.

of the two gifts asked for [148] some Frenchmen, to
go and pass the Winter in their Country; while the
other made request for some Fathers of our Society,
to teach all the Nations of those vast Regions the
way to Heaven. They were answered, in their own
way, by presents, and were very willingly granted
all that they asked. But, while those assigned to
this great undertaking are making their prepara-
tions, let us learn some news from the two French
Pilgrims and from their hosts.[11]

First, it is well to note that the Huron language
extends fully five hundred leagues toward the South,
and the Algonquin more than five hundred toward
the North. I know well that there are some slight
differences among these Nations; but they consist in
certain dialects, which are soon learned, and which
do not affect the fundamental principles of the two
languages.

In the second place, there are in the Northern
regions many Lakes which might well be called fresh-
water Seas, the great Lake of the Hurons, and
another near it, being as large as the Caspian Sea.

[149] In the third place, we were told of many
Nations surrounding the Nation of the Sea which
some have called '' the Stinkards,'' because its people
formerly lived on the shores of the Sea, which they
call *Ouinipeg*, that is, '' stinking water.'' The *Liniouek*, their neighbors, comprise about sixty Villages;
the *Nadouesiouek* have fully forty; the *Pouarak*, at
least thirty; and the *Kiristinons* surpass all the above
in extent, reaching as far as the North Sea.[12] The
Country of the Hurons, which had only seventeen
Villages, extending over about as many leagues,
maintained fully thirty thousand people.

Vn François m'a dit autrefois, qu'il auoit veu trois
mille hommes dans vne affemblée, qui fe fit pour
traiter de paix, au Païs des gens de Mer.   Tous ces
Peuples font la guerre à d'autres Nations plus éloignées; tant il eft vray, que les hommes font des
Loups à l'egard des hommes; & que le nombre des
fous eft infiny.   Ces fous fe tuent, fe voulant donner
la loy les vns aux autres.   Patience pour des Barbares, qui ne connoiffent pas [150] Dieu; mais ceux
qui font profeffion de le connoiftre, & qui fçauent
qu'il eft vn Dieu de paix, que fa demeure eft dans la
paix, & qu'il veut gouuerner les hommes, comme vn
Salomon pacifique: ceux-là, dis-je, font bien plus
coupables.   Les Sauuages Chreftiens demandent
pourquoy ceux qui font Baptizez, au de-là de la Mer:
c'eft à dire en Europe, fe font la guerre les vns aux
autres, au lieu de les venir fecourir contre ceux qui
les empefchent d'eftre inftruits, & de croire en Dieu
paifiblement, & qui font mourir les Croyants.

Difons en quatriéme lieu, que ces deux ieunes
hommes n'ont pas perdu leurs peines dans leur
grande courfe: Ils n'ont pas feulement enrichy quelques François à leur retour; mais ils ont donné
beaucoup de ioye à tout le Paradis dans leur voyage;
ayant Baptizé, & enuoyé au Ciel enuiron trois cents
petits enfants; qui ont commencé à connoiftre, & à
aimer & poffeder Dieu, en mefme temps qu'ils ont
efté lauez dans fon fang, par les eauës du Baptefme.
Ils ont reueillé dans l'efprit de ces Peuples, le fouue-
nir des beautez de [151] noftre Créance, dont ils
auoient eu vne premiere teinture au Païs des Hurons:
lors qu'ils alloient vifiter nos Peres qui l'habitoient,
ou que quelques-vns de nous autres s'approchoient
des Contrées voifines de leur Païs.

A Frenchman once told me that he had seen, in the Country of the people of the Sea, three thousand men in an assembly held to form a treaty of peace. All those Tribes make war on other more distant Nations,— so true is it that men are Wolves toward men, and that the number of fools is infinite. These fools practice mutual slaughter, each wishing to prescribe the law to the other. Let us be patient with Barbarians, who know not [150] God; but those who profess to know him, and who are well aware that he is a God of peace, that his abode is one of peace, and that it is his will to govern mankind as a peace-loving Solomon,— those, I say, are much more guilty. The Christian Savages ask why the people beyond the Sea,— that is, in Europe,— who are Baptized, make war on one another, instead of coming to help them against those who hinder them from being taught and from believing in God unmolested, and who put the Believers to death.

Let us say, in the fourth place, that these two young men have not undergone hardships for naught in their long journey. Not only have they enriched some Frenchmen upon their return, but they also caused great joy in all Paradise, during their travels, by Baptizing and sending to Heaven about three hundred little children, who began to know, love, and possess God, as soon as they were washed in his blood through the waters of Baptism. They awakened in the minds of those Peoples the remembrance of the beauties of [151] our Faith, whereof they had acquired the first tincture in the Country of the Hurons, when they visited our Fathers living there, or when some of us approached the Regions bordering on their Country.

CHAPITRE XV.

LE DEPART DES ALGONQUINS OUTAOUAK, & DE LEUR
DEFAITE.

PENDANT que ces Peuples faifoient leur petit
traficq, trente ieunes François s'équiperent,
pour les accompagner iufques en leur Païs, &
en raporter des peaux de beftes mortes. Ie leur
donnay pour guides, dans les voyes de leur falut, le
Pere Leonard Gareau, & le Pere Gabriel Dreuillettes,
anciens Ouuriers Euangeliques, bien verfez dans les
langues Huronne & Algonquine. Ils eftoient rauis
de fe voir choifis les premiers, pour porter Iefus-
Chrift dans vn Pays également remply de Croix, de
tenebres, [152] & de morts. Vn Frere de noftre
Compagnie, nommé Louys le Boëfme, defira d'eftre
de la partie, pour fecourir les Peres, auec lefquels fe
ioignirent trois ieunes hommes François, bien refolus
de viure & de mourir auec les Predicateurs de
l'Euangile.

Le iour du depart arrefté: cette efcoüade fe ioint
auec le gros des Sauuages. On met les canots en
l'eau, on s'embarque leftement, on fait ioüer les
auirons, & le dernier Adieu fe dit, à coups de fufils &
de canons. Mais ô mon Dieu, que les chofes humaines
font inconftantes. Tel eft remply de ioye au matin,
qui meurt de trifteffe auant la nuit.

A peine cette Flotte, compofée de plus de foixante
Vaiffeaux, auoit-elle vogué vne iournée fur le grand
fleuue, qu'elle fait rencontre d'vn Canot, conduit par

CHAPTER XV.

THE DEPARTURE OF THE OUTAOUAK ALGONQUINS, AND THEIR DEFEAT.

WHILE these People were doing their small trading, thirty young Frenchmen equipped themselves to bear them company to their Country, and to bring back furs. I gave them, as guides in the paths of their salvation, Fathers Leonard Gareau and Gabriel Dreuillettes, trained Gospel Laborers, and well versed in the Huron and Algonquin tongues. They were delighted at being the first ones chosen to carry Jesus Christ to a Country abounding equally in Crosses, in darkness, [152] and in death. A Brother of our Society, named Louys le Boësme, wished to be one of the party, as assistant to the Fathers, whom also three young Frenchmen joined, firmly resolved to live and to die with the Preachers of the Gospel.

On the day fixed for departure, this squad joined the main body, composed of Savages; the canoes were launched, and the men quickly embarked; paddles were set in motion, and the last Farewell resounded from the cannons' mouths. But alas for the mutability of all things human! Full of joy in the morning, a man dies of grief before night.

Scarcely had this Fleet of more than sixty Vessels accomplished one day's voyage on the great river, when it met two French Soldiers in a Canoe, who had been sent by the Governor of Three Rivers to

deux Soldats François, enuoyez par le Gouuerneur
des Trois Riuieres, pour donner aduis que l'Iroquois
Agneronon, grand ennemy des Algonquins, & des
Hurons, eftoit en campagne, & qu'il ne manqueroit
pas de leur dreffer des embufches dans leur voyage.
En effet, il [153] s'eftoit caché à l'abry d'vne pointe,
pour les furprendre au paffage; mais il fut trompé
pour ce coup: car nos gens redoublant leur courage,
firent ioüer fi fortement & fi adroitement leurs auirons,
qu'ils pafferent promptement à la faueur de la nuit,
fans eftre apperceus, & arriuerent fains & fauues au
Bourg des Trois Riuieres.

Nos trente François, qui s'eftoient équipez en vn
moment, pour vn voyage de cinq cents lieuës: voyant
par l'experience de vingt-huict lieuës qu'ils auoient
defia faites, qu'ils n'eftoient pas montez de bons
Canots, en ayant defia creué quelques-vns, & que
leurs prouifions eftoient bien courtes pour vn chemin
fi long. Que d'ailleurs ils feroient contraints de
mettre la main aux armes, fi l'Agneronon, auec
lequel nous auons vne paix de ie ne fçay quelle couleur, attaquoit leur Flotte, iugerent à propos de
remettre la partie au Printemps de l'année fuiuante.

Nos deux Peres, qui voyoient bien les dangers où
ils s'expofoient: mais qui n'ignoroient pas auffi que
le traficq des [154] Ames qu'ils alloient faire, eftoit
plus noble que celuy des peaux, que noftre Efcoüade
Françoife abandonnoit, ne voulurent iamais quitter
la partie. Ils s'embarquent auec le Frere, & auec
les trois François, qui s'eftoient ioints auec eux,
méprifans leur vie pour le falut de ces Peuples,
aufquels ils s'eftoient donnez pour l'amour de Iefus-
Chrift.

give warning that the Agneronon Iroquois, bitter
enemies of the Algonquins and Hurons, were in the
field, and would be sure to lay an ambuscade for
them on their journey. As a matter of fact, they
[153] had concealed themselves behind a point, in
order to surprise our Savages as they passed; but
this time they were outwitted. Our men, mustering
their courage, plied their paddles with such strength
and skill, that they passed swiftly in the darkness
without being seen, and arrived safe and sound at
the Village of Three Rivers.

Our thirty Frenchmen, who had equipped themselves at short notice for a journey of five hundred
leagues, seeing, from the experience of twenty-eight
leagues already accomplished, that their Canoes were
poor,— several leaking already,— and that their provisions were scarcely sufficient for so long a journey,— knowing, besides, that they would be forced
to resort to weapons if the Agneronons, with whom
we had at least the appearance of peace, should
attack their Fleet,— thought best to postpone their
expedition until the Spring of the following year.

Our two Fathers, though clearly perceiving the
dangers before them, were also well aware that the
traffic in [154] Souls, in which they were about to
engage, was nobler than that in skins, which our
Company of Frenchmen was abandoning; and they
were unwilling to turn back. They embarked with
the Brother and the three Frenchmen who had
joined them, holding their lives of no account as compared with the salvation of those Peoples to whom
they had, for the love of Jesus Christ, given themselves.

Behold them, then, on their way, with two hundred

Les voila donc fur les eaux, auec deux cents cinquante Sauuages Algonquins, à la referue de quelques Hurons, échapez du naufrage de leur ancien Païs. Ils fe font Barbares, pour ainfi dire, auec les Barbares, pour les rendre tous enfants de Dieu.

Les Iroquois Agneronons, qui n'étoient qu'enuiron fix vingts: voyant que leurs ennemis eftoient paffez, les fuiuent à la fourdine, à force de bras & de rames. Ils marchoient la nuit ferrez & fans bruit, fe cachant le iour dans les bois, enuoyant des Efpions, pour reconnoiftre la marche des Algonquins. Ce qu'ils firent bien-toft: car ces pauures gens, quoy qu'auertis de fe tenir fur leurs gardes, faifoient par tout vn [155] grand bruit. Quantité de ieunes gens, qui n'auoient iamais manié d'armes à feu, en ayant acheté des François, prenoient vn fingulier plaifir au petit tonnerre que leurs arquebufes faifoient rouler dans l'écho des forefts. On dit mefme qu'vn ieune Iroquois, amy de la paix, leur vint donner aduis de marcher en filence, & que fes gens eftoient aux aguets, pour les furprendre; mais ces ieunes étourdis fe fiant en leur courage, & en leur nombre, n'auoient des oreilles que pour le bruit qu'ils faifoient eux-mefmes, s'arreftant fort fouuent à tirer fur le gibier qu'ils rencontroient.

L'Iroquois prend le deuant, fe faifit d'vne pofte fort auantageux, au bord de la grande Riuiere, par où les Algonquins deuoient paffer. Il fe retranche premierement fur vne petite eminence, auec des arbres, qu'ils ont bien-toft mis à bas. Les Sentinelles, qu'il auoit placées en des lieux fort commodes, pour découurir de fort loin fur le grand fleuue, ayans auerty leur Capitaine que la flotte paroiffoit: Il iette

and fifty Savages, all Algonquins except a few
Hurons escaped from the wreck of their former
Country.   They turn Barbarians with the Barbarians,
so to speak, in order to make them all God's children.

The Agneronon Iroquois, who numbered only
about six-score, seeing that the enemy had slipped
by, followed them stealthily with all speed.   They
proceeded by night, in close order and without noise,
hiding in the woods by day, and sending out Spies
to reconnoiter the Algonquins.   Soon they discovered
them; for these unfortunate men, though cautioned
to be on their guard, were constantly making a [155]
great noise.   Many of the young men, who had
bought firearms of the French, having never handled
them before, took a singular pleasure in the mimic
thunder made by their arquebuses in the echoes of
the forest.   It was even said that a young Iroquois,
a friend of peace, came and warned them to proceed
quietly, saying that his companions were on the
lookout to surprise them.   But these young hot-
heads, trusting in their courage and their numbers,
had ears only for the noise made by themselves, halt-
ing very often to fire at game encountered on the
way.

The Iroquois went ahead and seized a very advan-
tageous position on the great River, in the path of
the Algonquins.   First, they intrenched themselves
on a slight eminence covered with trees, which they
soon felled.   The Sentinels, posted very advanta-
geously for commanding a long view of the great river,
gave their Captain warning when the fleet appeared,
and he placed a large number of brave Fusileers
among the rushes and [156] tall shrubbery, on a point

vn bon nombre de braues Fufeliers dans les ioncs, &
[156] dans de grands herbiers, en vne pointe que nos
gens venoient frifer. Six Canots de Hurons, &
quelques autres Algonquins, precedant le gros d'enuiron cinquante ou foixante pas, s'eftant venus ietter
dans les pieges fans y penfer, receurent vne grefle
de plomb, fi prompte & fi rude, que plufieurs furent
tuez, fans fçauoir qui leur auoit donné le coup de la
mort. Auffi-toft que les Iroquois eurent fait leur
décharge, ils fortent de leur embufcade comme des
Lyons de leur taniere, fe iettent fur ceux qui eftoient
encore en vie, & les traifnent dans leur fort. Le
Pere Leonard Gareau, qui eftoit dans cette auant-
garde, fut bleffé d'vn coup de fufil, qui luy rompit
l'épine du dos.

Ceux qui fuiuoient, voyant ce beau ménage, prennent les armes, fe iettent à terre, courrent apres
l'ennemy; mais ils rencontrent bien-toft vn retranchement, ou vn fort qui fait feu de tous coftez: Ils
l'enuironnent, ils l'attaquent, on en tuë, on en bleffe
de part & d'autre. L'Iroquois fe deffend fi bien, que
les Algonquins ne le purent enleuer, ny [157] porter
à fortir de fon fort pour venir au combat. Il fçauoit
bien qu'il n'eftoit pas égal en nombre, & que la peau
de Lyon luy manquant, il s'eftoit fort bien ferui de
celle du Renard.

Nos gens voyant cela, mettent la main à la hache,
font en peu de temps vn fort affez proche de celuy
des Iroquois, pour fe mettre à l'abry, & fe pouuoir
vn peu refraichir. Ils attendoient que les Iroquois
quittaffent leur Reduit, afin de les pouuoir pourfuiure;
mais ils fe tinrent clos & couuerts. Les Algonquins
voyant que la faifon les obligeoit de hafter leur retour

by which our men would pass. Six Canoes of Hurons, and some Algonquins, preceding the main
body by about fifty or sixty paces, heedlessly rushed
into the snare, and received so prompt and fierce a
shower of lead, that many were killed without knowing who dealt the blow. The Iroquois had no sooner
fired their pieces than they burst from their ambush
like Lions from their lair, rushing upon those who
were still alive, and dragging them into their fort.
Father Leonard Gareau, who was in this advance-
guard, was wounded by a musket-shot which broke
his spine.[13]

Those who followed, upon seeing the state of
affairs, seized their arms, leaped ashore, and pursued
the enemy, but soon came to an intrenchment, or
fort, which opened fire on all sides. They surrounded
and attacked it, and many were killed or wounded
on both sides; the Iroquois, however, maintained so
strong a defense, that the Algonquins could neither
take the fort by storm, nor [157] draw them out to
open combat. They well knew their enemy's inferiority in number, and that, the Lion's skin failing
him, he had very wisely assumed that of the Fox.

Our men, seeing this, took their hatchets, and
soon constructed a fort at no great distance from that
of the Iroquois, for shelter and recuperation. They
waited for the latter to leave their Fort, that they
might pursue them; but they held themselves under
close cover. The Algonquins, as the season compelled them to hasten their return Homeward, parleyed
with the Iroquois and made them a present, to induce
them to decamp, themselves retiring first in order to
leave the way clear. But the others refused to listen
and rejected the present, being resolved to attack our

en leur Païs, parlementêt auec les Iroquois, leur font
vn prefent à ce qu'ils décampent: fe retirent les
premiers, pour leur donner le paffage libre.   Les
Iroquois refufent le prefent, ils font la fourde oreille,
refolus de charger encore nos gens; mais ils furent
trompez: car les Algonquins feignant de fe vouloir
fortifier dauantage, pour attendre le depart de l'Iroquois, firent vn bruit comme d'vn abbatis de bois, à
grands coups de hache; & pendant ce tintamarre, les
Capitaines faifoient filer [158] doucement leurs gens
dans leurs Canots, à la faueur des tenebres de la
nuit.   C'eft ainfi qu'ils euaderent, laiffant dans leur
fort le Pere Gabriel Dreuillettes, & fon Compagnon,
& les trois François qui s'eftoient liez auec eux.   Le
Pere les vouloit fuiure; mais pas vn ne les voulut
embarquer.   Qui veut folidement prefcher le Crucifix,
ne doit attendre que des Croix.

party once more. They were outwitted, however;
for the Algonquins, feigning that they wished to
strengthen their fortifications, for the purpose of
awaiting the Iroquois' departure, made a noise like
that of felling trees with heavy strokes of the hatchet.
During this din, [158] and under cover of the night,
the Captains had their men file softly to their Canoes;
and thus they made their escape, leaving in their fort
Father Gabriel Dreuillettes with his Companion, and
the three Frenchmen who had joined them.   The
Father wished to accompany them, but no one would
take him into his canoe.   He who would be a stanch
preacher of the Crucifix must expect only Crosses.

CHAPITRE XVI.

DE LA MORT DU PERE LEONARD GARREAU.

DANS la déroute du Païs des Hurons, ces pauures Peuples ſe répandirent de tous coſtez. Les vns dans la Nation neutre : vne bonne bande ſe refugia à Kebec, dans le ſein des François : & quelques-vns ſe retirerent au Païs des Algonquins, nommez Outaouaᴋ, dont nous venons de parler. Vne partie de ces pauures fugitifs étoient [159] deſcendus à Kebec auec les Algonquins ; & comme ils auoient connû le Pere Leonard Garreau dans leur ancien Païs, & qu'ils auoient deſia receu de luy quelque teinture de noſtre Creance, il leur fut bien aiſé, inuitant leur ancien Paſteur, de le gagner. Il auoit plus d'enuie de leur preſcher Ieſus-Chriſt, qu'ils n'auoient encore de volonté de le receuoir. Il ſe lia donc auec eux dans la reſolution de donner ſon ſang & ſa vie, pour l'Euangile. Il voyoit quaſi vne morte inéuitable, dans les dangers d'vne entrepriſe auſſi ſainte qu'elle eſtoit penible. Il s'attendoit, ou d'eſtre maſſacré en chemin, comme il a eſté ; ou de mourir de faim dans vn Païs éloigné de cinq cents lieuës des François, ou d'eſtre mis à mort par le ſonge d'vn Barbare : toutes ces veuës ne l'effrayoient point.

Ce fut le Mercredy trentiéme d'Aouſt de cette année 1656. que les Iroquois eſtant en embuſcade, & faiſant vne décharge ſur ſix Canots Hurons, qui marchoient les premiers, comme nous auons dit au Chapitre precedent, [160] bleſſerent ce bon Pere à

CHAPTER XVI.

OF FATHER LEONARD GARREAU'S DEATH.

IN the devastation of the Country of the Hurons, those poor People were scattered in all directions,— some joining the neutral Nation, a large company taking refuge in the bosom of the French at Kebec, and others seeking a retreat in the Country of the Algonquins called Outaouak, of whom we have just been speaking. A part of these poor fugitives had [159] come down to Kebec with the Algonquins; and, as they had known Father Leonard Garreau in their own Country, and had already received some tincture of our Faith from him, it was very easy for them to obtain their former Pastor upon request. He was more eager to preach Jesus Christ to them than they were to receive him. Accordingly, he joined them, resolved to give his blood and his life for the Gospel, and seeing almost inevitable death in the dangers of an undertaking as holy as it was arduous. He expected either to be slain on the way,— as was the case,— or to perish with hunger in a Country five hundred leagues distant from the French, or to meet his death because of some Barbarian's dream. But none of these prospects frightened him.

On Wednesday, August thirtieth, of this year, 1656, the Iroquois, firing from their ambuscade upon six Canoes of Hurons, who were in the van, as we have described in the preceding Chapter, [160]

mort.   Vne balle luy ayant rompu l'épine du dos, le
renuerfa dans le Canot qui le portoit.   Auffi-toſt qu'il
fut bleſſé, les Iroquois le traiſnerent comme vn chien
dans leur fort : le dépoüillerent tout nud, luy rauiſſant
meſme ſa chemiſe, ne luy laiſſant qu'vn petit calleçon.
Ils le tournoient & retournoient, pour luy arracher
la balle du corps.   Ils luy preſenterent vn breuuage,
comme vne medecine, qu'il ne voulut point prendre.
Il fut trois iours couché ſur la platte terre, baigné dans
ſon ſang, ſans boire ny manger, ſans Medecin, ſans
Chirurgien, ſans autre ſecours que du Ciel.   Enfin
ayant eſté frappé le Mercredy, ils le porterent le
Samedy matin à Montreal, iettant deux méchants
petits preſens, ſelon leur couſtume ; l'vn pour
témoigner qu'ils eſtoient marris de l'accident qui eſtoit
arriué ; l'autre pour eſſuyer nos larmes, & appaiſer
nos regrets.   Tous les habitans de Montreal, regardoient & honoroient ce pauure Pere comme vn
Apoſtre, & comme vn Martyr, luy portant compaſſion
iuſques au profond du cœur.

[161] Ayant fait rencontre en ce lieu du Pere
Claude Pijart, Religieux de noſtre Compagnie, ſon
ame fut remplie de ioye, & il répandit ſon cœur dans
le cœur de ce bon Pere, qui nous a marqué les particularitez de ſa mort.   Au moment, dit-il, qu'il fut
bleſſé, il s'écria, *Domine, accipe ſpiritum meum*, Mon
Dieu, retirez mon eſprit. *Domine, ignoſce illis*. Seigneur, pardonnez leur.   Il dit ingenuëment au Pere,
qu'il n'auoit eu, ny dans l'attaque, ny dans ſa priſe,
ny dans les mauuais traitements de ſes meurtriers,
aucune indignation, ny meſme aucune froideur contre
eux ; mais au contraire, qu'il reſſentoit vn eſprit de
douceur, & de compaſſion pour ceux qui luy oſtoient
la vie.   Il dit auſſi, que ſe voyant dépoüillé tout nud,

mortally wounded this good Father. He fell back
into the Canoe that bore him, his spine broken by a
bullet. Forthwith, the Iroquois dragged him like a
dog into their fort, stripped him naked, taking away
even his shirt, and leaving him only a small pair of
drawers. They turned him over and over, to remove
the ball from his body, and gave him a drink, by
way of medicine, which he would not take. Three
days he lay flat on the ground, bathed in his own
blood, without food or drink, without Physician or
Surgeon, and with no help but that of Heaven.
Though wounded on Wednesday, he was not taken
to Montreal until Saturday morning, when they
offered two wretched little presents, according to
their custom. One of them was to show their regret
at the accident that had happened, and the other to
dry our tears and assuage our grief. All the people
of Montreal esteemed and honored this poor Father
as an Apostle and Martyr, giving him their heartfelt
compassion.

[161] Meeting there Father Claude Pijart, a Religious of our Society, his soul was filled with joy, and
he opened his heart to this good Father, who has
given us an account of his death. As soon as he was
wounded, as we are told, he exclaimed, *Domine, accipe
spiritum meum,*—" My God, receive my soul;" *Domine,
ignosce illis,*—" Lord, forgive them." He frankly told
the Father that he had felt, neither in the attack, nor
in his capture, nor during his ill treatment at his
murderers' hands, any indignation or even coldness
toward them; that, on the contrary, he had experienced a feeling of gentleness and compassion for
those who were taking his life. He also said that,
on seeing himself stripped naked, he felt a great joy

il reffentit vne grande ioye, & vne grande fatisfaction
d'efprit, fe voyant mourir dans la nudité de Iefus-
Chrift, fon Maiftre.   Mais cette ioye fenfible ne dura
pas long-temps, Dieu voulant acheuer en luy fon ouurage, & le purifier entierement, fe cacha, & le priua
de toute confolation.   C'eft, difoit-il, [162] la plus
grande peine que i'aye reffentie dans tous mes aban-
donnements, de me voir comme délaiffé de noftre Seigneur.   Il eft vray qu'il me fortifioit en la pointe de
mon efprit, par vne conformité amoureufe que i'auois
à fa fainte volonté, le remerciant de la faueur & de
l'honneur qu'il me faifoit, de donner ma vie pour luy.

Le Samedy qu'il nous fut apporté, il fe confeffa
trois fois fort exactement, & auec vne grande contri-
tion: Il receut le faint Viatique, & en fuitte l'Ex-
treme-Onction, répondant auec pieté aux paroles &
aux prieres de l'Eglife.   Ah! que ie fuis indigne des
faueurs que Dieu me fait, difoit-il!   Ie n'ay qu'vn
regret, c'eft de fouffrir fi peu: d'eftre trop à mon
aife: & de n'auoir pas recherché affez purement la
gloire de Dieu.   Il reïteroit fouuent ces paroles, *Ita
Pater, quoniam fic placitum fuit ante te! Fiat voluntas
tua.*   Oüy, mon Pere, puis que cette mort eft agreable
à vos yeux, Que voftre volonté foit faite.   Il parloit
de fa mort comme enchaffée dans la mort de Iefus-
Chrift.   Enfin fur les onze heures de nuit du [163]
mefme Samedy, le fecond iour de Septembre, vne
conuulfion l'emporta, nous laiffant à tous vne ioye au
cœur, & vne douce efperance, que fon fang produi-
roit vn iour des fruicts dignes de la gloire de Dieu.
On n'ômit rien pour honorer fes funerailles, & pour
luy témoigner l'affection qu'on luy portoit.   Son
corps fut mis dans le Cimetiere commun, en vn lieu
deftiné pour les Preftres, fur lequel on pretend de

and contentment, conscious that he was dying in the
nakedness of Jesus Christ, his Master.   But this vivid
satisfaction did not last long.   God, wishing to con-
summate his work in him, and to purify him wholly,
hid himself and left him bereft of all consolation.
" It was," he said, [162] " the greatest affliction I
experienced in all my destitution, to find myself
forsaken by our Lord.   It is true, he supported me
in the distress of my spirit, through my loving
compliance with his holy will, and my thankfulness
toward him for the favor and honor which he showed
me in letting me die for him."

On the Saturday when he was brought to us, he
confessed three times very minutely and contritely;
he also received the holy Viaticum and then Extreme
Unction, piously responding to the words and prayers
of the Church.   " Alas, how unworthy I am of God's
favors toward me!" he exclaimed.   " I only regret
that I suffer so little, and that I am too comfortable;
and that I have not sought God's glory with sufficient
singleness of purpose."   He often repeated the
words: *Ita, Pater, quoniam sic placitum fuit ante te, fiat
voluntas tua!* " Yea, my Father, since this death is
pleasing in thy sight, thy will be done."   He spoke
of his death as being enshrined in that of Jesus
Christ.   At length, toward eleven o'clock on the
night of the [163] same Saturday, the second of September, he died in convulsions, leaving all our hearts
full of joy and of a sweet hope that his blood would
one day bear fruits worthy of God's glory.   Nothing
was omitted to honor his obsequies, and to show the
affection in which he was held.   His body was
laid in the common Cemetery, in a spot set apart
for Priests, where we intend some day to raise a

faire vn iour paroiftre quelques marques du refpect
qu'on doit à fa memoire.

I'auois, dit le mefme Pere, connû tres-particuliere-
ment dans le Païs des Hurons, & admiré la haute
vertu de cét homme de Dieu.   Ie me fouuiens qu'hi-
uernant auec luy l'an 1644. en vn lieu nommé
Endarahy, & paffant fur vn étang glacé, le quatriéme
de Decembre, iour de faincte Barbe, la glace fe rom-
pant fous mes pieds, i'enfonçay dans l'eau; luy fans
penfer au danger, accourut à moy pour me fecourir,
la glace manquant fous luy, auffi bien que fous moy,
nous nous vifmes tous deux à deux doigts de la mort;
mais ayant fait vn [164] vœu en l'honneur de la
Sainte, dont nous honorions la memoire, elle procura
noftre déliurance: ce que i'attribuay à fes merites.

Il fit l'Efté fuiuant vn voyage auec moy au Païs
des Nipifiriniens, où les fatigues que fon zele luy
faifoit fouffrir, le ietterent dans vne maladie que nous
croyïons tous eftre mortelle: mais Dieu luy referuoit
vne morte plus genereufe.

I'ay particulierement remarqué & honoré en luy,
vn grand refpect, & vne attention exacte en toutes
les chofes de deuotion.   Vne humilité qui me confon-
doit, cherchant en toutes rencontres la foûmiffion, &
le mépris.   Vn amour ardent & vn infatigable zele
du falut des ames, qu'il a augmenté apres dans les
diuerfes Miffions où il a efté employé.   Il aimoit de
cœur & d'affection la faincte Vierge, qui comme ie
croy, luy a procuré vne mort fi glorieufe.

Voicy comme en parle vn autre Pere, à qui fon
ame eftoit affez découuerte.   Nous auons appris ce
foir quatriéme de Septembre, l'heureufe mort du
Pere Leonard Garreau, homme vrayement [165] felon
le cœur de Dieu, d'vne humilité tres-rare dans de

monument attesting the respect due to his memory.

" In the Country of the Hurons," said the same Father, " I had known very intimately and admired the exalted virtue of that man of God.   I remember that, when I was passing the winter with him, in 1644, at a place named Endarahy, we were crossing a frozen pond, on the fourth of December, saint Barbara's day, when the ice broke under my feet and I sank into the water.   Without thought of danger, he ran to my rescue, when under him, too, the ice gave way, and we found ourselves both within two finger-lengths of death.   But, making a [164] vow to the Saint whose memory we were honoring, we were delivered by her.   This I ascribed to his virtues.

" In the following Summer, he accompanied me to the Country of the Nipisiriniens, where the fatigues which his zeal led him to undergo, brought on an illness, which we all thought fatal; but God preserved him for a nobler death.

" I particularly observed and honored in him a profound respect and scrupulous care in all matters of devotion; a humility that put me to shame, ever seeking as it did submission and contumely; and an ardent love and tireless zeal for the salvation of souls, which afterward increased in the various Missions that he filled.   He loved the blessed Virgin with cordial affection, and she, as I believe, procured him so glorious a death."

Another Father, to whom he wholly unbosomed himself, speaks of him as follows: " We learned this evening, September fourth, of the happy death of Father Leonard Garreau, a man truly [165] after God's heart, of a very rare humility, joined with very rare talents which he always concealed; of a

tres-rares talens, qu'il a touſiours cachez: D'vn zele,
& d'vne ferueur ſi efficace, qu'il penetroit les cœurs
de ceux auec qui il conuerſoit: D'vne obeïſſance à
tout faire, & à ne rien faire, eſtant content de
tout.   Detaché entierement des creatures, & attaché
inuiolablement à Dieu, qu'il aimoit en eſprit & en
verité.   Il eſtoit remply de ſolides ſentimens de la
Foy, & pour l'ordinaire ſans aucun gouſt ſenſible; ce
qui n'empéſchoit pas qu'il ne fuſt tres exaƈt à tous
les deuoirs de la veritable deuotion.   Il y a enuiron
dix ou onze ans, qu'eſtant malade à la mort, ſelon
l'opinion de nos Medecins, qui l'auoient abandonné,
i'eus la conſolation de penetrer dans les plus ſecrettes
penſées de ſon cœur; ce n'eſtoit qu'vn perpetuel
amour, vn abandon total de ſoy meſme aux volontez
Diuines, auec tant de ferueur, auec vne force d'eſprit
ſi vigoureuſe, auec des tranſports d'vne ame ſi remplie de Dieu, qu'il n'appartenoit qu'à ſon eloquence
de les exprimer; ce qu'il faiſoit, à la verité, fort
energiquement, [166] mais auec des ſentiments de
ſoy-meſme auſſi humbles & auſſi profonds, que ſes
hautes vertus eſtoient releuées.   Et depuis ces dix
ans là, il a eſté toûjours croiſſant dans ce double eſprit
d'humilité & d'amour.
    Diſons pour concluſion que l'amour & le zele des
Ames, ont eſté ſon veritable caraƈtere.   Ce zele luy
a fait quitter le monde pour entrer en noſtre Compagnie.   Il luy a fait abandonner ſes parents, ſes
amis, & ſa patrie, pour ſe ietter dans le Canadas, non
parmy des Roys & des Princes, ou parmy des
Peuples bien policez; mais parmy des Barbares, dans
le milieu des foreſts, où la nourriture n'eſt quaſi pas
capable de ſuſtenter la vie; mais ſeulement d'empeſcher la mort.   Enfin le zele a eſté ſon element,

zeal and fervor so effective, that he penetrated the
hearts of those with whom he conversed; of an obedience ready to do all things or to do nothing, being
content with any lot; and entirely free from earthly
ties, and inviolably attached to God, whom he loved
in spirit and in truth.   He was thoroughly imbued
with the Faith, and ordinarily free from any sensible
consolation; this did not prevent him from being
very exact in all the duties of true devotion.   About
ten or eleven years ago, when he was mortally ill,
according to our Physicians, who had abandoned
hope, I had the consolation of penetrating his heart's
most secret thoughts.   I found only endless love and
total self-abandonment to God's will, together with
a fervor so ardent, a strength of mind so vigorous,
and transports of a soul so filled with God, that only
his own eloquence could express them — which,
indeed, he did very forcibly, [166] but with an
opinion of himself as humble and lowly as his distinguished virtues were exalted.   And, during these
ten years, he was ever increasing in this double
spirit of humility and love.''

Let us add, in conclusion, that love and a zeal for
saving Souls composed his real character.   This zeal
made him leave the world to enter our Society; it
made him forsake relatives, friends, and native land,
to hasten to Canadas, — not to the society of Kings
and Princes, or of highly civilized Peoples; but to
that of Barbarians buried in forests, where we may
almost say there is not food enough to sustain life,
but merely sufficient to prevent death.   In fine,
during his sojourn in this new World, zeal has been
his element, and the air that he last breathed in
dying.   Wounded by the Iroquois and dragged into

pendant ſon ſejour en ce nouueau Monde, & le
dernier air qu'il a reſpiré à ſa mort.   A meſme temps
que les Iroquois l'eurent bleſſé, & traiſné dans leur
Fort, s'oubliant de ſa nudité, mépriſant les playes
qui luy cauſoient la mort, il ſe traiſna vers quelques
Captifs Hurons, qu'il auoit engendrez à Ieſus-Chriſt
[167] par les Eaux du Bapteſme.   Il leur parla d'vne
voix, à la verité languiſſante, mais pleine de feu,
pleine d'amour, pleine de ſang.   Il les anima à
ſouffrir conſtamment pour Dieu, les tourmens qu'il
ſçauoit bien leur eſtre preparez, les aſſeurant qu'ils
ſe verroient bien-toſt au Ciel, s'ils perſeueroient dans
la Foy qu'ils auoient embraſſée.   Enfin les ayant
oüis en confeſſion, il les purifia dans le Sacrement de
Penitence.

Puis ayant ietté les yeux ſur vn ieune François,
qui par vn dépit remply de rage & de trahiſon,
s'eſtoit ietté parmy les Iroquois: Il l'appelle, luy
gagne le cœur, luy fait voir l'enormité de ſon crime;
il tire des regrets & des larmes de ce perfide, luy fait
confeſſer tous ſes pechez, & en luy donnant l'abſolu-
tion, il le diſpoſe à la mort, qu'il ne croyoit pas ſi
voiſine.   Vn Iroquois l'ayant découuert aux François
de Montreal, il fut pris & mené à Kebec, & condamné
au dernier ſupplice, qu'il ſupporta auec vne reſigna-
tion qui rauit tout le monde.   Il beniſſoit Dieu, de
ce qu'il auoit eſté pris & condamné, diſant hautement
que [168] c'étoit fait de ſon Ame, ſi on n'eût oſté la
vie à ſon corps.   Les Ames ſaintes ne vont quaſi
iamais toutes ſeules en Paradis, Dieu veut qu'elles
en menent ordinairement quelques-vnes auec elles,
qui leur tiennent compagnie dans la gloire.

FIN.

their Fort, forgetting his nakedness and making naught of the wounds from which he was dying, he dragged himself toward some Huron Captives whom he had caused to be born in Jesus Christ [167] by the Waters of Baptism, and addressed them in a voice weak indeed, but full of fire, of love, and of spirit. He encouraged them to suffer with firmness, for God, the torments which he well knew were awaiting them, assuring them that they should soon see each other in Heaven, if they stood fast in the Faith which they had embraced. Finally, after hearing their confessions, he purified them in the Sacrament of Penance.

He perceived a young Frenchman, who, from a feeling of spite, mingled with anger and treachery, had gone over to the Iroquois. Calling him, he won his heart, and made him see the enormity of his crime. Wringing regrets and tears from this faithless man, he made him confess all his sins, and, absolving him, prepared him for death, which he did not think was so near. Betrayed by an Iroquois to the French at Montreal, he was seized and led to Kebec, where he was sentenced to capital punishment, which he bore with a resignation edifying to all beholders. He blessed God for his capture and condemnation, declaring that [168] his Soul would have been lost if his body had not been sentenced to death. Saintly Souls scarcely ever go entirely alone to Paradise, as it is God's will that they should usually take others with them, to bear them company in glory.

END.

XCI — XCIII

Miscellaneous Documents, 1656

XCI.—Journal des PP. Jésuites, Octobre 25 à Decembre 27, 1656

XCII.—Mort du Frere Liegeois.   Anonymous; n.p., n.d.

XCIII.—Catalogve des Bienfaictevrs de N. Dame de Recourance de Kebec.   Various writers; 1632 – 57

SOURCE: Docs. XCI. and XCII. we obtain from the original MSS. in the library of Laval University, Quebec. Doc. XCIII. we obtain from a copy of the original MS., also in the archives of Laval University.

Journal des Pères Jésuites, Octobre 25 à Decembre 27, 1656.

1654.

febur. 5.

Le P. fr. Le Mercier Superieur general

Iournal interrompu.

vide 3. codices in quarto.

Le P. I. Lalleman vice supr. il continüe ce iournal

L E R P francois Le Mercier pour lors supe- rieur de toute La mission, au lieu de Continuer dans ce Liure en suitte du 5ᵉ. Iour de feburier 1654 dans L autre page cy deuant, Le Iournal, en a fait La continuation dans vn autre papier In *quarto*, detachè de celuycy *in folio*. Ie ne scay ni quoment ny pourquoy. Il continue ce Iournal le 10 feburier 1654. Iusques a L onziesme Iour de may Inclusiuè de L an 1656. auquel Iour Il fit le R P Hirosme Lallemant Vice superieur qui continüa le Iournal dans ce mesme papier du R. P Mercier in quarto cõmencant du 12 Iour de May 1656. Iusquez au 19. de Iuin de la mesme annee. Ledit pere Hirosme Lalle- mant me donna Ce Liure in folio, et les trois autres cayers in quarto du P francois le Mer- cier encore supr. et me pria de Continuer le Iournal. Ce que I ay fait cõmencant a escrire du 12 Iuillet Et continuant Iusques au 16° Iour d'octobre de la mesme annee 1656, auquel Iour les trois cayers in quarto ont finis Et ont Esté remplis. Ainsy I ay cõmence a escrire dans Ce Liure In folio Et continuer le Iour- nal. Comme vous verrez en la page sui- uante.

1656. octobre 25

Journal of the Jesuit Fathers, October 25 to December 27, 1656.

THE Reverend Father francois Le Mercier, at that time superior of The entire mission, instead of Continuing The Journal in this Book consecutively from the 5th Day of february, 1654, on The other page preceding this, wrote The continuation thereof in another document, In *quarto*, detached from this one, which is *in folio*,—I know not how or why. He continues this Journal on the 10th of february, 1654, Until The eleventh Day of may, Inclusive, of The year 1656. On that Day, He appointed the Reverend Father Hirosme Lallemant Vice-superior, who continued the Journal in that same quarto document of the Reverend Father Mercier, beginning with the 12th Day of May, 1656, Until the 19th of June in the same year. The said father Hirosme Lallemant gave me This folio Book, and the three other quarto books of Father francois le Mercier, who was still superior, and begged me to Continue the Journal. This I have done, beginning to write on the 12th of July, And continuing Until the 16th Day of october in the same year, 1656,— on which Day the three quarto volumes have come to an end, And Are filled. Accordingly, I have begun to write in This folio Book,

1654.

February 5.

Father françois Le Mercier, Superior general.

Journal interrupted.

Vide 3 codices in quarto.

Father J. Lalleman vice-superior; he continues this journal.

OCTOBRE 1656

25 Arriue des trois Riuieres a 8 heures du soir Vn canot a Quebec depeché par Mr Boucher qui nous apprend que 40 Oneiʃtchronnons en 7 canots sont arriuez aux trois Riuieres Le 20 d'octobre auec des Colliers a dessein d'emmener auec eux les hurons de quebec. lesquels oneiotchronons ont esté Inuitez a cela par Annahotaha a ce qu'on dit.

27 Monsieur Bourdon retourna de tadousac dans son bacq sans aucune lettre du pere Albanel, qu'il Laissa a tadoussac pour aller hyuerner de 1 autre bord auec les sauuages.

Mort de m^e. Charni.   30 A six heures du matin dieu appella a soy Madame Charni apres vne maladie de 16. Iours et vie tres pure et tres Innocente. Elle fut enterrée le 31 dans le nouueau cœur des Religieuses hospitalieres.

Cemetiere beni.   31 a 6 heures du matin le P. Supr benit auec les Ceremonies accoustumées de L eglise le Cemetiere des Meres hospitalieres dans le Nouueau Cœur.

Sur les 9 heures on fit a la paroisse le seruice de Madame Charni lequel estant acheué, le corps fut portè & enterrè dans le nouueau Cemetiere des Meres hospitalieres qui n'estoit encor dans la Closture. Cette faueur fut accordée a Mad^e. Charni qui 1 auoit fort souhaitee et demandée.

And to continue the Journal; As you will see
on the following page.

1656, october 25.

OCTOBER, 1656.

25. At 8 o'clock in the evening, A canoe,
despatched by Monsieur Boucher, arrives at
Quebec from three Rivers; it brings us information that 40 Oneioutchronnons, in 7 canoes,
arrived at three Rivers on The 20th of october
with Collars, intending to take away with
them the hurons of quebec. These oneiotchronons were Invited to do so by Annahotaha, as is said.

27. Monsieur Bourdon returned from tadousac in his boat, without any letter from father Albanel, whom he Left at tadoussac to go
and winter on the other shore with the savages.

30. At six o'clock in the morning God
called to himself Madame Charni, after an
illness of 16 Days, and a life most pure and
Innocent. She was buried on the 31st, in the
new choir of the hospital Nuns.[14]

*Death of
madame Charni.*

31. At 6 o'clock in the morning, the
Father Superior blessed, with the customary
Ceremonies of The church, the Cemetery of
the hospital Mothers in the New Choir.

Cemetery blessed.

About 9 o'clock, the service for Madame
Charni was held in the parish church; at its
end, the body was borne to and buried in the
new Cemetery of the hospital Mothers, which
was not yet Enclosed. This favor was granted
to Madame Charni, who had greatly desired
and requested it.

Morües peschées a La malbaye.

a 3 heures apres midy arriua de tadoussac dans son bac le sieur Lepinè qui nous apporta Nouuelle du p Albanel: et nous dit que luy sieur Lepinè auoit peschè vn milier de molüe en vn Iour a la malbaye, a 8 lieües au dessous de L isle aux Coudres ce qui ne s'estoit encor fait en Canada.

A 9 heures du soir arriua N f pierre feautè dans vne Chalouppe des trois Riuieres sans Nouuelles.

NOUEMBRE

2 arriua a quebec des trois Riuieres a 10 heures du soir le pere Ragueneau auec 4 oneiotchronons. et Mr Charni qui ne fut qu'a mi Chemin de son voyage.

3 au soir fut tenu conseil dans la Cabane d'Anotaha huron par les 4 Oneiotchronons qui firent 4. presens pour leur faire scauoir quils les venoient querir et les emmener en leur pais ce fut en presence des francois et Algon.

Presens des onnei-outs aux Hurons....

1 present. Ie te prends par le bras pour t'emmener. tu scay toy huron qu'autrefois nous ne faisions qu'un Cabane et vn païs. Ie ne scay par quel accident nous nous sommes separez. Il est temps de nous reünir. Ie te suis desia venu querir deux fois Vne fois a Montreal parlant au francois En ton absence, la 2°. a quebec. Cest pour la troisiesme fois que ie viens a present. Vn Collier.

2 Ie te metz vne natte dans ma Cabane.

At 3 o'clock in the afternoon, sieur Lepinè arrived in his boat from tadoussac, and brought us News of father Albanel. He also told us that he,— sieur Lepinè,— had caught a thousand cod in one Day at malbaye, 8 leagues below The isle aux Coudres; this had not yet been done in Canada.

Cod caught at malbaye.

At 9 o'clock in the evening, Our brother pierre feautè arrived in a Shallop from three Rivers, without News.

NOVEMBER.

2. There arrived at quebec from three Rivers, at 10 o'clock in the evening, father Ragueneau with 4 oneiotchronons and Monsieur Charni, who was only half-Way in his journey.

3. In the evening, a council was held in the Cabin of Anotaha, a huron, by the 4 Oneiotchronons, who made 4 presents in order to give the Hurons notice that they were coming to seek them and take them away to the Iroquois country. This was in the presence of the french and Algonquins.

1st gift. " I take thee by the arm to lead thee away. Thou knowest, thou huron, that formerly we comprised but one Cabin and one country. I know not by what accident we became separated. It is time to unite again. I have twice before come to seek thee,— Once at Montreal, speaking to the french In thy absence; the 2nd time, at quebec. It is for the third time that I now come." A Collar.

Gifts from the onneiouts to the Hurons.

2nd. " I put a mat in my Cabin for thee."

3 Ie te donne de la terre pour faire du bled d'inde.

4 Ie te leue de terre

P. Lemoyne.

5 Le pere le Moine Arriua a quebec auec St. Iaques soldat, de son voyage des Agniengeronons nous portans Nouuelles que la paix continuoit entre eux & le françois; qu'ils la faisoit auec le huron et que si 1 algonquin vouloit enuoyer des ambassades chez Eux qu'ils la fairoient aussy

Profession de Mlle.
Bourdon hospre

7 Mr de lepinè partit pour la seconde fois pour tadoussac. Item Sœur Marie therëse de Iesus hospitaliere fit sa profession. le P Sup officia le P Vimon prescha. Mr bourdon y assista et fut a l'offrande et Madame bourdon et sa fille d'Auteil entrerent dans la maison des hospitalieres auec La permission du p. Supr.

17 Kahiĸohan arriua du bicq au soir dans vne chalouppe.

17. Ie receu lettres des trois Riuieres par lesquelles I'apris que le P. Ragueneau auoit fait les presens qui suiuent aux oneiotchronons.

1 pour leur graisser les Iambes et les bien vaigner de leur arriuée 3 capots pour leur trois familles:

2 pour leur dire qu'ils seront tousiours les bien venus icy pourueu qu'ils viennent en petit nombre, y ayant trop de difficultez trop de larcins Et trop peu de place En nos maisons en vn grand nombre. Vn Collier.

3rd. " I give thee some land for raising indian corn."

4th. " I lift thee from the ground."

5. Father le Moine Arrived at quebec with St. Jaques, a soldier, from his journey to the Agniengeronons, bringing us News that the peace was continuing between them and the french; that they were making peace with the hurons; and that, if the algonquins would send embassies to Them, they would make it also with them.

Father Lemoyne.

7. Monsieur de lepinè started for the second time for tadoussac. *Item*, Sister Marie therèse de Jesus, hospital nun, made her profession. The Father Superior officiated; Father Vimon preached. Monsieur bourdon was present, and was at the offering; and Madame bourdon and her daughter d'Auteil [15] entered the hospital nuns' house, with The permission of the father Superior.

Profession of Mademoiselle Bourdon, hospital nun.

17. Kahikohan arrived from bicq in the evening, in a shallop.

17. I received letters from three Rivers, by which I learned that Father Ragueneau had made the following gifts to the oneiot-chronons:

1st. To grease their Legs, and to welcome them on their arrival, 3 cloaks for their three families.

2nd. To tell them that they will be always welcome here, provided they come in small number,— as there are too many difficulties, too many thefts, And too little room In our houses, for a great number. A Collar.

3   pour Leur dire que 1 on leur refera leurs armes comme ils ont demandè. 2000 grains de porcelain.

4   pour leur dire que ce qu'ils ont demandè que l'on allast demeurer chez eux a Oneiȣt: Cela dependoit d'Achiendace, qui est a Onon-tae, Et qu'ils debuoient s'adresser a luy.   Vn Collier.

5   pour les reprimender de ce qu'ils sont sortis de quebec dans vne fausse crainte des Algonquins, qui n'ayant que des pensees de paix ne sont pas pour faire vn mauuais coup, principalement dans le sein d'onontio.   Vn collier.

6   pour leur faire scauoir que L Onnotaero-non lors qu'il traitta de paix auec Nous au nom des quatre Nations Superieures y compris les Hurons Et Algonquins Et qu'ainsy ils ne debuoient rien craindre de ce cotè La.

7   pour mettre vne natte en leur pais, ou ils nous ont desia allumé vn feu lorsque les francois Hurons ou Algonquins y voudront aller visiter.   Vn Collier.

8ᵉ de 8 castors pour les exhorter a aller a la chasse sans crainte en quelque endroit que ce soit et que s'ils rencontroient les Algonquins ils se fassent chaudiere et se donnent de la viande.

9ᵉ Vn peau d'orignac pour leur faire scauoir que l'Algonquins ayant parlè depuis peu a l'Agnieronon   Il y a paix de tous costez.

3rd. To tell Them that their weapons will
be repaired, as they have requested,—2000
porcelain beads.

4th. To tell them that, concerning what
they have asked,—that we should go to live
with them at Oneiout,—That depended upon
Achiendace,[16] who is at Onontae; And that
they must address him. A Collar.

5th. To reprove them because they left
quebec in a false dread of the Algonquins,
who, having only thoughts of peace, are not
disposed to commit a hostile act, especially in
the bosom of onontio. A collar.

6th. To let them know that The Onnon-
taeronon, when he negotiated a peace with
Us in the name of the four Upper Nations,
included therein the Hurons And Algonquins; And that they should, therefore, fear
nothing from That quarter.

7th. To place a mat in their country,—
where they have already kindled a fire,—
when the french, Hurons, or Algonquins
shall choose to go and visit it. A Collar.

8th. Of 8 beavers, to exhort them to go to
the chase without fear, wherever it be; and
that, if they should meet the Algonquins,
they shall prepare a kettle, and give one
another meat.

9th. A moose-skin, to let them know that,
the Algonquins having recently spoken to the
Agnieronon,[17] There is peace on all sides.

The Algonquins have Contributed the
following presents.

Les Algonquins ont Contribué aux susdits presens.

Le 7ᵉ le 8ᵉ le 9ᵉ Et le 3ᵉ. qui font 4 presens.

fidelité promise.   Le tout a estè bien receu de L Oneiotchronon qui a promis Vne foy Inuiolable

P. albanel au bicq.   20   Kahiкohan qui estoit venu du bic le 17 au soir s'en retourna au mesme Lieu. Il auoit apportè lettres du p Albanel.

Le froid cõmença rudement.

DECEMBRE.

5.   Ie visitè La cote de beauport ou ie fus 3 iours.

11   Ie visitè La cote de beauprè, ou ie demeurè Iusques au 18 inclusiuè.   Le chemin Et le temps furent tres mauuais.

24   Le p poncet dit la messe de minuict auec Diacre Et sousdiacre.

Noel.   25   Mr Vignart fit le diacre, Et Mr le bé le soudiacre.   Il y eut trois Confesseurs les pp. Vimon, Chastelain et Mr Sᵗ Sauueur.   I as-

fetes de Noël.   sistè au Lutrain.   le P le moine dit la messe de minuict a 1 hospital & Mr Sᵗ Sauueur aux Vrsulines.   Item le dit p le moine dit la grande Messe au mesme lieu Et Moy aux Vrsulines   Cest ordre ne fut pas bien concertè Il ne faut plus doresnauant retirer les Chappelains de leurs chappelles pour faire diacre Et soudiacre en les priuan de dire.   La messe de minuict en leurs monasteres.   C'est vn subiet de murmur raisonable.   La Nuict fut fort douce par vn degel.   On sonna le premier

The 7th, the 8th, the 9th, And the 3rd,
which make 4 presents.

All has been well received by The Oneiot-   *Fidelity promised.*
chronon, who has promised An Inviolable
faith.

20. Kahikohan, who had come from bic   *Father albanel*
on the evening of the 17th, returned to the   *at bicq.*
same Place. He had brought letters from
father Albanel.

Keenly cold weather begins.

DECEMBER.

5. I visited cote de beauport, where I spent
3 days.

11. I visited cote de beauprè, where I
remained Until the 18th, inclusive. The
road And the weather were very bad.

24. Father poncet said the midnight mass,
with Deacon And subdeacon.

25. Monsieur Vignart served as deacon,   *Christmas.*
And Monsieur le bé [18] as subdeacon. There
were three Confessors: fathers Vimon and
Chastelain, and Monsieur St. Sauveur. I
assisted at the Lectern. Father le moine said   *Christmas festivals.*
the midnight mass at the hospital, and Mon-
sieur St. Sauveur at the Ursulines'. *Item*,
the said father le moine said high Mass at the
same place, And I at the Ursulines'. This
order was not well planned. The Chaplains
must not again be henceforth withdrawn from
their chapels in order to serve as deacon And
subdeacon,— being thus deprived of saying
The midnight mass in their monasteries.
This is a cause of reasonable complaint. The

coup de Matines a 9 heures le 2^d a 9 et $\overline{}$ et le
3° a vn peu deuant dix heures.   On comẽca
Imediatemen a 10 heures.   La messe du Iour
a 7. la grande Messe a 9 $\underline{^2}$.   le sermon se fit
apres vespres, en suitte le salut.

ordre des jours de
nöel.

Le 24 on sonne [le] premier coup du souper
(la vieille de Noel estant en vn dimanche) a 5
heures le 2 a 5 heures et vn quart. les litanies
a 6 heures et vn quart lexamen a 6 heures
Et $\overline{_2}$.   le lendemain le leuer a 5 heures.   le
1^r du souper a 5 heures du soir & le second a
5 heures & vn quart.   Les Litanies a 7 heures.

St Estienne

26   A 3 heures du soir Retournerent a quebec Les 3 Ambassadeurs hurons qu'on auoit
enuoyè a Agniè.   Ils sont accompagnez de 5
Agnieronons dont 4 sont venus a quebec le
5e est restè aux 3 Riuieres.   Le fruit de leur
ambassade a estè qu'au printemps prochain
les Agnieronons viendront en nombre querir
les hurons a quebec.

On dit La grande Messe auec diacre Et
soubdiacre.

St Jean.

27   On dit La grande Messe sans diacre et
soubdiacre.   Ie Croy que la maladie du pere
poncet en fut cause.

Night was very mild, on account of a thaw. The first bell for Matins was rung at 9 o'clock, the 2nd at 9½, and the 3rd a little before ten o'clock. We began Promptly at 10 o'clock. The mass for the Day at 7, high Mass at 9½. The sermon occurred after vespers; next, the benediction.

On the 24th, the first bell for supper was rung (Christmas eve being on a sunday) at 5 o'clock, the 2nd at a quarter past 5, the litany at a quarter past 6, the examination at 6½. Next day, the rising bell at 5 o'clock; the 1st bell for supper at 5 o'clock in the evening, and the second at a quarter past 5. Litany at 7 o'clock.

Order for the christmas days.

26. At 3 o'clock in the evening, The 3 huron Ambassadors who had been sent to Agniè Returned to quebec. They are accompanied by 5 Agnieronons, 4 of whom have come to quebec; the 5th remained at 3 Rivers. The result of their embassy was, that next spring the Agnieronons will come in force, to seek the hurons at quebec.

St. Stephen's day.

High Mass is said, with deacon And subdeacon.

27. High Mass is said without deacon and subdeacon. I Think father poncet's sickness was the reason.

St. John's day.

Mort Du Frere Liegeois.

L ES Iroquois avoient deja tüé ou brulé Les peres
    Daniel, de Brebeuf, Lallemant, et Buteux: Ils
    avoient massacré Le Pere Iogues, auec deux
donnez; La Lande, et robert dit Le bon.   Iusque
La ils sembloient avoir épargné nos freres Coädju-
teurs; quoiqu'ils accompagnassent nos peres, par tout
ou ils alloient.   Mais L'année 1655. ils etendirent
Leur cruauté jusqu'a eux: ils en tüerent Vn, proche
de Quebec; et blesserent L'autres de deux bales,
vers Le platon sainte Croix.   Ce dernier etoit Le Fr.
Loüis Le Böesme, Et L'autre Le Frere N. Liégeois;
tous deux françois de nation, Et dignes d'une sorte
de martire.

Les Iroquois, acharnez a La perte des Algonquins
et hurons Chrêtiens, dont nous conservions Les
debris dans Le fort de Sillery: rodoient incessament
autour de ce Village; pour Leur tendre des Embus-
ches, et a ceux qui Leur servoient d'asile.   Le 29me.
de May Vne troupe de sept ou huit agniez, ayant
apperçu notre Frere Liégeois dans Les champs, Voi-
sins de Sillery; ou il s'occupoit vtilement et coura-
geusement au service des Missionnaires Et de Leurs
Neophytes, dans des temps fort dangereux: ils L'in-
vestirent tout a coup, Le prirent sans resistance, Lui
percerent Le Cœur d'un coup de fusil, et L'etendirent
mort a Leurs pieds: L'un d'eux Lui Enleva La
Chevelure; et L'autre Lui coupa La teste, qu'il Laissa
sur La place.

Death Of Brother Liegeois.

THE Iroquois had already killed or burned fathers Daniel, de Brebeuf, Lallemant, and Buteux; They had murdered Father Jogues, with two donnés,— La Lande, and robert, called " The good." Until Then, they seemed to have spared our brother Coadjutors, although these accompanied our fathers wherever they went.   But in The year 1655 they extended Their cruelty even to them; they killed One of them, near Quebec, and wounded The other with two balls, toward The platon sainte Croix. This latter was Brother Louis Le Böesme; And The other, Brother N. Liégeois,— both french by nation, And worthy of a sort of martyrdom.[19]

The Iroquois, bent on The destruction of the Christian Algonquins and hurons, whose shattered remnant we preserved in The fort of Sillery, were incessantly prowling about this Village, in order to lay Ambushes for Them, and for those who furnished Them an asylum.   On the 29th of May, A band of seven or eight agniez, having perceived our Brother Liégeois in The fields Near Sillery,— where he was usefully and courageously engaged in the service of the Missionaries And of Their Neophytes, in very dangerous times,— all at once surrounded Him, took Him without resistance, pierced His Heart with a gunshot, and stretched Him dead at Their feet.   One of them Carried off His Scalp, and The other cut off His head, which he Left on The spot.

Le Lendemain Les algonquins trouverent son corps, et L'apporterent a Sillery, d'ou il fut transporté en chaloupe a Québec. Nos peres et nos freres allerent processionnellement, Le prendre au bord de L'eau: Les pères en robbe, avec Le bonnet quarré sur La tete, et vn cièrge a La main; Nos freres avec quelques Vns des donnez ou des hommes de La maison, apporterent Le corps dans notre Chapelle; ou L'on dit Vepres des morts Et d'autres prieres après. Le soir nos ff accommoderent Le Corps du defunt, a La maniere de La Compagnie: Et La 31. de May il fut inhumé, aprés L'office et La messe; tous nos peres et nos ff., avec beaucoup de personnes du dehors, assisterent a ses obseques. Il fut Enterré au bas de La Chapelle: c'est a dire dans L'un des deux costez, ou se trouve aujourdhui L'autel de la congregation des messieurs.

Le F. Liégeois a passé plusieurs années dans Le Canada, Et il a rendu de bons services a La mission; Et specialement au collége de Québec; qui avoit brulé tout recemment, Et qu'on releva de son temps: nous avions ici de neuf sortes d'ouvriers, emploïez a La batisse de La maison et d'une Chapelle nouvelle, sur Lesquels il etoit chargé de veiller. De québec il passa aux trois Rivieres: ou il bastit vne maison Commode avec vne chapelle pour nos missionnaires et Leurs sauvages. De la il revint a Québec, ou il s'occupa a perfectionner Les ouvrages, qu'il y avoit conduit autrefois. Enfin Durant Le fort de la guerre des Iroquois Il fut envoïé a Sillery, pour aider ou conduire Les Sauvages dans La Construction d'un nouveau fort, qu'ils faisoient dans Les Champs. C'est ou il trouva La recompense de ses travaux: Je

On the Next day, The algonquins found his body
and brought It to Sillery, whence it was conveyed in
a shallop to Québec.   Our fathers and brethren went
in a procession to receive It at the edge of The
water,— The fathers robed, with birettas on Their
heads, and tapers in Their hands.   Our brethren,
with some of the donnés, or household servants,
brought The body into our Chapel, where We said
Vespers for the dead, And afterward other prayers.
At evening, our brethren made ready The Body of
the deceased after The manner of The Society; And
on The 31st of May he was buried, after The office
and The mass.   All our fathers and brethren, with
many persons from without, were present at his
obsequies.   He was Buried in the lower part of The
Chapel,— that is to say, on The side where to-day
stands The altar of the congregation of messieurs.

Brother Liégeois spent many years in Canada, And
rendered good service to The mission,— especially
to the college of Québec, which had quite recently
burned, And which was rebuilt in his time.   We had
nine kinds of workmen here, employed in The building of The house and of a new Chapel,— Whom he
was charged to oversee.   From québec he went to
three Rivers, where he built a Convenient house, with
a chapel, for our missionaries and Their savages.
Thence he came back to Québec, where he was
occupied in completing The enterprises which he had
formerly directed.   Finally, During The height of
the war with the Iroquois, He was sent to Sillery,
to aid or direct The Savages in The Construction of
a new fort which they were making in The Fields.
It is there that he found The recompense of his
labors,— I mean, a precious death,— while he was

veux dire vne mort précieuse; tandis qu'il travail-
loit, a garentir nos neophytes des Insultes de L'Iroquois.

Il paroist par nos memoires, que Le f Liégeois fut
considére des Gouverneurs de son temps: et que nos
peres avoient en Lui vne Confiance particuliere;
puisque pour Le service de La mission, Et a L'occasion de nos diverses batisses, il a plusieurs fois
traversé Les mers.   .   .   .   Ie ne trouve point dans
Les annales; quel etoit son nom de batême, ni de
qu'elle province il etoit. quoiqu'il en soit, je ne
doute pas que Dieu n'ait recompensé son Zéle, son
courage, et ses travaux.

laboring to protect our neophytes from the Outrages of The Iroquois.

It appears by our records that brother Liégeois was esteemed by the Governors of his time; and that our fathers had a special Confidence in Him, since for The service of The mission, And in connection with our various buildings, he repeatedly crossed The seas. . . . I do not find in The annals what his baptismal name was, or from what province he came. However this be, I doubt not that God has rewarded his Zeal, his courage, and his labors.[20]

Catalogve des Bienfaictevrs de N. Dame
de Recouurance de Kebec, povr qvi
il favt prier et les recom-
mander avx prieres
dv pevple.

L'an 1632.

L'AN 1632. le 5. iuillet, les François arriuerent à Kebec, et 8. iours apres ren-
trerent dans le fort, que l'Anglois
Les P.P. Jesvites. leur remiſt entre les mains. Les peres de la
Compagnie de Iesus qui vinrent en ceste flotte,
entretinrent de leurs ornements l'autel qu'on
dressoit au fort tous les dimanches et festes
pour dire la saincte messe, et administrer les
sacrements aux François iusques à ce que la
chapelle fust bastie.

1633.
Mʳ. de Champlain.
L'an 1633, Mʳ. de Champlain fist bastir la
chapelle de Nostre Dame de Recouurance aux
frais de Messieurs de la Compagnie. Les
peres de la Compagnie de Iesus l'entretinrent
d'ornements et de cire iusques au mois de
Iuin de l'année 1634.

Les P.P. Jesuistes.
L'Image de Nʳe
Dame de
Recouurance.
Item ils donnerent l'Image de Nostre Dame
en relief qui est sur l'autel; ceste Image
s'appelle Nostre Dame de Recouurance tant à
cause que la chapelle porte ce nom à raison
[que] Mʳ. de Champlain auoit faict vœu de la
faire bastir soubs ce tiltre si on recouuroit le

List of the Benefactors of Nostre Dame de Recouvrance at Kebec, for whom prayers should be offered, and who should be commended to the prayers of the people.

IN the year 1632, on the 5th of july, the French arrived at Kebec; and 8 days afterward they entered the fort, which the English had handed over to them. The fathers of the Society of Jesus who came with that fleet supplied with their own ornaments the altar that was erected in the fort every sunday and festival for the celebration of holy mass, and for administering the sacraments to the French, until such time as the chapel was built. *In the year 1632.*

The Jesuit Fathers.

In the year 1633, Monsieur de Champlain caused the chapel of Nostre Dame de Recouvrance to be built at the expense of the Gentlemen of the Company. The fathers of the Society of Jesus supplied it with ornaments and wax until the month of June in the year 1634.[21] *1633. Monsieur de Champlain.*

Item, they gave the Image of Our Lady in relief which is above the altar. This Image is called Nostre Dame de Recouvrance [Our Lady of Recoverance], both because the chapel bears that name,— on account of Monsieur de Champlain having made a vow to *The Jesuit Fathers, The Image of Nostre Dame de Recouvrance.*

pays, ce qu'il a accomply la chose estant arriuée, que pour autant que ceste Image a esté
recouurée d'vn naufrage, que fist vn pere de
la Compagnie de Iesus venant en ces contrées.

1634
.Messievrs.
L'image de St.
Ioseph.

L'an 1634 Messieurs de la Compagnie ont
enuoyé pour 100. escus de Meubles et ornements, entre autres l'Image de St. Ioseph en
bosse qui est sur l'autel.

M. Du Plessis
Les 2. tableaux sur
cuiure de la Natiuité
et de St. Ioseph.

Mr. du Plessis Bochart, pour lors General
de la flotte, a donné deux tableaux en cuiure
de mediocre grandeur, l'vn de la Natiuité de
Nostre Seigneur, l'autre qui represente Nostre
Dame, St. Ioseph, et l'Enfant Iesus au millieu.

M. de Castillon.
Les 4. petits tableaux
de nos Saincts.

Item, Mr. de Castillon a donné deux petits
tableaux des Sts. Ignace, Xauier, Louys de
Gonzague et Stanislas.

1635
M. De Champlain.

L'an 1635, Mr. de Champlain, Gouuerneur
du pays laissa par testament à la Chapelle
quelques meubles, dont la vente a faict la sõe
d'enuiron 900₶.

De ceste somme on a
eü le soleil et calice
vermeil doré, auec
les burettes et le
bassinet.

Item vn grand coffre de bois,

Item quelques seruiettes,

Item enuiron 2 douzaines de seruiettes,

Item vn petit coffre garny de peintures
qui a esté vendu 16₶.

M. De Castillon.
Le grand tableau de
Nostre Dame.
1636
.Messievrs.

Monsieur de Castillon a donné le grand
tableau de Nostre Dame sans encastillement.

L'an 1636. Messieurs de la Compagnie ont
enuoyé vne aube de toile commune,

Item vne nappe d'autel,

Item deux amicts,

Item sept purificatoires,

build it under that name if the country were recovered, which he did when that event took place,—and because this same Image was recovered from a shipwreck that befell a father of the Society of Jesus, while on his way to these countries.[22]

In the year 1634, the Gentlemen of the Company sent Furniture and ornaments to the value of 100 écus,—among other things the Image of St. Joseph in relief that is above the altar.

Monsieur du Plessis Bochart, then General of the fleet, gave two brass pictures of medium size: one of the Nativity of Our Lord; the other representing Our Lady and St. Joseph with the Infant Jesus between them.

Item, Monsieur de Castillon gave two small pictures of Sts. Ignatius, Xavier, Louys de Gonzague, and Stanislas.[23]

In the year 1635, Monsieur de Champlain, Governor of the country, left by his will to the Chapel some furniture, the sale of which realized the sum of about 900 livres.[24]

Item, a large wooden chest;

Item, some napkins;

Item, about 2 dozen napkins;

Item, a small chest ornamented with pictures, which was sold for 16 livres.

Monsieur de Castillon gave the large picture of Our Lady without the frame.

In the year 1636, the Gentlemen of the Company sent an alb of common linen;

Item, an altar-cloth;

Item, two amices;

1634.
The Gentlemen,
The image of
St. Joseph.

Monsieur Du Plessis,
The 2 pictures on
brass of the Nativity
and of St. Joseph.

Monsieur de
Castillon,
The 4 small pictures
of our Saints.

1635.
Monsieur De
Champlain.

With this sum were
purchased the gilded
sun and the silver-
gilt chalice, with the
wine-pitchers and
tray.

Monsieur De
Castillon,
The large picture of
Our Lady.
1636.
The Gentlemen.

Item vn surplis,

Item vn pauilon de camelot vert ondé,

Item vn pauilon de droguet à fleurons rouges,

Item trois ou 4 liures d'encens,

Item dix liures de cire iaune en cierges,

Item dix liures de cire blanche en cierges.

Vn des peres de la Compagnie de Iesus donna, auec la permission de son Superieur, vne ceinture pour l'Aube, vne boëte de petit taffetas pour hosties, & 1 palle.

1640.

En l'année 1640. l'eglise de Kebec ayant esté bruslée et consommée du feu auec la maison des peres Iesuistes, on sauua quasi tous les ornements d'Eglise.

Messievrs.

Es annees suiuantes, Messieurs de la Compagnie ont cessé de faire des dons pour les ornements d'Eglise, laissants le soin de ceste affaire à la charité des habitants, se contentants de la pension de 600ll. pour deux peres en chaque Residence.

1642
Mʳ. de L'Isle.
Les tapis qui ont esté mis en plusieurs pieces.

En l'année 1642. Mʳ. De l'Isle, lieutenant de Mʳ. le Gouuerneur a donné vne robe de castor, dont on achepta les deux pieces de tapisserie qui sont autour de l'Autel.

Amendes.

Mʳ. le Gouuerneur a faict applicquer ès dites années suiuantes quelques amendes à l'Eglise de Kebec, qui ont esté employées en ornements.

1643 & 1644.

Es annees 1643. & 1644. on fift vne cueillette parmy les habitants pour quelques ornements & meubles de l'Eglise.

Item, seven purificators;

Item, a surplice;

Item, a curtain of green watered camlet;

Item, a curtain of drugget with red flowers;

Item, three or 4 livres' weight of incense;

Item, ten livres of yellow wax in tapers;

Item, ten livres of white wax in tapers;

One of the fathers of the Society of Jesus gave, with the permission of his Superior, a girdle for the Alb, a box of small taffeta for wafers, and 1 palla [chalice-cover].

In the year 1640, the church of Kebec was burned and destroyed by fire, together with the house of the Jesuit fathers.[25] We saved nearly all the Church ornaments.

1640.

In succeeding years, the Gentlemen of the Company ceased to make donations for Church ornaments, leaving the care of that matter to the charity of the habitants, and contenting themselves with paying the pension of 600 livres for two fathers at each Residence.[26]

The Gentlemen.

In the year 1642, Monsieur De l'Isle, lieutenant of Monsieur the Governor, gave a robe of beaver-skins, with which were purchased the two pieces of carpet that lie around the Altar.

1642.
Monsieur de L'Isle,
The carpets laid in
several pieces.

Monsieur the Governor in the following years caused certain fines to be applied to the Church of Kebec; they were expended in purchasing ornaments.

Fines.

In the years 1643 and 1644, a collection was taken up among the habitants for some ornaments and furniture for the Church.[27]

1643 and 1644.

Mr. De Montmagny.
Le petit Tabernacle
tout doré.

M^r. de Montmagny, Gouuerneur, donna 25. escus, qui ont esté employez au tabernacle doré qui est à present sur le grand autel, apporté en l'an 1644. auec quelques autres aumosnes des particuliers, dont on a aussi achepté deux chasubles de satin, l'vne rouge, l'autre verte, à fleurs toutes deux.

Item vne grande chape de satin blanc à fleurs.

Item 4 chandeliers de cuiure, apportés ceste année présente 1645.

1644 & 1646.
Mr. de Montmagny.
Le vase de l'eau
baptismale.
1645.
Le fond de la
bastisse de l'Eglise.

M^r. de Montmagny, Gouuerneur, a donné le vase de cuiure cizelé qui sert pour l'eau baptismale.

En l'an 1645. M^r. de Montmagny Gouuerneur, et les habitants, ont applicqué douze cents cinquante castors prouenants des soldats venus des Hurons, pour faire bastir vne Eglise à Kebec, en l'honneur de Nostre Dame de la Paix.

1646.
Mr. de Montmagny.
La tapisserie grande
pour le marchepied
de l'autel.

En l an. 1646. Monsr. de Montmagni, Gouuerneur de la nouuelle france, a donné à l'eglise de Quebec vne piece de tapisserie neufue et assez grande pour seruir au marchepied de l'Autel les bonnes festes de l'année.

Messieurs.
La cloche de 100ℓℓ.

Item en mesme temps il a declaré qu'il donnoit à l'église, de la part de Messieurs de la Comp. de la Nouuelle France, la cloche qu'on a penduë au clocher en l'automne dernier, pesant enuiron 100ℓℓ; elle restoit des meubles des dicts Messieurs de la Compagnie.

Mlle De Tilly.
tauaiole.

Le 9. d'auril 1646. Melle Tilli a donné à la Chapelle de Québec vne tauaiole d'enuiron 2

Monsieur de Montmagny, the Governor, gave 25 écus, which,—together with some other alms, from private individuals,—were expended on the gilded tabernacle which is now on the main altar, brought in 1644. With these sums have also been purchased two satin chasubles,—one red, the other green, and both flowered.

Item, a large cope of flowered white satin;

Item, 4 brass candlesticks, brought this present year, 1645.

Monsieur de Montmagny, the Governor, gave the chased brass vessel for the baptismal water.

In the year 1645, Monsieur de Montmagny, the Governor, and the habitants gave twelve hundred and fifty beaver-skins, brought by the soldiers who came from the Huron country, to have a Church built at Kebec in honor of Our Lady of Peace.[28]

In the year 1646, Monsieur de Montmagni, the Governor of new france, gave to the church of Quebec a piece of new carpet sufficiently large to cover the Altar-steps on all the great feasts of the year.

Item, at the same time he declared that he gave to the church, on behalf of the Gentlemen of the Company of New France, the bell that was hung in the steeple last autumn, weighing about 100 livres; and that remained from the effects of the said Gentlemen of the Company.

On the 9th of april, 1646, Mademoyselle Tilli[29] gave to the Chapel of Québec an altar-

Monsieur De Montmagny, The small Tabernacle, all gilt.

1644 and 1646. Monsieur de Montmagny, The vessel for baptismal water.

1645. The fund for the building of the Church.

1646. Monsieur de Montmagny, The large carpet for the altar-steps.

The Gentlemen, The bell of 100 livres.

Mademoyselle De Tilly, altar-cloth.

aulnes de long, qui a desia serui, et n'est pas neufue.

En dec. 1646. Made. Giffard a donné 4 aulnes de passement noir.

En Ian. 1647. Madelle de Repentigny a donné vn corporal à dentelle.

Item 3. corporaux et 2. mouchoirs.

Item vn dessus de nappe d'autel de toile d'Hollande.

Et Madelle Godefroy vn corporal à dentelle.

Monsr. de la Tour a donné 100₶. qui ont serui à fournir le payement du grand ciboire apporté ceste année, auec la Croix et 4 chandeliers d'argent.

Monsr. de Repentigny a donné 40₶. pour commencer le grand tabernacle, pour lequel la communauté a fourny 400₶. qui est arriué icy l'an 1649. au mois d'aoust.

Robert Hache a donné vne cloche pesant 1000₶. qui est arriuée l'an 1651.

Monsr. Ménoil a donné vne petite tasse godronnée et cizelé d'argent vermeil doré

Item vne couppe basse couuerte de cristail.

Mr. Zacharie Cloustier a donné vne regle d'Ebene pour le Bedeau.

Monsr Gloria a donné la somme de 33₶. 6s. 6d.

Monsr de St Martin, Chantre a donné la somme de 60₶. pour estre employée en liures d'Eglise pour le chœur.

Jean Joliet Charron, a laissé à sa mort par testament la sõe de 38₶.

cloth about 2 ells long, which has already been used and is not new.

In december, 1646, Madame Giffard gave 4 ells of black lace.

Monsieur Giffard, black lace.

In January, 1647, Mademoyselle de Repentigny gave a corporal edged with lace;

Item, 3 corporals and 2 handkerchiefs;

Item, an upper altar-cloth of Holland linen;

And Mademoyselle Godefroy a corporal edged with lace.

1647. Mademoyselle De Repentigny, Corporals, Handkerchiefs.

Mademoyselle Godefroy.

Monsieur de la Tour gave 100 livres, which sum was employed in paying for the large ciborium brought this year, with the Cross and 4 silver candlesticks.

Monsieur de la Tour, a large ciborium.

Monsieur de Repentigny gave 40 livres to commence the large tabernacle, for which the community gave 400 livres. It arrived here in 1649, in the month of august.

1648. Monsieur De Repentigny, a large tabernacle.

Robert Hache gave a bell weighing 1000 livres, which arrived in the year 1651.

1650. Robert Hache, Bell.

Monsieur Ménoil gave a small cup, carved around the edge and chased, of silver gilded over;

Item, a low cup covered with crystal.

1651. Monsieur Menoil, a silver-gilt cup.

Monsieur Zacharie Cloustier gave an Ebony staff for the Beadle.

Zacharie Cloustier, Beadle's Staff.

Monsieur Gloria gave the sum of 33 livres, 6 sous, 6 deniers.[30]

Monsieur Gloria, Money.

Monsieur de St. Martin, Chanter, gave the sum of 60 livres to be expended in purchasing Church books for the choir.

Monsieur St. Martin, Money.

Jean Joliet, a Wheelwright, left by will at his death the sum of 38 livres.

Legacy, Joliet.

Barbe Hebou — formerly the wife of Jean

Leg.
Barbe Hebou.

Barbe Hebou iadis femme de Jean Miloüer dict Du maisne, a legué par testament la somme de 66℔. 13s. 8d.

Mlle. de Repentigny.

Mad^{elle}. de Repentigny et Mad^{elle}. Godefroy sa fille ont presté à l'Eglise, toutes les festes solennelles de l'année depuis le iour de Noel 1650. leurs tentures de tapisserie et autres choses qu'on leur a demandé, non sans preiudice et incommodité notable.

1651 et 1652.
Prests.

Item, Mad^{elle}. de Repentigny fit à son fils Charles vn fort beau surplis à dentelle, lequel ne luy ayant serui qu'vne fois, fut bruslé dans l'incendie des Meres Vrsulines.

Item elle a donné la sotanne rouge auec le bonnet quarré qui sert à Charles son fils.

Dvquet.
argent.

Mad^e. Duquet a donné 22℔. qui luy estoient dues pour des ouurages de toile faicts pour l'Eglise.

R. P. Sup^r.
Droguet.

Le R. P. Sup^r. à la requeste du P. Ierosme Lalemant, a donné vne piece de droguet d'enuiron 8. aulnes; c'est vne espece de toile imprimée de fleurs rouges.   On en a fait, de 7 aulnes enuiron vn pauillon.

Cuuette.

Item vne petite cuuette pour les burettes, d'estain.

Mad^e. Marsolet.
1652.
pierre.

Vne grosse pierre pretieuse en ouale percée d'argent auec vn ruban bleu pour la clef du grand tabernacle.

Mad^{elle}. de
Repentigny.
Chappelet
1652.
Mad^e. d'Emery.
1651.
Chappelet.

Vn beau chappelet d'Ambre pour N. D. de Recouurance le 14 d'aoust 1652.

A enuoyé de France par Mad^e. de Monceaux vn gros chappelet de cornaline pour la mesme Image de N. D. de Recouurance.

Milouer, called Du maisne — bequeathed by will the sum of 66 livres, 13 sous, 8 deniers.

Mademoyselle de Repentigny and Mademoyselle Godefroy, her daughter, lent to the Church on all the solemn feasts of the year from Christmas day, 1650, all their tapestry hangings, and other articles which were asked from them, — not without considerable trouble and inconvenience.

Item, Mademoyselle de Repentigny gave to her son Charles a very handsome surplice, trimmed with lace, which was used but once by him, and was burned in the fire that destroyed the house of the Ursuline Mothers.

Item, she gave the red soutane with the biretta used by her son Charles.

Madame Duquet gave 22 livres that were due her for linen articles which she had made for the Church.

The Reverend Father Superior gave, at the request of Father Jerosme Lalemant, a fine piece of drugget, about 8 ells long; it is a kind of linen, with red flowers printed on it. With about 7 ells a canopy was made.

Item, a small basin of pewter for the wine-pitchers.

A large oval precious stone, pierced with silver, with a blue ribbon, for the key of the large tabernacle.

A beautiful Amber rosary for Our Lady of Recoverance, on the 14th of august, 1652.

Sent from France by Mademoyselle de Monceaux, a large rosary of carnelian for the same Image of Our Lady of Recoverance.

Legacy,
Barbe Hebou.

Mademoyselle de Repentigny.

1651 and 1652.
Presents.

Duquet,
money.

Reverend Father Superior,
Drugget.

Basin.

Madame Marsolet,
1652,
stone.

Mademoyselle de Repentigny,
Rosary,
1652.

Madame d' Emery,
1651,
Rosary.

Madelle. De l'Isle.
Sept. 1652
tauiolles.

A donné à la paroisse; vne pente de ray-seau d'enuiron 2. aulnes; 2. rideaux de toile a bandes de rayseau; vne toilette d'enuiron vne aulne & demie à 4. bandes.

Madelle. de
Repentigny.
Ian. 1653.
Mad. de la Pelterie.

Vne belle dentelle deliée large de 3 doigts. 4. aulnes pour le tour de la nappe.

Vn grand tableau de S^t. Joseph, mis au costé gauche de l'autel ou retable de la paroisse.

Mad. d'Ailleboust.

Vne nappe de credence le 1er. de Ianu. 1654.

Mad. de la Pelterie.

Madame de la Pelterie dix escus p^r ayder à accomplir la Chape et la dalmatique et tunique des ornements pour les morts.

Elle a de plus donné depuis six mois ce 15e. de Ianuier 1654. p^r. l'entretien des officiers de l'Eglise la valeur de plus de 40₶.

Item la mesme 21₶. 10s. pour ayder à ache-pter la tapisserie de Madame de Monceaux.

Item depuis le dict temps iusques au 3. may à diuerses rencontres, en estoffe p^r. habiller les enfants, et autres choses selon le memoire plus de 100₶.

Madem. Manse.

Mademoys. Manse enuoya en may 1654. vne belle estoffe de satin de la Chine p^r. faire vne escharpe p^r. S^t. Sacrement.

Mademoyselle de
Repentigny.

Mademoyselle de Repentigny en mesme temps donna un beau tableau du rosaire.

La r. m. Eugenie des
fontaines.

L'an 1654. la m. Eugenie des Fontaines de la maison de S^{te}. Marie à Paris, rue S^t An-toine, enuoya vne belle chasuble de satin à fleurs auec vn amy, la bourse, corporal etc.

Gave to the parish church a lace hanging of about 2 ells; 2 linen curtains with lace borders; and a table-cover about an ell and a half long, with 4 stripes.

Mademoyselle De l'Isle, September, 1652, altar-cloths.

Beautiful fine lace, 3 fingers wide, and 4 ells long, as a border for the altar-cloth.

Mademoyselle de Repentigny, January, 1653.

A large picture of St. Joseph placed on the left side of the altar or altar-screen of the parish church.

Madame de la Pelterie.

A credence-cover, on the 1st of January, 1654.

Madame d'Ailleboust.

Madame de la Pelterie, ten écus toward completing the Cope, dalmatic, and tunic of the vestments for the dead.

Madame de la Pelterie.

She has given during six months up to this 15th of January, 1654, for the maintenance of the officers of the Church, more than 40 livres.

Item, the same, 21 livres, 10 sous toward the purchase of the tapestry of Madame de Monceaux.

Item, from the said date to the 3rd of may, on various occasions,— in cloth for dressing the children, and other articles, according to the memorandum,— over 100 livres.

Mademoyselle Manse sent in may, 1654, a fine piece of Chinese satin to make a scarf for the Blessed Sacrament.

Mademoyselle Manse.

Mademoyselle de Repentigny at the same time gave a fine picture of the rosary.

Mademoyselle de Repentigny.

In the year 1654, mother Eugenie des Fontaines of the house of Ste. Marie in Paris, rue St. Antoine, sent a fine chasuble of flowered satin with an amice, burse, corporal, etc.

The reverend mother Eugenie des fontaines.

Paris.

En mesme temps le R. P. Charles Lalemant obtint vne aumosne p^r payer à Monsr. Quenet 142₶. que la paroisse luy deuoit, & 40₶. p^r. des cierges.

M^r. Bourdon.

Monsr. Bourdon a donné p^r la Chapelle de St Ioseph, où il a son banc la valeur de plus de 50. escus, soit en argent ou en clous.

M. Grouuel.

Monsr. Martin Grouuel enuiron autant la pluspart en bois, planches et madriers; outre de l'huile à brusler deuant le S^t. Sacrement, et vne petite pente [de tapisserie p^r. mettre à l'entour de la chaire.

M^e. de Monceaux.

En 1655. Mad. de Monceaux, vn parement d'Autel de reseau en couleur.

La R. M. Eugenie des Fontaines cy-dessus énoncée, vne belle dalmatique.

La R. M. Marguerite Doniat.

La R. M. Marguerite Doniat de l'Assomption à Paris, trois beaux surplis.

M^r. l'Espine.

Monsr de l'Espine, vne robe de loutre et de plus ces deux années dernières nous a fait valoir bien à profit quelques rets qu'on luy auoit données p^r. porter à Tadoussac.

M^r. de Maure.

Monsr. de Maure quelques minots de blé.

M. de la Pelleterie.

Madame de la Pelleterie 100₶. ⎱ pour encensoir d'argent,

R. P. Pierre le Clerc.

R. P. Pierre le Clerc de Paris 100₶. ⎰ or à brunir &c.

le P. Roy.

Le P. Roy de Paris 30₶.

M^r. Bourdon.

M^r. Bourdon p^r. le clocher 20₶.

M^r. De Charny.

M^r. de Charny 30₶.

M. Godefroy.

M^r. Godefroy vn escu d'or.

At the same time, Reverend Father Charles Lalemant obtained an alms to pay Monsieur Quenet [31] 142 livres that the parish church owed him, and 40 livres for tapers.

Paris.

Monsieur Bourdon gave for the Chapel of St. Joseph where his pew is situated, the value of over 50 écus, either in money or in nails.

Monsieur Bourdon.

Monsieur Martin Grouvel, about as much,— chiefly in timber, boards, and planks; besides oil to be burned before the Blessed Sacrament, and a small tapestry hanging to be placed around the pulpit.

Monsieur Grouvel.

In 1655, Madame de Monceaux, an Altardrapery of colored network.

Madame de Monceaux.

Reverend Mother Eugenie des Fontaines, mentioned above, a handsome dalmatic.

The Reverend Mother Marguerite Doniat, of the Assumption in Paris, three fine surplices.

The Reverend Mother Marguerite Doniat.

Monsieur de l'Espine, a robe of otter-skins; and, moreover, during the past two years he has enabled us to derive great profit from some nets that had been given him to take to Tadoussac.

Monsieur l'Espiné.

Monsieur de Maure, several minots [32] of wheat.

Monsieur de Maure.

Madame de la Pelleterie, 100 livres,

Reverend Father Pierre le Clerc, of Paris, 100 livres,

Father Roy, of Paris, 30 livres,

} for a censer of silver, burnished gold, etc.

Madame de la Pelleterie.

Reverend Father Pierre le Clerc.

Father Roy.

Monsieur Bourdon, for the steeple, 20 livres.

Monsieur Bourdon.

Monsieur de Charny, 30 livres.

Monsieur De Charny.

Monsieur Godefroy, a gold écu.

Monsieur Godefroy.

M. Daudeuille.

Mad. Seuestre.

Mr. Daudeuille 27ħ. 10. s.

Madame Seuestre 12ħ. ou 15ħ.

Monsr. de Lauson Gouuernr. nous a fait tomber entre les mains en diuerses rencontres plus de 300ħ.

Le R. P. Paul Ragueneau,

Est à remarquer que depuis 1651. les Superieurs de la maison de ñre Compie ont grandement assisté la paroisse.

le. P. Fr. le Mercier.

1° faisants subsister vn seminaire d'enfants la pluspart à leurs despens. 2° fournissants vn de nos Freres pr. auoir soin de la sacristie de la paroisse. 3° nous prestants Mre. Charles Boiuin, charpentier, trois moys durant, pour conduire l'ouurage de ñre clocher. 4° retirants en ceste maison St Martin, principal Chantre de l'Eglise. 5° nous fauorisants en tout en plusieurs autres façons et manieres.

DEPUIS LA TOUSSAINTS 1655.

1655.
Mr. Martin Grouuel et sa femme.

Le Sr. Martin Grouuel et sa femme ont fait don de leur terre située au lieu dict La grande Riuiere, au dessus du Cap de Tourmente, dans la seigneurie de Beaupré; mais les Seigneurs, n'ayants pas voulu laisser cela en main morte, obligerent la paroisse de s'en deffaire, & elle fut venduë sept cents ħ à Charles Cadieu dit Couruille.

Les Srs. Bourdon et l'Espiné.

Le Sr. l'Espine et le Sr. Bourdon, associés pr. la traite de Tadoussac, vne barique d'huile à brusler.

Me. Buissot.

Madame Buissot, vne belle escharpe de soye rouge.

Monsieur Daudeville,[33] 27 livres, 10 sous.

Madame Sevestre, 12 or 15 livres.

Monsieur de Lauson, the Governor, gave into our hands on various occasions, more than 300 livres.

It should be observed that, since 1651, the Superiors of the house of our Society have greatly assisted the parish church.

1. They maintain a seminary for children, chiefly at their own expense. 2. They provide one of our Brethren to take care of the sacristy of the parish church. 3. They lent us Master Charles Boivin, carpenter, for three months to direct the work on our steeple. 4. They lodge in that house St. Martin, the principal Chanter of the Church. 5. They aid us in everything in many other ways and fashions.

SINCE ALL SAINTS' DAY, 1655.

Sieur Martin Grouvel and his wife donated their land situated at the place called La grande Riviere above Cap de Tourmente, in the seigniory of Beaupré; but as the Seigniors [34] did not wish to leave the property in mortmain they compelled the parish to dispose of it, and it was sold for seven hundred livres to Charles Cadieu, called Courville.[35]

Sieur l'Espine and Sieur Bourdon, who are partners for the Tadoussac trade, a barrel of lamp oil.

Madame Buissot, a handsome scarf of red silk.

Monsieur Daudeville. Madame Sevestre.

Reverend Father Paul Ragueneau.

Father François le Mercier.

1655. Monsieur Martin Grouvel and his wife.

Sieurs Bourdon and l'Espiné.

Madame Buissot.

Monsr. De Charny.

Monsr de Charny vne piece de taf[e]tas noir de vingt aulnes, à 8₶ l'aulne.

La Mere Eugenie de la Visitation.

Nous ẽ venu de Paris par les vaisseaux arriués en 1656. six beaux vases de fayance figurée auec leurs bouquets de la part de la M^e. Eugenie des Fontaines de la Visitãon de Paris

La Mere Marguerite de l'Assomption.

Item 6. autres de la part de la M^e. Marguerite Doniat de l'Assomption.

Le R. P. Gvill. Thiersan.

Item vne belle chasuble de damas noir, dont prés de la moitié a esté donnée par charité par le soin du R. P. Guill. Thiersant.

DEPUIS LA TOUSSAINCTS 1656.

1656. Monsr. Grovvel.

Le S^r. Martin Grouuel a donné vn deuant d'Autel, deux pauillons droguet blanc à fleurs rouges; quatre chasubles, deux blanches, vne rouge et vne noire, vn voile rouge et vn blanc, deux bourses, deux Agnus Dei, vn petit tableau, deux encensoirs, vne nauette de cuiure, trois corporaux, deux voiles de reseau, vn petit benitier de cuiure, deux breuiaires, vne nappe d'autel, vne aulbe & un amict.

Made. Morin.

Madame Morin, vn escharpe de cotton barriollé de iaune, pour la chapelle S^te. Anne.

Monsr. Vignal.

Monsieur Vignal, vne nappe pour la chapelle S^te. Anne.

Le P. Svperievr.

Le R. P. Superieur, vn pupiltre de bois noir à missel.

DEPUIS LA TOUSSAINCTS 1657.

1657. Mr. Gloria.

M^r. Gloria a donné vne petite boëtte dorée pour mettre des hosties.

Monsieur de Charny, a piece of black taffeta twenty ells long, worth 8 livres the ell.

Monsieur De Charny.

We have received from Paris, by the ships that arrived in 1656, six beautiful vases of faience figured with bouquets from Mother Eugenie des Fontaines, of the Visitation at Paris.

Mother Eugenie of the Visitation.

Item, 6 others from Mother Marguerite Doniat, of the Assumption.

Mother Marguerite of the Assumption.

Item, a fine chasuble of black damask, nearly one-half the cost of which was given out of charity through the efforts of Reverend Father Guillaume Thiersant.

Reverend Father Guillaume Thiersan.

SINCE ALL SAINTS' DAY, 1656.

Sieur Martin Grouvel gave an Antependium; two canopies of white drugget with red flowers; four chasubles,—two being white, one red, and one black; a red veil and a white veil. He has also given two burses, two Agnus Dei, a small picture, two censers, a brass incense-boat, three corporals, two lace veils, a small copper vessel for holy water, two breviaries, an altar-cloth, an alb, and an amice.

1656. Monsieur Grouvel.

Madame Morin,[36] a scarf of cotton checkered with yellow, for St. Anne's chapel.

Madame Morin.

Monsieur Vignal, an altar-cloth for St. Anne's chapel.

Monsieur Vignal.

The Reverend Father Superior a missal-desk of black wood.

The Father Superior.

SINCE ALL SAINTS' DAY, 1657.

Monsieur Gloria gave a small gilt box to hold wafers.

1657. Monsieur Gloria.

Pierre Paradis.   Pierre Paradis a donné un grand cousteau pour coupper le pain benit.

Noël L'Anglois.   Noël l'Anglois a donné vne nappe de toille iaune d'vne aulne ou enuiron, pour s'en seruir à coupper le pain benit.

Le R. P. Poncet.   Le Reuerend Père Poncet a enuoyé de France deux iolies scapulaires pour la Vierge et le petit Iesus de ceste paroisse, en l'année mil six cent cinquante huict. Recuës le septiesme aoust.

DEPUIS LA TOUSSAINCTS 1658.

DEPUIS LA TOUSSAINCTS 1659.

En 1660 . . . .

(Reliqua desiderantur.)

Pierre Paradis[37] gave a large knife where-with to cut the blessed bread.

Pierre Paradis.

Noël l'Anglois gave a napkin of yellow linen, about an ell in length, to be used when the blessed bread is cut.

Noël L'Anglois.

Reverend Father Poncet sent from France two pretty scapulars, for the Virgin and Infant Jesus of the parish church, in the year one thousand six hundred and fifty-eight. Received on the seventh of august.

Reverend Father Poncet.

SINCE ALL SAINTS' DAY, 1658.

SINCE ALL SAINTS' DAY, 1659.

In 1660 . . . .

(Reliqua desiderantur.)

XC

In reprinting the *Relation* of 1655 – 56 (Paris, 1657), by Jean de Quen, we follow a copy of the original Cramoisy edition in the Lenox Library. The " Priui-lege " was " Donné à Paris le 23. Decembre 1656," and the " Permifsion " was " Fait à Paris ce 28. Decembre 1656." The prefatory letter of Jean de Quen is dated " A Kebec ce 7. Septembre 1656." This annual is no. 109 of Harrisse's *Notes*.

Collation: Four preliminary leaves, consisting of one blank leaf; title, with verso blank, 1 leaf; " Table des Chapitres," pp. (2); " Priuilege," with " Permifsion " on the verso, 1 leaf; prefatory letter from Jean de Quen to the French provincial, Louis Cellot, pp. 1 – 6; text (16 chaps.), pp. 7 – 168. Signatures: Four preliminary leaves without signature mark, A – L in eights. The last four leaves of sig. L are blank, one of which is usually pasted on the cover. There is no mispaging.

Copies have been sold or priced as follows : Leclerc (1878), no. 2601, priced at 200 francs; O'Callaghan (1882), no. 1237, sold to Library of Parliament of Canada for $21, and had cost him $32.50 in gold; Barlow (1890), no. 1305, sold for $9; and Lenox Duplicate Sale, sold by Bangs & Co., of New York, April 29, 1895, no. 176, to Charles D. Marshall, of Buffalo, for $27.50. Copies are preserved in the following libraries: Lenox, Harvard, Brown (private), Marshall (private), Ayer (private), Library of Parliament (Ottawa), Laval University (Quebec), British Museum, and Bibliothèque Nationale (Paris).

XCI–XCII

For bibliographical particulars of the *Journal des Jésuites,* see Vol. XXVII.

An anonymous MS. sketch of the murder by the Iroquois (May 29, 1625) of the Jesuit brother, Jean Liégeois, lies within the old MS. volume of the *Journal.* This we reproduce from the original.

XCIII

The *Catalogve des Bienfaictevrs de N. Dame de Recouurance de Kebec,* was a contemporary list of those who, from time to time, between the years 1632 and 1657, made gifts to the chapel built by Champlain. The entries were in the handwriting of several of the Jesuit missionaries — among them, Jerome Lalemant, De Brébeuf, Ragueneau, and De Quen. The original MS. of this interesting document long rested in the archives of the Seminary of Quebec. In *L'Abeille,* a literary journal conducted by the teachers and students of the Petit Séminaire, the *Catalogve* was published for the first time, commencing in the number for April 14, 1859, and concluded in the issue for May 18 following. To this publication were appended numerous explanatory and biographical notes by the Abbés C. H. Laverdière and H. R. Casgrain, editors of the *Journal des Jésuites.*

It is possible that the original MS. was used as printers' "copy," for it cannot now be found. In the library of Laval University is what Mgr. T. E.

Hamel, the librarian, considers a " very accurate " copy. We have corrected the *L'Abeille* version by the MS. transcript in Laval, and have reproduced such of the notes of Laverdière and Casgrain as convey information not already given in our own notes in previous volumes of this series.

Note:— We take pleasure in introducing, with the present volume, the collection of *Relations* formed by the late Orsamus Holmes Marshall, and now owned by his son, Charles D. Marshall, of Buffalo, N. Y. The elder Marshall was one of the pioneer collectors of these volumes, and among the first to recognize their value as sources of history. The collection now comprises twenty-one annuals. Those represented, and previously published by us, are: 1635 (Harrisse, no. 63), 1636 (H. 65), 2nd issue of 1637 (H. 68), 2nd issue of 1638 (H. 70), 2nd issue of 1639 (H. 75), 1640 (H. 76), 1640–41 (H. 77), 1642 (H. 80), 1642–43 (H. 81), 1643–44 (H. 83), 1645–46 (H. 86), 1st issue of 1648–49 (H. 90), 2nd issue of 1648– 49 (H. 91), 1650–51 (H. 97), 1652–53 (H. 101), and 1653–54 (H. 103). Subsequent ones will be duly noted in order.

NOTES TO VOL. XLII

(Figures in parentheses, following number of note, refer to pages of English text.)

1 (p. 71).— Otihatangué is identified by Beauchamp, Clark, and others as the Salmon River, N. E. of Oswego. Beauchamp defines the meaning of this word as "large clearing;" he also mentions other names (*Ind. Names*, p. 65) applied to this locality. One of these appellations was La Famine (Anglicized as Famine Bay), doubtless given on account of the sufferings endured by the French on their way to Onondaga in 1656. The place is mentioned by Le Moyne, in 1654, as "a resort of all nations." Coronelli's map (1688), says that there "most of the Iroquois disembark to trade their beaver." See Clark's excellent note identifying Otihatangué, in *Early Cayuga History*, p. 17. Cf. *note* 6, vol. xli. of this series.

2 (p. 71).— The *poisson doré* here mentioned is probably the common yellow or American perch *(Perca americana* or *flavescens).* The *achigen* is the black perch or black bass; the name is of Algonkin origin (Clapin's *Dict. Canad.-Français*, p. 343). Both these kinds of perch abound in fresh-water lakes and in rivers, in Canada and the Northern States.

3 (p. 75).— *Neds percés:* the Beaver tribe (vol. x., *note* 6). The rapids referred to are probably those of St. Louis (Lachine).

4 (p. 83).— *Tethiroguen:* the Oneida River, issuing from Oneida Lake (Goienho). The village of Oneiout (Oneida) was probably on the eastern side of Oneida Creek, near the present Munnsville.

5 (p. 109).— Charles Garman (Garemand) was captured by the Iroquois in June, 1653, at which time he was eight years old (vol. xxxviii., p. 175).

6 (p. 149).— A version of the Huron myth of Ataentsic (vol. x., pp. 127 – 129, 323).

7 (p. 163).— Concerning the manufacture and uses of mats by North American aborigines, see *U. S. Bur. Ethnol. Rep.*, 1891 – 92, p. 18 – 21. The use of mats for catching fish seems somewhat unusual; but, when fastened across a narrow stream, a coarse mat of plaited rushes might well serve as a net.

8 (p. 179).— Cf. the description of this feast with those given by Brébeuf (vol. x., pp. 175 – 177) and Lalemant (vol. xvii., pp. 167 – 187).

9 (p. 197).— Regarding Taronhiaouagui (Tha-ron-hya-wä'-kon), see vol. viii., *note* 36; vol. x., *note* 12.

10 (p. 213).— Upon the name Otondiata, Beauchamp says (*Ind. Names*, p. 72): "It was interpreted for me as *Stone stairs*, an appropriate name. It was applied to Grenadier island [St. Lawrence Co., N. Y.] as early as 1673, and with slight variations was always prominent."

11 (p. 221).— The identity of these two French explorers was long unknown; but recent historical researches sufficiently confirm the opinion that they were Radisson and Groseilliers (vol. xxviii., *note* 32). This is the first mention (so far as known), in contemporary documents, of their discoveries. Radisson wrote several narratives of his voyages; the MSS. of these are preserved in the archives of the Bodleian Library and British Museum; they first appeared in print in the *Prince Soc. Pubs.*, vol. xvi. (Boston, 1885). Parts of the relation of Radisson's third and fourth voyages are republished, with annotations, in *Wis. Hist. Colls.*, vol. xi., pp. 64 – 96; cf. *Id.*, vol. xiv., p. 5, *note*, and *Parkman Club Pubs.*, no. 2. The first of these narratives relates his experiences while a prisoner among the Iroquois (1652 – 53). During this time he met, at Fort Orange, the Jesuit Poncet, who also had been captured by the Iroquois. A little later, Radisson made his escape, and was sent by the Dutch to Holland. Returning to Canada in May, 1654, he seems to have departed with Groseilliers (his brother-in-law) in the following August, upon the voyage referred to in our text. In July, 1657, he went with the Jesuits to Onondaga, and wrote an account of that enterprise, much longer and more circumstantial than Ragueneau's.— See his *Voyages* (Prince Soc.), pp. 86 – 134.

The discoveries of Radisson and Groseilliers mentioned in our text are again referred to in the *Relation* of 1658 (vol. xliv. of this series), where Druillettes gives information — regarding the routes to Hudson Bay, and the tribes of the Northwest — derived partly from these two explorers, partly from the roving Indians.

12 (p. 221).— The tribe here called *Puants* were the Winnebagoes (vol. xv., *note* 7); the *Liniouek*, the Illinois (vol. xxiii., *note* 9); the *Nadouesiouek*, the Sioux (vol. xxiii., *note* 8); the *Kiristinons*, the Crees (vol. xviii., *note* 15).

Pouarak (Poualac): an abbreviated form of *Assinipoualak*, which, according to the *Relation* of 1658, means "warriors of the rock," modernized as Assiniboin. A tribe of Siouan stock, dwelling west of the Crees, on the Saskatchewan and Assiniboin rivers.

13 (p. 231).—A letter (dated 1656) by Claude Pijart, in the archives of l'École Ste. Geneviève, Paris, gives a similar account of Garreau's death. Pijart states that the Algonkin fleet numbered some 300 people; also that Garreau was assigned as their spiritual instructor, at their own request. A copy of the *Elogium*, or obituary notice, sent out by his superior upon the death of Garreau, is in the archives of St. Mary's College, Montreal. See sketch of his life, and reference to Perrot's account of his death, in vol. xxiii., *note* 13.

14 (p. 251) —Regarding Madame de Charny, see vol. xxxvii., *note* 6.

15 (p. 255).—The Madame Bourdon here referred to was Anne de Monceaux (vol. xxxv., *note* 3); she married (Aug. 21, 1655) Jean Bourdon (vol. xi., *note* 11), as his second wife. For mention of her daughter, see vol. xxxvi., *note* 38.

16 (p. 257).—The name Achiendasé had been given by the Iroquois to Lalemant, as superior of the missions; in accordance with their custom, it was also conferred upon Le Mercier as his successor.

17 (p. 257).—In the original MS., the *Mort du Frere Liégeois* is inserted at this point, thus interrupting the sentence.

18 (p. 259).—The MS. annals of the Hôtel-Dieu of Quebec mention this priest (Le Bey) as chaplain of that institution.

19 (p. 263).—"All which follows, regarding the death of Brother Liégeois, is written upon a detached sheet, somewhat smaller in size than the rest of the folio MS. This notice is from the hand of the person whose writing appears on the margins of the entire Journal."

"Robert le Coq (called 'the good') was killed, not with Father Jogues, but four years later."

"Brother Liégeois's name was Jean."

The above notes are taken from Quebec ed. of *Journal*, p. 196.

20 (p. 267).—The spot where Liégeois was interred is thus identified by Faucher de St. Maurice, in his brochure entitled *Relation . . . des fouilles faites . . . dans . . . les fondations du Collège des Jésuites* (Quebec, 1879), p. 38: "The excavations of Sept. 6, 1878, made in the Jesuit barracks . . . lead us to believe that the foundation walls surrounding the place where the excavations were made were those of the old sacristy of the chapel, designated in the *Journal des Jésuites*, p. 197, by the name of 'Congrégation des Messieurs.' The chapel which bears this name — or, rather, as Abbé Ferland says in his *Notes sur les registres de Notre-Dame*, p. 90, 'the room which served the Jesuits as a chapel' from the end of 1650 — was included in the main building, and could not have been far from this sacristy."

The excavations above referred to were made by order of the Canadian government, and most of the work was done under the direction of St. Maurice. On August 21 (1878), human bones were uncovered, which were decided by local antiquarians to be those of the Jesuit priests Jean de Quen and François du Peron, and the brother Jean Liégeois. A full account of this discovery is given by Rochemonteix in *Jésuites*, t. i., pp. 456–465. Cf. St. Maurice, *ut supra*.

It may be added here that the reference made, in the next paragraph of the text, to the burning of the College of Quebec is somewhat ambiguous. "The college of Quebec, properly speaking, had never been burned. It is true, the residence of Nôtre Dame de Recouvrance was consumed by fire in 1640; but it was not until several years later that the foundations were laid for the college (now 'the Barracks')."— Quebec ed. *Journ. des Jésuites*, p. 197, *note*.

21 (p. 269).— The original MS. of the *Catalogve des Bienfaictevrs* was long preserved in the archives of the Seminary of Quebec, but now cannot be found there, only a copy of it remaining. Its publication in *L'Abeille* (see Bibliographical Data of this volume) was accompanied with notes; such of these as we here use will be distinguished by their numbers and the initials of the editors,— as, "L. & C., 11;" i.e., "note 11, by Laverdière and Casgrain."

At the time when this document begins, "Canada had just been restored to France, by the treaty of Saint Germain-en-Laye, Mar. 29, 1632." The Jesuits mentioned in the text were Fathers Anne de Noué and Paul le Jeune, and Brother Gilbert Burel. The chapel of Nôtre Dame de Recouvrance, "which was the first parochial church at Quebec, must have been built upon the site or in the neighborhood of the present Anglican cathedral."— L. & C., 2, 3, 5.

22 (p. 271).— Cf. mention of this incident in Lalemant's letter describing his shipwreck (vol. iv., p. 245).

23 (p. 271).— Ignatius Loyola was the founder of the Jesuit order, and François Xavier, his most eminent disciple. For notice of Luigi di Gonzagua, see vol. xviii., *note* 3. Stanislas Kostka, belonging to a noble Polish family, was born in 1550. A student in the Jesuit college at Vienna, he desired to enter that order, but his family would not allow this step; he obtained, however, a position in the college at Dillingen. Being afterward sent to Rome, he assumed the monastic habit in 1567, and died Aug. 15, 1568. He was beatified in 1604, and afterward canonized.

24 (p. 271).— Regarding this legacy by Champlain, see vol. xiii., *note* 1.

25 (p. 273).— See Le Jeune's description of this fire, vol. xix., pp. 65 - 67. The Jesuit residence thus consumed was built in 1635.

26 (p. 273).— The Jesuits had then six residences in Canada: two at Quebec— Notre Dame des Anges, and Notre Dame de Recouvrance (that is, the lodging that was lent to them after the fire, until the new building was erected); the residence of La Conception, at Three Rivers; that of Sainte Anne, at Cape Breton; that of Saint Joseph, at Ihonatiria; and that of La Conception, at the village of Ossossané.— L. & C., 13.

27 (p. 273).— Another MS. of the same period, preserved in the Archiepiscopal archives, assigns a different use to the proceeds of this collection. "In 1643 and 1644," this MS. says, "collections were taken among all the parishioners, for the erection of the church."— L. & C., 16.

28 (p. 275).— The manuscript above cited says: "In 1645, Monsieur de Montmagny, the Governor, and the parishioners gave, in addition to the collections mentioned above, 1,270 beaver-skins, which might then be worth 8,000 livres, to build the said church, which was called Notre Dame de la Paix. . . . That church was built in the form of a cross,— 30 feet wide by 100 feet long, including the walls,— on the site which it now occupies, which was given for the purpose by Guillaume Couillard and his wife" (1645). That gift must have been merely verbal; for the same manuscript adds, a little farther on: "On the 15th of January, 1652, by deed before Audouart, notary, Guillaume Couillard [and his wife], gave to the church of Quebec aforesaid the ground on which the said church is built, 80 perches in superficies."

"There were," it adds, "two chapels: that on the epistle side was called Saint Joseph's, and that on the gospel side was called Saint Anne's. From that time, this church has been the parish church of Quebec; it has been maintained by the charity of the parishioners."

Proceedings of the church wardens, October 8, 1645: "Resolved that, in view of the destruction by fire, five and a half years ago [in 1640], of the first parish church of the said habitants, a new one be built in honor of the most Blessed Virgin, the Mother of God, under the title of Notre Dame de la Conception, who is the Patroness and Titular of the Parish of Quebec." And inasmuch as, through the intercession of the most Blessed Virgin, peace had that year been obtained with the Iroquois, it was resolved that that church should bear the name of Notre Dame de la Paix. It was also decided that a clergy-house be built near the church. Reverend Father Lalemant, Superior of the Jesuits, and Monsieur de Montmagny, the Governor, laid the first stone of the said church.— L. & C., 17.

Concerning the above-mentioned gift of the habitants, cf. vol. xxvii. of this series, p. 89; vol. xxviii., pp. 225–227.

29 (p. 275).— Geneviève Juchereau, daughter of Jean Juchereau, sieur de More, and wife of Charles Le Gardeur de Tilly.— L. & C., 18. See vol. xxvii. of this series, *notes* 5, 15.

30 (p. 277).— Jean Gloria was born in 1639, near Dieppe. He is mentioned in 1650 as an employé in the Jesuit residence at Quebec; but in January, 1652, he married Marie Bourdon, a niece of Jean Bourdon. By her he had six children, two of whom became hospital nuns. In 1658, he was procuror, or agent, for the habitants of Quebec. He died in October, 1665.

31 (p. 283).— Reference is made to Jean Guenet (vol. xxxv., *note* 12).

32 (p. 283).— The minot is an old measure of capacity, equivalent to 39 liters, or 1.11 Winchester bushels.

33 (p. 285).—*Daudeville:* Nicolas le Vieux de Hauteville, lieutenant-general of the seneschal's jurisdiction, (vol. xxxvi., *note* 52); he came to Canada with De Lauson (1651). He married (September, 1654) Marie Renardin de la Blanchetière; they had two daughters, one of whom became a hospital nun.

34 (p. 285).— The inhabitants of the Côte de Beaupré still give the stream that name. On the maps it is called River Sainte Anne.

The company of the Hundred Associates conceded the Côte de Beaupré to Antoine Cheffault, sieur de la Renardière, and the Island of Orleans to sieur Jacques Castillon, on January 15, 1636. But we observe, by a declaration of February 29 following, that the sieurs Cheffault and Castillon had not acquired those two seigniories for themselves alone,— because they acknowledge that they are for themselves and for Messieurs François Fouquet and Charles de Lauson, councilors of state; for Monsieur Berruyer, seignior of Manselmont; and for Messieurs Jean Rozé, Jacques Duhamel, and Juchereau, merchants ; the eight associates owning each one-eighth in the partnership. This company, which generally took the name of the Company of Beaupré, sold those two seigniories, by various deeds passed between the years 1662 and 1668, to Monseigneur de Laval, who bequeathed them to the Seminary of Quebec in 1680.— L. & C., 51, 52.

35 (p. 285).— Charles Cadieu (also named Courville) was born in 1628. At the age of twenty-six, he married Michelle Macard, by whom he had eight children. In 1650, he was engaged with

L'Épinay and others in the Tadoussac trade. His death occurred in 1715.

36 (p. 287).— Hélène Desportes, widow of Guillaume Hébert; she was married a second time to Noël Morin, a wheelwright; he was the father of Germain Morin, who was the first Canadian priest, and one of the members of the Seminary of Quebec.— L. & C., 54.

37 (p. 289).— Pierre Paradis, a native of Perche, born in 1605, married Barbe, daughter of Jean Guyon (vol. xxvii., *note* 16), by whom he had nine children. He died in January, 1675.

Trieste

Trieste Publishing has a massive catalogue of classic book titles. Our aim is to provide readers with the highest quality reproductions of fiction and non-fiction literature that has stood the test of time. The many thousands of books in our collection have been sourced from libraries and private collections around the world.

The titles that Trieste Publishing has chosen to be part of the collection have been scanned to simulate the original. Our readers see the books the same way that their first readers did decades or a hundred or more years ago. Books from that period are often spoiled by imperfections that did not exist in the original. Imperfections could be in the form of blurred text, photographs, or missing pages. It is highly unlikely that this would occur with one of our books. Our extensive quality control ensures that the readers of Trieste Publishing's books will be delighted with their purchase. Our staff has thoroughly reviewed every page of all the books in the collection, repairing, or if necessary, rejecting titles that are not of the highest quality. This process ensures that the reader of one of Trieste Publishing's titles receives a volume that faithfully reproduces the original, and to the maximum degree possible, gives them the experience of owning the original work.

We pride ourselves on not only creating a pathway to an extensive reservoir of books of the finest quality, but also providing value to every one of our readers. Generally, Trieste books are purchased singly - on demand, however they may also be purchased in bulk. Readers interested in bulk purchases are invited to contact us directly to enquire about our tailored bulk rates. Email: customerservice@triestepublishing.com

You May Also Like

Results of Astronomical Observations Made at the Sydney Observatory, New South Wales, in the Years 1877 and 1878

H. C. Russell

ISBN: 9780649692613
Paperback: 120 pages
Dimensions: 6.14 x 0.25 x 9.21 inches
Language: eng

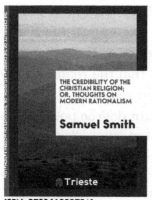

The Credibility of the Christian Religion; Or, Thoughts on Modern Rationalism

Samuel Smith

ISBN: 9780649557516
Paperback: 204 pages
Dimensions: 5.83 x 0.43 x 8.27 inches
Language: eng

www.triestepublishing.com

You May Also Like

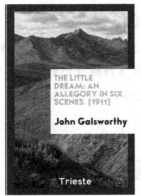

The Little Dream: An Allegory in Six Scenes. [1911]

John Galsworthy

ISBN: 9780649637270
Paperback: 50 pages
Dimensions: 6.14 x 0.10 x 9.21 inches
Language: eng

Report of the Second Annual Meeting of the Maryland State Bar Association, Held at Ocean City, Maryland, July 28-29, 1897

Conway W. Sams

ISBN: 9780649724185
Paperback: 130 pages
Dimensions: 6.14 x 0.28 x 9.21 inches
Language: eng

www.triestepublishing.com

You May Also Like

ISBN: 9780649420544
Paperback: 108 pages
Dimensions: 6.14 x 0.22 x 9.21 inches
Language: eng

1807-1907 The One Hundredth Anniversary of the incorporation of the Town of Arlington Massachusetts

Various

ISBN: 9780649194292
Paperback: 44 pages
Dimensions: 6.14 x 0.09 x 9.21 inches
Language: eng

Biennial report of the Board of State Harbor Commissioners, for the two fiscal years commencing July 1, 1890, and ending June 30, 1892

Various

You May Also Like

Biennial report of the Board of State Harbor Commissioners for the two fisca years. Commeneing July 1, 1884, and Ending June 30, 1886

Various

ISBN: 9780649199693
Paperback: 48 pages
Dimensions: 6.14 x 0.10 x 9.21 inches
Language: eng

Biennial report of the Board of state commissioners, for the two fiscal years, commencing July 1, 1890, and ending June 30, 1892

Various

ISBN: 9780649196395
Paperback: 44 pages
Dimensions: 6.14 x 0.09 x 9.21 inches
Language: eng

Find more of our titles on our website. We have a selection of thousands of titles that will interest you. Please visit

www.triestepublishing.com